Aesthetics, Organization, and Humanistic Management

This book is a reaction to the reductionist and exploitative ideas dominating the mainstream contemporary management discourse and practice, and an attempt to broaden the horizons of possibility for both managers and organization scholars. It brings together the scholarly fields of humanistic management and organizational aesthetics, where the former brings in the unshakeable focus on the human condition and concern for dignity, emancipation, and the common good, while the latter promotes reflection, openness, and appreciation for irreducible complexity of existence. It is a journey towards wholeness undertaken by a collective of management and organization theorists, philosophers, artists, and art curators.

Reading this book's contributions can help both academics and practitioners work towards building organizational practices aimed at (re) acquiring wholeness by developing aesthetic awareness allowing for more profound understandings of performativity, insights into the dynamics of power, appreciation of ambiguity and ambivalence, and a much needed grasp of complexity. The varied ways of engaging with art explored by the authors promote imaginative insights into and reflection on the beauty and vicissitudes of organizing of management knowledge and collective expression.

It will be of interest to researchers, academics, practitioners, and students in the fields of organizational theory and practice, business and management history, human resource management, and culture management.

Monika Kostera is Professor Ordinaria and Chair in Management at the Jagiellonian University, Poland and Professor in Management and Organization at Södertörn University, Sweden.

Cezary Woźniak is a philosopher and Professor in Institute of Culture at Management and Social Communication Department, Jagiellonian University, Poland.

Humanistic Management
Series Editors: Michael Pirson, Erica Steckler, David Wasieleski, Benito Teehankee, Ricardo Aguado and Ernestina Giudici

Humanistic Management draws together the concepts of social business, sustainability, social entrepreneurship, business ethics, conscious capitalism and cooperative capitalism to present a new humanistically-based research paradigm. This new paradigm challenges the prevailing neoliberal "economistic" approach that dominated twentieth-century management theory and practice, and instead emphasises the need to protect human dignity and wellbeing as well as economic drivers.

Aesthetics, Organization, and Humanistic Management
Edited by Monika Kostera and Cezary Woźniak

Aesthetics, Organization, and Humanistic Management

Edited by
Monika Kostera and
Cezary Woźniak

Routledge
Taylor & Francis Group
NEW YORK AND LONDON

First published 2021
by Routledge
605 Third Avenue, New York, NY 10017

and by Routledge
2 Park Square, Milton Park, Abingdon, Oxon, OX14 4RN

First issued in paperback 2022

Routledge is an imprint of the Taylor & Francis Group, an informa business

Publisher's Note
The publisher has gone to great lengths to ensure the quality of this reprint but points out that some imperfections in the original copies may be apparent.

Library of Congress Cataloging-in-Publication Data
Names: Kostera, Monika, 1963– editor. |
Woźniak, Cezary, editor.
Title: Aesthetics, organization, and humanistic management /
edited by Monika Kostera and Cezary Woźniak.
Description: New York, NY : Routledge, 2021. |
Series: Humanistic management | Includes bibliographical
references and index.
Identifiers: LCCN 2020022907 | ISBN 9780367550073 (hardback) |
ISBN 9781003091530 (ebook)
Subjects: LCSH: Management—Psychological aspects. |
Management—Social
aspects. | Management—Moral and ethical aspects.
Classification: LCC HF5548.8 .A59 2021 | DDC 658.001—dc23
LC record available at https://lccn.loc.gov/2020022907

ISBN: 978-0-367-55010-3 (pbk)
ISBN: 978-0-367-55007-3 (hbk)
ISBN: 978-1-003-09153-0 (ebk)

DOI: 10.4324/9781003091530

Typeset in Sabon
by codeMantra

Contents

Contributors

Elizabeth Carnegie currently teaches museum and heritage management at the University of Sheffield. She came to academic work from practice having been a museum curator specializing in the representation of peoples and cultures within localities. Her research focuses on how complex institutions such as museums construct and frame themselves for external and tourist audiences within the "political present." She has published extensively on how museums in Turkey and the Near East are interpreted. Her recent work is also concerned with the notion of the "virtual artefact," here framed as the marked body (tattoos) as a site/sight for public and private remembering and mourning. She is particularly interested in how objects and memories are combined, drawing on individuals' life histories and present values to shape collective memory and to make group identity "truth" claims. Her current work with Prof. Jerzy Kociatkiewicz focuses on the representation of the recent political past within post-communist and memorial museums in Eastern and Central Europe.

Matilda Dahl is Assistant Professor at the Department of Business Studies, Uppsala University. Her research revolves around organizational orders and dreams in society. She is currently exploring how to write research and meet research participants in a poetic way.

Alessandra Di Pisa has worked as an artist and a lecturer for 15 years in Sweden and internationally, engaging with a wide range of expressions such as video, performance, sound art, robotics, artificial intelligence, and artists' books. Di Pisa is a lecturer at Linköping University and has been teaching at the KTH Royal Institute of Technology since 2007. Her previous exhibitions include Hyper Design – Shanghai Biennale (2006), Living in a Modern Society, Kaliningrad State Art Gallery (2009), and Swedish Conceptual Art, Kalmar Art Museum (2010). She has given lectures on art, creativity, and design thinking at Linköping University, Nordic Summer University, Lithuania, Konstfack, Octa Pharma, Socialstyrelsen, The Swedish International Development Cooperation Agency (SIDA), Historiska Museet, KTH Royal Institute of Technology, Färgfabriken, IBM Sweden, Moderna

Museet, Skandia, Bonniers Konsthall, Berghs School of Communication, and Kalmar Konstmuseum, among others.

Daniel Ericsson received his PhD from the Stockholm School of Economics and is currently Associate Professor at Linnaéus University. He is particularly interested in understanding how entrepreneurship is constructed and organized in society, as well as the unforeseen consequences of entrepreneurship. In his latest project, he studies how entrepreneurship is enacted in the cultural sector.

Mateusz Falkowski, PhD, is a philosopher, Assistant Professor in the Institute of Culture at the Jagiellonian University (Kraków), and lecturer at the School of Form (Poznań). He is the author of three books – *Kryteria sprzedajnej manifestacji* (Criteria of Venal Demonstration, together with Marek Sobczyk), *O maszynach* (On Machines), and *Twórca i perspektywy* (Creator and Perspectives), and co-author of the *Cinema of Gravity.* Since 2011, he has been the President of the Managerial Board of the Barbara Skarga Foundation for Thinking.

Yannick Fronda is senior lecturer at Institut Mines-Telecom. He makes regular use of films and arts in his teaching. His research focuses on vulnerability and suffering in the face of the brutality of certain managerial practices, in both their psychological and social dimensions. He also studies what is innovative in organizations and creative and artistic performances. He highlights the role of the imaginary and the paradoxical tensions in management, as well as the identity effects of resistance to change. He has contributed to *Artiste et entrepreneur* and *Petit bréviaire des idées reçues en management.*

Piotr Graczyk received his PhD from the Graduate School for Social Research at the Polish Academy of Science in Warsaw in 2001. He is currently working as Associate Professor at the Institute of Culture in the Faculty of Management and Social Communication of Jagiellonian University (Kraków). His main fields of interest are contemporary art and art theory, especially the intersection of aesthetics and political philosophy. He writes about literature as a political factor. In 2015, he received the Barbara Skarga Prize for the best essay.

Pierre Guillet de Monthoux is Professor of Philosophy and Management at Copenhagen Business School, Denmark. He is engaged in research on aesthetics, art, and curating in organizations and management. He is currently guest professor at the Stockholm School of Economics (SSE), where he is also the Director of the SSE Art Initiative.

Jenny Helin is Associate Professor at the Department of Business Studies, Uppsala University. In her current research, she investigates a poetic understanding of organizational life. She is passionately inquiring into generative ways of developing collaborative research methods and academic writing practices.

Jerzy Kociatkiewicz is Professor of Human Resource Management at the Institut Mines-Télécom Business School. His research interests cover a wide gamut of organization theory and include organizational space and experience, sense-making, and narrative processes within and around organizations. He has published in a variety of journals including *Management Learning*, *Organization*, *Organization Studies*, and *Annals of Tourism Research*. With Zygmunt Bauman, Irena Bauman, and Monika Kostera, he co-authored *Management in a Liquid Modern World*.

Monika Kostera is Professor Ordinaria and Chair in Management at the Jagiellonian University in Kraków, Poland and Professor in Management and Organization at Södertörn University, Sweden. She has also been Professor and Chair at Durham University, UK. She is the author, co-author, and editor of over 40 books in Polish and English and of numerous scientific articles. Her current research interests include organizational imagination, disalienated work, and organizational ethnography. She is a member of the Erbacce Poets' Cooperative.

Marta Kudelska is curator and author of texts about art. She has published numerous articles in journals dedicated to art, as well as in catalogues for exhibitions. She graduated in contemporary culture and art history from the Jagiellonian University in Krakow. Currently she is a PhD student at the Jagiellonian University, where she deals with the activities of young curators in Silesia and Krakow.

Marcin Laberschek is an employee of the Culture Institute of the Jagiellonian University. He is a lecturer, researcher, and author of scientific publications on management and marketing in the area of culture, media, and advertising. His interests are focused on (1) research methodology in humanistic management, (2) management of organizations engaged in cultural activities, (3) symbolic and cultural meanings of management processes in marketing and advertising, and (4) critical marketing, postmarketing, and management on the postmodern market.

Hugo Letiche is Adjunct Professor in Institut Mines: Telecom Business School, Evry (FR) and Professor of Management and Organization, School of Business, University of Leicester, UK. He has a Drs. in clinical and social psychology (Leiden) and a PhD in pedagogy (Free University, Amsterdam). Previously, he was the Director of the practitioner PhD program at the Universiteit voor Humanistiek, Utrecht (NL). His book publications include (author/co-editor) *L'Art du sens* PUL (2019), *Turn to Film*: Brill (2019), *Post-Formalism* Peter Lang (2017), and *Demo(s)*: sense publishing (2016); he has published articles in *Organization Studies*, *Organization*, *Revue Française de Gestion*, *Management Learning*, *JOCM*, *Culture & Organization*, *Journal of Curriculum and Pedagogy*, *ephemera*, *E:CO*, *Society*

Business Review, etc. His current research interests are in the turn-to-affect, the ontological turn in ethnography, and object-oriented ontology.

Philippe Mairesse is Associate Professor and responsible for the Unesco chair "Arts, Science and Sustainable Development Goals" at ICN-Artem (Nancy, France). He has extensive experience in research and publication in the field of organizational aesthetics and the relationship between art and organizations. As early as 2004, he became actively involved in this area, both through his practice of artistic intervention in companies and training, and through his research and publications. In 2018, he created the academic and artistic journal *Dysfunction*, and in 2019, the international forum "Dysfunction Day" on the issue of the dissemination of research through art. In recent years, he has organized or participated in several national (ANR) or European research projects on the theme of Art and Organization, a subject on which he also co-organizes workshops and tracks in international conferences (EGOS, AoMO).

Jean-Luc Moriceau is Professor of Research Methods at Institut-Mines Télécom Business School and is in charge of doctoral students' training at LITEM (a joint research laboratory of IMT-BS and University of Evry Val d'Essonne). He defends a humanistic and creative approach to research, reflecting on its aesthetic, ethical, and political dimensions and emphasizing the role of affects, performance, and writing. A member of the SCOS board, he has made several academic performances. He has co-edited *Demo(s): Philosophy, Pedagogy, Politics; Turn to Film*, *Méthode qualitative de recherche en sciences sociales*, and *L'art du sens dans les organisations*, and six special issues of journals.

Luc Peters is a philosopher and writer. His books include *Cliché & Organization: Thinking with Deleuze and Film*, *On Mirrors! Philosophy–Art–Organization* (together with Dr Anthony R Yue), *On Noise!* (Release 2020), and *Frank Lloyd Wright – NOMAD* (together with Huubke Rademakers) (release 2020). He is a regular at various conferences like EGOS, APROS, and SCOS and co-organizer of the 2016 CORPORATE BODIES Film Fest. Besides writing, he works as a manager, guest lecturer, and consultant and hardrock-drummer and torturer of guitars creating horrendous noise. Between his travels and adventures, Luc lives and works in the Netherlands.

Marja Soila-Wadman, PhD, is a senior lecturer and researcher associated with Södertörn University, Stockholm, Sweden. Her research interests are creativity and aesthetics in organizations, management and entrepreneurship in art- and culture-creating organizations, and organizational development and change. The case study that the text in this volume refers to was conducted when she was the Director of Business and Design Lab at the University of Gothenburg, a cooperation between the School of Business, Economics and Law and the School of Design and Crafts (HDK). Before moving to business administration studies, she worked 12 years as a dentist, where aesthetics in everyday practice was important to take into account.

Robert Stasinski has worked as an artist, writer, editor, and curator for fifteen years. He is Editor and Communications Director of Art Initiative, Stockholm School of Economics, and Course Leader in Arts Management at the International Master Program in Curating at Stockholm University. He was the editor-in-chief of *Konstnären* and *Nu-E – The Nordic Art Review*, as well as editor of several books including *Felix Gmelin – The Aging Revolution* (2006; Daniel Birnbaum, Ronald Jones, and David Rimanelli), *The Synthetic Supernatural* (2011), *The Board Room* (2016; Therese Bohman, Dragana Vujanović Östlind, and Ingrid Elam), and *The Heckscher-Ohlin Room* (2018; Mats Lundahl, Lars Strannegård, Pierre Guillet de Monthoux, Erik Wikberg, Bella Rune, Isak Nilson, Jens Fänge, and Charlotte Gyllenhammar). He has written and lectured on topics such as artificial intelligence, arts management, cultural policy, neuroaesthetics, body image/body politics at Stockholm University, Akademi Valand, Linköping University, Nordic Summer University, Konstfack, KTH, Färgfabriken, IBM Sweden, Moderna Museet, and the Stockholm School of Economics, among others.

Antonio Strati, Senior Professor at the Department of Sociology and Social Research, University of Trento, Italy, and *chercheur associé* (Visiting Professor) at the Centre de Recherche en Gestion (i3-CRG), CNRS, École polytechnique, IP Paris, is both a sociologist and an art photographer. He is a founder member of the Research Unit on Communication, Organizational Learning and Aesthetics (RUCOLA) at Trento and of the Standing Conference on Organizational Symbolism (SCOS). His book *Organization and Aesthetics* (Sage, 1999) has been translated into several languages. He is also the author of *Theory and Method in Organization Studies* (Sage, 2000) and has recently published *Organizational Theory and Aesthetic Philosophies* (Routledge, 2019).

Anke Strauß, PhD, is a critical management and organization researcher working on the intersection between art and economy. Being interested in changing forms and politics of organizing contemporary work lives, she writes about solidarity, affect, aesthetics, practices of collaborating, and alternative ways of organizing. Currently she is research fellow at Zeppelin University in Friedrichshafen at the chair of art theory and curating. Together with Christina Ciupke, she is working on a project founded by the VW foundation on artist-run organizations and the performativity of utopian thinking for (re-)organizing cultural labor.

Cezary Woźniak studied History of Art and Philosophy at Jagiellonian University, where he is now working as Professor in the Institute of Culture at Management and Social Communication Department. His publications include *Martin Heidegger's Thinking on Art* (1998, 2004) and *Augenblick: Primordial Experience and Limits of Philosophy* (2008, 2013). He works widely on a variety of philosophical themes, but with particular focus on phenomenology, Buddhist studies, culture studies, hermeneutics, and aesthetics.

1 Introduction

Understanding Organizing and the Quest for Wholeness

Cezary Woźniak and Monika Kostera

Against Reductionism

Contemporary management and organization studies are often based on ideological premises: instead of pursuing an explorative study into how organizations are managed, they try to produce knowledge useful to managers, and, above all, create and disseminate the conviction that the current socio-economic system is the best, or even the only possible. Martin Parker (2018) notes that much of the current managerial knowledge is limited and presented in a seductively simple form that does no justice to complexity and diversity in the area. Organizations are reduced to one type only (business corporations), and management is presented as a strictly goal-oriented activity. The philosophical approach can be best described as dramatically simplified utilitarianism (Dierksmeier, 2011). Parker calls for research that broadens our knowledge and shows possible and actual alternatives to this narrowed down world of ideas and practices. We need more and broader knowledge relevant for complex organizations to counteract the raging reductionism that dominates in the contemporary approach to all management problems, producing serious problems such as irreversible damage to the planet and erosion of social institutions and structures. If we fail, humanity may no longer be able to cope with problems towards what is it: ecological, cultural, economic, and political. The solutions that have worked so far are no longer helpful because they applied to radically different contexts and situations. Insisting on them creates even further serious problems and damage to nature and society, as Zygmunt Bauman (2017) points out in his last book, *Retrotopia*.

These concerns correspond well with the relatively new but already vibrant humanistic turn in management (for an overview, see Orzechowski, 2009; Pirson, Spitzeck, Amann, Khan, & Kimakowitz, 2009; Pirson, Steinvorth, Largacha-Martinez, & Dierksmeier, 2014). The *Humanistic Management Manifesto* published by the Humanistic Management Network states the following:

> The Humanistic Management Network defends human dignity in the face of its vulnerability. The dignity of the human being lies in

her or his capacity to define, autonomously, the purpose of her or his existence. Since human autonomy realizes itself through social co-operation, economic relations and business activities can either foster or obstruct human life and well-being. Against the widespread objectification of human subjects into human resources, against the common instrumentalization of human beings into human capital and a mere means for profit, we uphold humanity as the ultimate end and key principle of all economic activity

(Humanistic Management Network, 2014)

For Aesthetics

One of the ways of looking at organization and management, without resorting to reductionism, is one that is informed by art and the philosophy of aesthetics. Antonio Strati (1999) upholds that aesthetics in organizational life is a form and a part of human knowledge and excluding it leads to epistemological blindness. If aesthetics is eliminated from organization and management studies, the latter cease to have relevance for organizational life and become sterile. It is a kind of idealization, albeit one devoid of meaning, because it implies disembodiment and thus obscures, rather than makes visible, vital aspects of the studied realities. These aspects include management of symbols, organizational ceremonies, and the physical settings of work. Strati welcomes the (re-) introduction of the aesthetic dimension into the study of organization, and calls for an increased attention to aesthetics as epistemology, practice, and feature of organization. This call concerns both theoretical and methodological issues, which may result in insights and knowledge beyond the logico-rational, narrowly defined boundaries of the field, which still (now as at the time of the writing of Strati's book) dominate the discourses. It demands new metaphors, a new language and consciousness, enriching management studies with the contributions from philosophy and anthropology. Only then the knowledge in and of organization can truly claim completeness, touching upon and using understandings about such central issues as emotions and feelings in organizations, the importance of symbol, the dynamics of culture, and, last but not least, the embodied and emotional aspects of learning and cognition.

This view is also supported by another of the early proponents of the aesthetic perspective in organization studies, Guillet de Monthoux (1998). He proposes to recognize management itself as a kind of art: an approach that appreciates the complexity of the organizational world. It uses philosophy, as well as aesthetic reflection and sensibility, to problematize organizational issues and to gain understanding on them beyond the simplistic utilitarian preoccupation. Management is a "journey in the aesthetic space" (Guillet de Monthoux, 1993, p. 4), the pursuit of what is possible. As such it needs a language and a sensibility to grasp and express this space.

> We are not able to understand management without understanding art. It is impossible to understand economic development without an aesthetic perspective.
>
> (ibid., p. 1)

Yet, there is often a gap between economic and humanistic knowledge. The divide is not a given and certainly not historical. Guillet de Monthoux (1993) points to the origins of modern economic thought – the writings of Adam Smith – and calls attention to the broader humanistic perspective that is already present in his way of understanding economics, as part of human and moral sciences. The market, social communication and self-management are all related to morality and aesthetics, even if many contemporary managers are unaware of this dimension. The now so dominating reductionism is not due to the lack of insight handed down by the classics, but rather due to omissions and an ideologization of management theory and education, and to the rupture with philosophy and the humanities that took place only a few decades ago.

Guillet de Monthoux proposes to return to another important classic, Immanuel Kant, for insights about the aesthetic sphere, which, according to the philosopher, is located in the space between scientific truth and the moral sphere. Art can be treated as a kind of practical moral compass that helps with ethical and moral questions, and it can also be an inspiration for managers who seek new ideas in relation to internal problems of the organization as well as to market activities. Aesthetics offers a rich epistemological framework for research and description, thanks to which it is possible to study the phenomena of an organization without the radical simplification of their complexity. Finally, art produces tools to reflect on the presence of the aesthetic dimension, which is often overlooked in the rationalistic discourse on management. Every human activity has an aesthetic dimension; thus, an important aspect of the success of an organization's functioning is its aesthetic value (Guillet de Monthoux, 1993).

Not aiming at a complete review of relevant literature, rather trying to provide an outline of what we consider to be the most relevant markers of the area from the perspective of this book, we will now briefly present a few key advantages provided by the inclusion of an aesthetic dimension in organization studies, addressing some of the most popular topics present in the mainstream of organization studies and what they gain by aesthetic awareness.

First, such awareness brings about a profound understanding of performativity, suggests Jean-Luc Moriceau (2018), which is now considered one of the major themes of interest in organization studies. Performative arts bring many valuable understandings and tools: they produce aesthetic experiences by organizing expressions and impressions. These arts also have many political aspects, by providing poetic moments with emancipative and problematizing potential. The material they utilize is strictly social and organizational: places, roles, structures, and norms. These configurations and reconfigurations trigger affects that may help to interpret organizational phenomena.

Another important blind spot addressed by the adoption of an aesthetic perspective is the dynamics of power distribution (Moriceau, 2016). The topic of power is one of the most constant presences in organization studies; however, without a holistic perspective emphasizing the embodied and physical motion, we lack a sufficient understanding of certain power dynamics that influence, among other things, organizational learning. Movement is restricted and directed by power, thus enabling or disabling learning. Power propagates and defines itself in part by physical restriction. Learning from artistic productions, such as theatre, we are able to gain knowledge about both the unfolding of the dynamics and some of its sources.

Furthermore, art enables learning. Through its ambiguity and ambivalence, it could be useful in knowledge-creation processes in organizational contexts marked by dynamism and uncertainty (Berthoin Antal, 2014). Artistic intervention is a way of organizational learning that involves organizational actors and settings and allows artists to engage with them, making space for refreshing and changing the one's experience with the re-imagination of what seems to been taken as immutable, as given. Artistic interventions invite multiple ways of knowing, in particular, embodied senses and are intercultural in a very practical sense: they provide opportunities to explore new ideas in the workplace, within the work context, in a way that is, at the same time, highly imaginative and experimentally practical.

Thanks to an aesthetic perspective, it becomes viable to link an oft-postulated complexity perspective with an experienced and experiential narrative of organizing. Hugo Letiche (2000) suggests that concepts derived from complexity theory, such as self-organization, may have a reductionist effect on organizational thinking and research, even though it aspires against anti-reductionism. This happens because of the inability to cope with the variety of consciousness and self. A broader humanistic perspective enables the emergence of a phenomenal complexity theory. A text-based consciousness, including art and music, is part of a complexity involving "a multi-dimensional ecology of world and consciousness, objects and perception, opportunities and language" (Letiche & Lissack, 2009, p. 61).

Finally, art can, argues Antonio Strati (1999), provide a language, a way of seeing, and cognitive tools derived from the humanities that allow to more accurately and directly address topics such as emotions, beauty, and disgust; teach and develop the creativity and sensitivity of the human being; and contribute to the building of interpersonal relations at work. Indeed, an aesthetic perspective can help end the body–mind divide in management practice and reflection. The corporality of human participants of organizations is, in many dominating approaches to management and to business, regarded as a mere tool that should be subjected to mental functions. Art makes it possible to bring back a balance that is a better representative of human experience of organizational reality, and thus fill the gap that arose between reductionist and narrowly rationalistic knowledge and the perception of the world and being human (Linstead & Höpfl, 2000).

The chapters of this book address all of these key issues – performativity, structure, learning, and complexity – all embedded into larger contexts and nets of ideas and practices and relying on a language that opens communication towards wholeness without descending into cacophony and chaos – art and the aesthetic.

Towards Wholeness?

This wholeness is one that we can name as phenomena coming into being, lasting, transforming themselves, and disappearing. Some of them can also somehow still live on in the human memory, even for generations, as the historical sources of our present situation. However, in what appears from the history as the wholeness, we can also pick out some ideas and senses, things and structures, different activities and processes – what creates our human world. We try to understand and to describe it; we try to understand and describe the present shape of time.

The first thinker to raise and develop those questions in the Western thought was unquestionably Heraclitus, who already to the ancient Greeks was a "dark" thinker, hard to understand. Speaking very generally, according to Heraclitus, the world is characterized by constant arising and fading, and the "constant" feature of this process would be change. Arising and fading would then be the result of constant grinding of isolated opposites, such as darkness and light, cold and heat. In Heraclitus's thought, we can list four kinds of them, which would constitute their dialectic of some kind, explaining that all events originate in the tension occurring between the opposites.

If one is to understand this radically, that is, contradictions are not qualities of a substantially monistically understood reality or being of some sort, but rather merely concurrent forces (*coincidentia oppositorum*), tensions yielding unsubstantial arising or appearing, then Heraclitus offers us not only a dynamic, variabilistic vision of reality, but also the lesson that reality has no being or substance at all and that it's impossible to say anything *a fortiori* about it. A possibility of such an interpretation of his thought appears already in antiquity, as recounted by Aristotle, who so writes in *Metaphysics* about the Heracliteans:

> they observed that all nature around us undergoes change and held that one cannot speak the truth about that which is undergoing change. So *a fortiori* nothing true could be said about what was changing at all points in all ways. It was from the seed-bed of such thinking that there flowered the most extreme of the views we went through above. This is the position of those who appropriated the legacy of Heraclitus, notably of Cratylus. His mature position was that speech of any kind was radically inappropriate and that expression should be restricted exclusively to the movement of the finger. He was appalled that Heraclitus had claimed that you could not step twice into the same river. In his, Cratylus', opinion it was already going far too far to admit stepping into the same river once.
>
> (Aristotle, 1998, p. 101)

It seems that, on the one hand, for this dialectic of change, or opposites, there is no alternative, and, on the other, this dialectic ultimately abolishes itself as something impossible to establish because in order to do that some ground is needed, some basis, a substance, in other words, some presence, which is bound to be instantly abolished by this very dialectic. All in all, this dialectic turns out to be something no longer dialectical. Opposites work probably on the relative, mereological, ontic, phenomenal level, and that's probably why Heraclitus says only that, only as much, and at the same time so much, as in the fragments B 8 and B 122. The first can be translated as "opposite convergents"; the other consists of one word only: *αγχιβασίη*, which can be translated as "approaching" (Kahn, 1981, p. 289). These fragments can perhaps be understood as utterances on the threshold of language which wants to express the elusive becoming, the happening of the unsubstantial change. The coupling of opposites would be, as it were, earlier than any preconceived whole, and that whole, as a product of that coupling, still remains something impossible to conceptualize, something that denies any possibility of understanding it monistically. In the fragment B 10, Heraclitus so says about those couplings, or connections, as that's another way of translating the Greek *συνάψιες:*

> Connections
> Whole and unwhole,
> Convergent divergent, consonant dissonant,
> And one out of all,
> And all out of one
>
> (Kahn, 1981, p. 54)

This Heraclitean dialectic has yet another moment, which needs to be stressed here. That moment is already signalled by the very semantic range of the word *συνάψιες* as coupling, connection, fusion, and bond. Namely, the oppositions are not oppositions in the strict sense, as they are mere elements, poles of a coupling, a bond, a relation, and as such they are in a sense fluid, transitive. For one cannot, for example, abstract death from life, or separate life from death, as one cannot set the border between life and death, because life and death form an inseparable unity. By the same token, one cannot set the borderline between being and nothingness, or between activity and passivity. In other words, those opposites cannot be substantialized, which would already define the possibilities and limits of language trying to express them without at the same time assuming, and falling into, the metaphysics of presence, to use a Derridean term for a shortcut. That's why Aristotle's charge against Heraclitus is pointless. We read in *Metaphysics*:

> No one can believe that the same thing both is and is-not. On one interpretation, this is the point that Heraclitus was making.
>
> (Aristotle, 1998, p. 88)

One may say that whereas for Aristotle, contradiction doesn't express anything and is only a nonsense, for Heraclitus, it describes, or relates, the way phenomena come into being, or appear, which can still be expressed only to a limited extent, if it can be expressed at all. Yet again Heraclitus, fragment B 49:

> Into the same rivers we step and do not step, we are and we are not.
>
> (Kahn, 1981, p. 289)

Where does this Heraclitean dialectic of opposites lead us, what is it that Cratylus, moving his finger, is trying to tell us? What can be the significance of all this for the project of philosophy, including phenomenology? Diogenes Laertius, in his *Lives and Opinions of Eminent Philosophers*, thus describes Heraclitus:

> He was nobody's pupil, but he declared that he "inquired of himself," and learned everything from himself.
>
> (Diogenes Laertius, 1965, p. 413)

It is certainly possible to see some description of the philosopher's attitude here, an attitude that is aimed at experience and is based on the exploration of that experience, while forgoing any ready-made concepts that would somehow predefine that exploration. Heraclitus's work might be called critical, even destructive, with respect to the designs of metaphysics, which would like to substantialize that field, positing, one way or another, the existence of some beings or things – that's why probably the greatest critic of Heraclitus would be Aristotle, who, perhaps even more than Parmenides and Plato, contributed to the establishing of the Western tradition of thought. It seems as though Heraclitus's anti-metaphysical dialectic of opposites brought thought even at its birth to a standstill – a stalemate that would consist in the primary ineffability of arising, the silence of logos, which, however, earlier did its critical job, thus defining its own possibilities and limits, a thought with which, incidentally, Hegel would certainly disagree. To put it differently, less radically, Heraclitus already asks the question about the sense and the limits of thought.

Structure of the Book

This book is a collective journey towards wholeness, undertaken by a collective of management and organization theorists, philosophers, artists, and art curators, as well as what we see and write into the experience of art and organization. We have decided to organize the chapters according to their mode of engagement with key themes, as addressed at the beginning of this chapter: reflection, imagination, practice, and expression.

The part dedicated to reflection opens with Antonio Strati's personal reflection on the meaning of art and organizing, with the gripping illustration of the narrative of Ambrogio Lorenzetti's frescos in the "Sala della Pace" of the Palazzo Pubblico in Siena. The language of art is presented to be the medium of all engagements with organizing – through reflecting, imagining, practicing, and expressing. The third chapter of the book, and second in this part, authored by Jerzy Kociatkiewicz, offers a reflection on how the language of arts can help to recontextualize and open up the way social science research is regarded and practised.

The second part concerns imagination and contains three chapters. In Chapter 4 of the book, Luc Peters and Anke Strauß narrate the story presented in a well-known film, *The Hudsucker Proxy*, to both imagine and reconsider organizational structure and control. The narrative unfolds as a combination of shapes: lines and circles around the possibility to image vision and being visionary through blindness. Matilda Dahl, Jenny Helin, and Pierre Guillet de Monthoux draw a poetic picture of reverie in the countryside in the book's fifth chapter. They inquire into how dreamt realities play a role in today's organizations and propose both a framework and a language for evoking poetic aspects of organizing. Piotr Graczyk's text, Chapter 6, outlines utopias that can be imagined, dreamt, and organized into being in a field of various tensions of and between social traditions.

The third part addresses practice and holds as many as six of the contributions. Chapter 7, by Marta Kudelska, is a description of a curatorial experience in an imaginative, alchemical language that both communicates and is the artistic expression itself. In Chapter 8, Jean-Luc Moriceau, Philippe Mairesse, and Yannick Fronda, likewise, simultaneously create a text that engages with Tino Sehgal's performative artwork in the Palais de Tokyo. On the basis of this artefact they consider how spacing happens and what role it plays in organizing. Marja Soila-Wadman also focuses on an artistic intervention in Chapter 9. Her topic of interest is the interplay between the artistic dimension and organizational learning. She followed artistic workshops for one year and muses on the relationship between emotional tensions and artistic expressions in the learning process. Chapter 10, by Robert Stasinski and Alessandra Di Pisa, presents a transdisciplinary art project with an artificial intelligence system core. They study the connections between the artistic and the (purely?) technical, and ponder the role of management epistemologies in these complex processes. Marcin Laberschek, in Chapter 11, focuses on old monuments from the state communism era in Poland that used to symbolize the enterprises and their identity, but nowadays for the most part are at best forgotten, if not dismantled. He reflects on the role of these statues, as well as the meanings they carry – and the ones they have ceased to carry. Some artefacts to be found in today's museums reflect a problematic period with colonial and orientalist connections. The chapter muses on the implications of this in terms of identity and structure.

The fourth and final part concerns expression and primarily focuses on the forms and language suitable for research of art and organizing. Daniel Ericsson's Chapter 13 grapples with the ideas of what writing about management and organization does and what it could do by engaging in a highly imaginative writing process that draws attention to knowledge. How can language create a meaningful whole? The author considers different elements such as plot and sense-making as part of the narrative knowledge expression (and creation). Chapter 14, by Mateusz Falkowski, ponders conditions of establishing of a relationship between art and management in the light of expression understood as art creation. This is presented as an interaction, a bond and relationship, with many practical and philosophical consequences. In Chapter 15, the final chapter of the book, Hugo Letiche considers the possibility of research expression decentered from the usual authorial focus. Such multilayered expression, which he labels the "filmic," informed by the art of film, is able to convey a complexity that the study of organization requires.

References

Aristotle (1998). *Metaphysics, trans. with an introduction by Hugh Lawson-Tancred.* London, UK: Penguin Books.

Bauman, Z. (2017). *Retrotopia.* Cambridge, UK: Polity.

Berthoin Antal, A. (2014). When arts enter organizational spaces: Implications for organizational learning. In P. Meusburger (Series Ed.) & Ariane Berthoin Antal, P. Meusburger, & L. Suarsana (Eds.) *Knowledge and space: Vol. 6. Learning organizations: Extending the field* (pp. 177–120). Dordrecht, Netherlands: Springer.

Dierksmeier, C. (2011). Reorienting management education: From the homo economicus to human dignity. *Humanistic Management Network Research Paper*, 13/05.

Guillet de Monthoux, P. (1993) *Det sublimas konstnärliga ledning: Estetik, konst och företag*. Stockholm, Sweden: Nerenius & Santerus.

Guillet de Monthoux, P. (1998) *Konstföretaget: Mellan spektakelkultur och kulturspektakel*. Stockholm, Sweden: Korpen.

Humanistic Management Network (2014) *Promoting human dignity, promoting human well-being*. Retrieved on 17-10-2014 from http://www.humanetwork.org/

Kahn, C. (1981). *The art and thought of Heraclitus*. Edition of the fragments with translation and commentary by Charles H. Kahn. Cambridge, UK: Cambridge University Press.

Laertius, D. (1965). *Lives of eminent philosophers*, ed. and trans. by R. D. Hicks, vol. II. Boston, MA: Harvard University Press.

Letiche, H. (2000). Phenomenal complexity theory as informed by Bergson. *Journal of Organizational Change Management, 13*(6), 545–557.

Letiche, H., & Lissack, M. (2009). Making room for affordances. *E:CO, 11*(3), 61–72.

Linstead, S., & Höpfl, H. (2000) Introduction. In S. Linstead & H. Höpfl (Eds.), *The aesthetics of organization* (pp. 1–11). London, UK: Sage.

Moriceau, J. L. (2016). An apprenticeship to pleasure: Aesthetics dynamics in organizational learning. *Society and Business Review, 11*(1), 80–92.

Moriceau, J. L. (2018). Écrire le qualitatif: écriture réflexive, écriture plurielle, écriture performance. *Revue Internationale de Psychosociologie et de Gestion des Comportements Organisationnels, ESKA, 24* (57), 45–67.

Orzechowski, E. (2009). *Dziś nawet żebrak musi być sprawnym menedżerem: O zarządzaniu kulturą i szkolnictwem wyższym*. Kraków: Attyka.

Parker, M. (2018). *Shut down the business school: What's wrong with management education*. London, UK: Pluto Press.

Pirson, M., Spitzeck, H., Amann, W., Khan, S., & Kimakowitz, von E. (Eds.). (2009). *Humanism in business*. Cambridge, UK: Cambridge University Press.

Pirson, M., Steinvorth, U., Largacha-Martinez, C., & Dierksmeier, C. (Eds.). (2014). *From Capitalistic to Humanistic Business*. London, UK: Palgrave Macmillan.

Strati, A. (1999). *Organization and aesthetics*. London, England, Thousand Oaks, CA and New Delhi, India: Sage.

2 Art and Organizing

A Brief Personal Reflection

Antonio Strati

Introduction

In my aesthetic approach (Strati, 2019), art is just one of the many social phenomena under study, as it is for various other scholars of the aesthetic dimension of organizing (Carr & Hancock, 2003; Gagliardi, 1990; King & Vickery, 2013; Kostera, 1997; Linstead & Höpfl, 2000). My aesthetic approach, in fact, has its foundations in reflections on social practice theory in organizations (Gherardi & Strati, 2012), in the aesthetic sociology of Georg Simmel (1908), in the phenomenology of Merleau-Ponty, in the personalistic hermeneutics of Luigi Pareyson (1954), and in post-humanist awareness (Braidotti, 2013).

I have also addressed, on various occasions, some critical concerns about art and its connections with organizing: (a) art is a phenomenon whose beauty and perfection can sometimes be even anesthetizing and dull our critical–sensorial knowledge (Strati, 1999; Strati & Guillet de Monthoux, 2002), and (b) the philosophy of art itself can constitute a problem that has the same relevance assumed by rationality in organizational theories (Strati, 2019, pp. 66–74) for contemporary everyday aesthetic philosophies (Yuedi & Carter, 2014), which emphasize that, while on the one hand aesthetics goes far beyond the art world, on the other hand art emerges from a wide range of non-artistic activities, experiences, and performances (Sartwell, 2003).

However, I consider art very important in various ways to understand and manage organizational life (*Aesthesis. International Journal of Art and Aesthetics in Management and Organizational Life*, 2008; *Human Relations*, 2002; *Organization Studies*, 2018). What, moreover, the studies on organizational aesthetics most circumscribed to the sphere of artistic phenomena illustrate well (Guillet de Monthoux, 2004; Johansson Sköldberg, Woodilla, & Berthoin Antal, 2016; *Organizational Aesthetics*, 2016; Scalfi Eghenter, 2018; *Scandinavian Journal of Management*, 2014; Taylor & Ladkin, 2009).

In this brief personal reflection on "art and organizing" I will focus on the frescoes that decorate the Palazzo Pubblico (public palace) where the government of the Tuscan city of Siena in Italy has been sitting for more than seven centuries. I have always found them of an extraordinary charm; I often noticed depictions on which I had not previously dwelt; I usually came out with a feeling of inner satisfaction for the great depiction of the ideals of Good Government and republican citizenship that distinguished the Italian Renaissance of the city state of Siena in the fourteenth century.

Usually, I entered the room and stayed there for a long time. The cycle of frescoes by Lorenzetti is an excellent work of art, of extraordinary beauty, but also of extreme complexity. I have always looked at it slowly, guided by natural light in the study of figurations, colours, architecture, and, also, of the interior lights of the frescoes. Step by step I immersed myself in the painting of the Sienese Renaissance with all my senses, picking up the smells; moving now here, now there; taking quick notes from time to time – as we shall see in this brief personal reflection on the interconnections between art and organizing.

The Cycle of Frescoes of Buon Governo

The Palazzo Pubblico of Siena is one of the main icons of the city. Together with its tower, the Torre del Mangia, which is of an extraordinary height to be able to emerge over all the other towers of Siena, this palace occupies, in fact, a strategic position in the scenography of Piazza del Campo, which is the main square of the city.

This palace is, therefore, constitutive of the aesthetics of the organizational communication of the city. In other words, it represents the city of Siena. However, at the same time, for more than seven centuries it has been a place of daily life in the city because it is the seat of the town hall of the city, that is, the site of the administrative government and the place of maximum representation of the Sienese community.

Ambrogio Lorenzetti, one of the great masters of Renaissance painting, frescoed the council chamber of elected citizens governing the city between 1338 and 1339. This is the Sala dei Nove (https://en.wikipedia.org/wiki/The_Allegory_of_Good_and_Bad_Government), so called because at that time nine were the magistrates elected (Consiglio dei Nove) to the government of the Republic of Siena, a predominantly Ghibelline city state that was allied with the emperor and also consisted of the surrounding Tuscan territory and that had rivaled with Florence, the Guelph Duchy allied with the Papal State for more than four centuries, that is, from 1125 to 1555.

It was the Sienese government that commissioned the frescoes by Lorenzetti, and that carefully followed the design. Again, the nine magistrates carefully supervised the implementation and paid for its realization, "just as they had sponsored and paid for the reconstruction of Palazzo Pubblico," points out the historian Quentin Robert Duthie Skinner (2003, p. 164).

A public commission of the city of Siena was, therefore, at the origin of the cycle of frescoes of the Allegory of Good and Bad Government and constituted the humus of symbologies, values, and ideals that Ambrogio Lorenzetti would paint. It is not a question of art that celebrates religions or divinities, nor of art that aims to represent the nobility and the rich gentlemen. Instead, it is art aimed at making the ideals of republican "citizenship" immortal in the secular social life of the Sienese Renaissance. An art, therefore, closely interrelated with the earthly organization, worldly, deadly and that is realized in the frescoing of the walls of the council chamber of the city of Siena.

Was this what fascinated me so much about Lorenzetti's pictorial art? Certainly, the republican ideals, the symbols of daily work life, the values of democracy and social justice constituted an integral part of my aesthetic appreciation of the pictorial representation of the cycle of frescoes of Good and Bad Government.

Although I was aware that it was not a question of republican citizenship and democracy in the current sense of the term because it concerned essentially the upper classes of the city, thinking that every year in the Magistracy of the Nine, fifty-four citizens succeeded each other, and that the statutes that ordered the government of the city created opportunities for hundreds of others to be part of the councils and commissions – figures of republican democracy that, as the historian Randolph Starn (1994; Italian trans. 1996, p. 28) remarks, would not find a comparison in many of our cities today or even in the Athens of Pericles – I found the organizational communication and the educational project inherent in these frescoes beautiful.

My scepticism regarding the illusion of the goodness of all these republican virtues represented in the frescoes was not due to my aesthetic appreciation of the frescoes, but rather my intellectual knowledge and critical attitude. The work of art, on the contrary, was fascinating, persuasive, and convincing: a great artistic interpretation of the republican experiment that constituted this grandiose political and organizational project of the Italian municipalities that marked the Renaissance.

The goodness of the allegorical representation was thus intimately linked to the beauty of the work of art created by this great master of the Renaissance. The close connection between art and organizing of these frescoes was, in fact, still capable of giving form and charm to the "social memory" of the ideal city of the Renaissance. Also for the choice of the fresco as the specific art form to constitute the aesthetic material of this social memory.

Randolph Starn (1994; Italian trans. 1996, pp. 7–8) writes about this and notes that there is no art form that can be said to be more typically Italian than the fresco and that the cycle of Good and Bad Government by Lorenzetti represents one of the most beautiful results. Consider, just to get an idea of the spread of this form of art, the frescoes of the same period by Giotto in the Scrovegni Chapel in Padua or those painted in later times by Michelangelo in the Sistine Chapel in Rome.

Fresco painting was a form of art closely interrelated with the organizing, of art intimately connected with the reasons of power – even when it is in artistic controversy with the secular or religious power – and, above all, of art aimed at public communication of values, ideals, and symbologies.

Imagine that from 1300 to at least 1600, in Italy, public buildings, castles and stately homes, civic loggias, and churches and chapels scattered throughout the entire peninsula were covered with frescoes. It was the golden age of fresco painting, a pictorial form made with pigments dissolved in water and applied to a layer of freshly laid plaster – notes Starn (1994; Italian trans. 1996, p. 103) – for which the plaster and the painting, with drying, were completely integrated.

Sensitive Construction of the Aesthetic Path

It is during a two-year period of the first half of the fourteenth century, therefore, that Ambrogio Lorenzetti frescoed three walls of the rectangular hall where meetings of the Government of the Nine were held – three frescoed walls that constitute a single cycle of frescoes that receive light from the window of one of the two shorter walls, the one to the left of entrants. On the opposite side and, therefore, on the right of entrants, there is the other short wall on which Lorenzetti painted the Allegory of Good Government. On the long wall facing those who enter, instead, Lorenzetti has depicted the allegorical illustration of the Bad Government and its Effects on the urban and rural environment. On the other long wall, the one behind entrants, Lorenzetti represented the Effects of Good Government both in the city and the country.

In her anthropological essay, Maria Luisa Meoni (2001, p. 14) observes that already the arrangement of the representations that make up the cycle of frescoes

> indicates precise conceptual and pictorial choices: the surface most illuminated by the natural source – the window – contains the Allegory of Good Government; in front of those who enter, there are painted the allegory and the effects of the Bad Government, which communicate an immediate sense of unease due to the desolation of devastation and war, the dark and livid hues that mark sterility and disorder, moral and civil. We are therefore urged to turn to the other two walls, in spatial succession from left to right, for the viewer, where the allegorical representation of the Good Government unfolds and the illustration of its Effects on society takes place. The reading of this fresco requires a vision of the whole, precisely because each of the walls of the cycle is – as we have seen – closely

related to the others, from the point of view of spatial dislocation, for the conceptual structure, and for the artistic choices.

To complete the picture related to the cycle of Good Government, it should be added that the three frescoed walls are separate and, at the same time, connected to each other by the fictitious architecture of frames, inscriptions, and the movement of the painted light, which goes from left to right, as does that of the window.

Taken together, therefore, these frescoes are too large to be captured at a glance and from a single vantage point. Precisely for this reason I went several times to look at them. These frescoes impose the sensitive construction of a path, the comprehension through the images of the flow that, from the obscure oppression of tyranny – the winged harp "Timor," that is, terror – leads to the visual experience of the philosophical and political organizing of the social ethics of the city.

This visual experience illustrates the importance of the interconnections between the "beautiful" and the "good" and between aesthetic philosophies and moral philosophies that I have discussed in a recent essay on the beauty of responsible management (Strati, 2020). I wrote it with reference to the "Italian industrial design" created at the Olivetti, a leading company in the production of typewriters and computers, for the intimate link between aesthetics and ethics (Gaut, 2007) that characterizes the social practices of this project of organizing industrial design.

Olivetti's design has become the emblem of Italian design (De Fusco, 2002) and still symbolizes Italian design, despite the relevance of Italian postmodernist design, Radical Design, and Anti-Design (Fiell, Fiell, & Rossi, 2013). Even a typewriter, in fact, is able to evoke the specific style of living the daily working life and the particular form of feeling the relationship between work time and non-working time (Sudjic, 2008, p. 49) which characterized the responsible and humanistic management in Olivetti, from the work process and organizational communication to the company library, the company canteen, the company kindergarten, and the workers' housing.

Also the working life represented by Lorenzetti in the cycle of Good and Bad Government shows the relevance of the relationship between the aesthetic dimension and the social ethics, as I will illustrate in the next section.

Citizenship and the Aesthetic Redemption of Working Life

In the cycle of frescoes of Buon Governo, the fact that the depictions are marked by writing responds to the republican dream and to the ideal of social justice and citizenship. These are epigraphs, quotations, and inscriptions designed to explain literally – and in two languages, Latin and Italian – the figurative apparatus.

The explanatory inscriptions that bind the image symbolically represent the writing that the Sienese citizen appropriates to the detriment of the monopoly that, at that time, both the clergy and the lawyers, and the aristocracy, had on writing (Starn, 1994; Italian trans. 1996, pp. 20–21). The cycle of frescoes by Buon Governo maintains, in fact, the communication project of the ideal and philosophical dream of the republican political cause.

This dream is rendered in the allegories of the cycle of frescoes without the presence of the nobility and the clergy. "The idealized city of Lorenzetti and its *contado* [countryside] are places where life is not only prosperous but also remarkably secular" – Quentin Skinner (2003, p. 137) writes – and we do not see any more the representation "of the lives of these thousands of monks, nuns, friars and other parish priests who lived in Siena at the time."

Instead, we see useful and necessary activities, those of work in the city and in the fields: "the attention of Ambrogio Lorenzetti to the moments of work, to the possession of the necessary expertise to effectively perform a technical operation, expresses a sort of redemption, even aesthetic" – observes Maria Luisa Meoni (2001, p. 55) – which must be connected to an enhancement of their social function, for which the accuracy, elegance, and subtlety of some depictions of work situations seem destined "to enhance their built-in skills and competences."

> High up, at the top of a building, a group of masons, to document the care in architectural interventions in an expanding city. The attention with which Ambrogio [Lorenzetti] paints the workers goes beyond the simple narrative element: as we will also be able to detect on other occasions, the figures of the operators – including a woman – acquire elegance from being fixed in precise postures and technical gestures; almost a trait of "nobility" that enhances the aspects of social utility of the work, and at the same time emphasizes in an original way the knowledge, skills and bodily attitudes of those who perform it.
>
> (Ibid., p. 34)

Lorenzetti is the "artist–philosopher" of this aesthetic redemption of work through the artistic interpretation of micro-working practices and atmospheres and of the conditions of the world of work.

But we must not run into the error of getting out of symbolism and allegory. These frescoes do not document the life of work in the Siena of the fourteenth century. Rather, they depict the republican dream of citizenship and aesthetic redemption of the work, putting into action concrete elements between them. How the painter Dosso Dossi will do two centuries later, frescoing the halls of the Castello del Buon Consiglio in Trento, "they do not correspond to any precise concept of reality" but "remain convincing, engaging, moving" – the art historian Claudio Strinati (2009, p. 94) underlines – precisely because they are part of a "realm of painting," which constitutes "the sovereign realm of a convincing fantasy in itself, and at the same time is explicitly not true," nor even likely, and which has an "unstable equilibrium" while it leads us to immerse ourselves in a fascinating and mysterious world.

It is within this framework that we understand how Ambrogio Lorenzetti manages to place two ethical–political themes at the centre of his ideal of good governance: that of justice and that of the subordination of private interest to the common good. It is always within this framework that, as Meoni (2001, p. 16) points out, the representation of the Municipality of Siena is explicit on the level of the allegories of republican citizenship and that, moreover, this representation presents a very significant ambivalence. It

> symbolically represents the Bene *del* Comune [Good *of the* Municipality] and at the same time, by a happy coincidence, the Bene *comune* [*common* good] of all citizens. The reference to the concrete situation in Siena is intertwined with the ideal ethical-political message.

The relationship between the aesthetic dimension and the ethical dimension of the "organizing" is enhanced. After all, observes Pierre Guillet de Monthoux (2008, p. 74), art

> has always been considered an aesthetic gateway to ethical reflection and judgement. Although art provides subjective pleasure and sensuous experience, its philosophical task is to engage in the great quest for objective common truth. Kant emphasizes that the strength of aesthetics is that people organize around a work of art that charms them in ways impossible to grasp by theoretical concepts. In the same way Friedrich Schiller saw art – in this case, the role of a court theater – as the organizer of morality through the aesthetic judgement of the spectators of a play.

At the end of this section, I return to the fact that the cycle of frescoes in the Sala dei Nove, now called Sala della Pace, or the pictorial art of Ambrogio Lorenzetti, fascinated me so much, but not only for its aesthetic beauty. The social ethics, the civic ethics, the republic that the artist depicts with so much beauty has its beauty in its turn: the aesthetic dimension and the ethical dimension turned out to be intimately connected to each other (Strati, 2020), and it is like if painting should "depict rather than beauty in itself, rather than the triumph of the aesthetic dimension, the ethical dimension" (Strinati, 2009, p. 130).

With the warning that, as I have already observed, with Ambrogio Lorenzetti – one of the great Tuscan painters who, together with Giotto, owed the invention of perspective, that is, the organization of space in painting "according to which a surface gives the sensation of depth" (Strinati, 2009, p. 95) – we are in the presence of

> a work of *self-representation*: that [the work of self-representation of the Sienese republican value] commissioned for political propaganda purposes by the Government of the Nine and that [again the work of self-representation] of the ideals of the artist who, for a happy convergence, depicts the utopian aspiration for a Siena that is joyful, serene, festive and laborious, safe and reassuring in relation to its territory, because it is orderly and well governed.
>
> Therefore, it is worth stressing that Ambrogio Lorenzetti builds the masterpiece by harmonizing the concrete elements in a grandiose and ideologically structured design that depicts an ideal vision through real references.
>
> (Meoni, 2001, pp. 12–13)

Art Reveals the Philosophical Foundations of Organizing

At this point, I could put an end to my brief reflections on art and organizing because I have already clarified the aesthetic sentiments and philosophical considerations that the cycle of frescoes of Buon Governo has gradually aroused in my fifteen years of teaching at the University of Siena. But the fact is that there is more: the frescoes of Buon Governo constitute an artistic document that corrects the interpretation of what is itself a philosophical foundation of the Sienese republican dream.

Lorenzetti, in fact, is not only the artist–philosopher of whom Giorgio Vasari wrote already – he is the author of a work of art that "demonstrates that the emergence of the new principles of civic ethics at work in the pre-humanist republican ideology predates the diffusion of scholastic Aristotelianism, and in any case is independent of it," writes Olivier Christin (2003, p. 12).

It is a precious artistic–philosophical revelation (Skinner, 1986) because it illustrates "a special view of citizenship" and, observes Skinner (2003, p. 114), it is "from these modest origins, rather than from the impact of Aristotelianism, that the classical republicanism of Machiavelli, Guicciardini, and their contemporaries was born. The political theory of the Renaissance owes more to Rome than to Greece." This "philosophy of republican freedom," comments Christin (2003, p. 12) at the close of the Preface to Skinner's writings on the frescoes of Good and Bad Government,

> borrows in fact first of all from the Roman authors, Cicero first, but also Sallust or Seneca. The history of political philosophy prior to the British revolution and the formation of liberal ideology can no longer ignore this other conception, neo-Roman, of the freedom that then emerges. The interpretation of the iconographic program of the Lorenzetti frescoes is, in this, the starting point for a profound re-reading of the foundations of modern political thought.

Epilogue

Perhaps my desire to look repeatedly at the cycle of Good and Bad Government and to breathe the atmosphere of aesthetics (Strati, 2009) of the Sala dei Nove – or Sala della Pace – lies precisely in this mixture of aesthetic feelings originating from art and philosophy, from painting and writing, from aesthetic beauty and ethical beauty, from the aesthetic materiality of the frescoes that is capable of organizational communication even centuries later.

The art we are leaving now – that of Lorenzetti – was great and led me to reflect on fundamental aspects of the moral philosophy and the political philosophy that characterized the relationship between art and organizing in the Republic of Siena in the 1300s. This art, so decidedly immersed in political ideals, was able to respond to its commission with an artistic–philosophical perspective.

It was, that is, a "practical" art that had its own foundations in the "practical" philosophy that originated in ancient Rome and then developed with Niccolò Machiavelli, with Giambattista Vico, and, more recently, with the Italian thought always oriented in the world of historical and political life (Esposito, 2010). It is an art of great civic value, that of Ambrogio Lorenzetti and the cycle of frescoes of Buon Governo, because it is art that, in describing the organizing – imaginary and ideal – of the Republican democracy of the Municipality of Siena, creates community, that is, performs the "organizing."

References

Aesthesis. International Journal of Art and Aesthetics in Management and Organizational Life (2008). Special themed issue on "Aesthetics / The Construction and Re-construction of Memories of Organizational Life", 2/1. Edited by P. Guillet de Monthoux and A. Strati. (A selection of articles is available at the Aesthesis Archive: https://digitalcommons.wpi.edu/aesthesis)

Braidotti, R. (2013). *The posthuman*. Cambridge, UK: Polity Press.

Carr, A., & Hancock, P. (Eds.). (2003). *Art and aesthetics at work*. Basingstoke, UK: Palgrave Macmillan.

Christin, O. (2003). Preface. In Q. Skinner (Ed.), *L'artiste en philosophe politique: Ambrogio Lorenzetti et le Bon Gouvernement* (pp. 7–12). Paris, France: Éditions Raisons d'Agir.

De Fusco, R. (2002). *Storia del design*. Roma, Bari, Italy: Laterza.

Esposito, R. (2010). *Pensiero vivente. Origine e attualità della filosofia italiana*. Torino, Italy: Einaudi. (English trans.: *Living Thought. The Origins and Actuality of Italian Philosophy*. Stanford, CA: Stanford University Press, 2012).

Fiell, C., & Fiell, P. with Rossi, C. (2013). *Masterpieces of Italian design*. London, UK: Goodman Fiell.

Gagliardi, P. (Ed.). (1990). *Symbols and artifacts: Views of the corporate landscape*. Berlin, Germany: de Gruyter.

Gaut, B. (2007). *Art, emotion and ethics*. Oxford, UK: Oxford University Press.

Gherardi, S., & Strati, A. (2012). *Learning and knowing in practice-based studies*. Cheltenham, UK, Northampton, MA: Edward Elgar Publishing.

Guillet de Monthoux, P. (2004). *The art firm: Aesthetic management and metaphysical marketing from Wagner to Wilson*. Stanford, CA: Stanford Business Books.

Guillet de Monthoux, P. (2008). Arts and organizations. In S. Clegg & J. R. Bailey (Eds.), *International encyclopedia of organization studies* (pp. 72–74). London, UK: Sage.

Human Relations (2002). Special issue on "Organising aesthetics", 55/7. Edited by A. Strati & P. Guillet de Monthoux.

Johansson Sköldberg, U., Woodilla, J., & Berthoin Antal, A. (Eds.). (2016). *Artistic interventions in organizations: Research, theory and practice*. London, UK: Routledge.

King, I. W., & Vickery, J. (Eds.). (2013). *Experiencing organisations: New aesthetic perspectives*. Faringdon, England: Libri Publishing.

Kostera, M. (1997). The Kitsch-Organization. *Studies in Culture, Organization and Societies, 3*(3), 163–177.

Linstead, S., & Höpfl, H. (Eds.). (2000). *The aesthetic of organization*. London, UK: Sage.

Meoni, M. L. (2001). *Utopia e realtà nel Buon Governo di Ambrogio Lorenzetti: tipologie formali nella rappresentazione dell'agire dell'uomo. Un'analisi* antropologica. Firenze: Edizioni IFI.

Organization Studies (2018). Special issue on "Organizational creativity, play and entrepreneurship", 39/2–3. Edited by D. Hjorth, A. Strati, S. Drakopoulou Dodd & E. Weik.

Organizational Aesthetics (2016). Special issue on "Dance", 5/1. Edited by B. Biehl-Missal & C. Springborg.

Pareyson, L. (1954). *Estetica. Teoria della formatività*. Torino: Edizioni di "Filosofia". Reprinted 1988, Milano, Italy: Bompiani. (Partial English trans.: *Existence, interpretation, freedom: Selected writings*. Edited by PD Bubbio. Aurora, CO: The Davies Group, 2009).

Sartwell, C. (2003). Aesthetics of the everyday. In J. Levinson (Ed.), *The Oxford handbook of aesthetics* (pp. 761–770). Oxford, UK: Oxford University Press.

Scalfi Eghenter, A. (2018). Organizational creativity, play and entrepreneurship. *Organization Studies, 39*(2–3), 169–190.

Scandinavian Journal of Management (2014). Special issue on "Art and Management", 30/1. Edited by S. Meisiek & D. Barry.
Simmel, G. (1908). *Soziologie. Untersuchungen über die Formen der Vergesellschaftung*. Leipzig, Germany: Dunker & Humblot. (English trans.: *Sociology. Inquiries into the construction of social forms*, Vol. I–II. Edited by A. J. Blasi, A. K. Jacobs & M. Kanjireathinkal. Leiden, Netherlands: Brill, 2009).
Skinner, Q. (1986). Ambrogio Lorenzetti: The artist as political philosopher. *Proceedings of the British Academy, 72*, 1–56.
Skinner, Q. (2003). *L'artiste en philosophe politique: Ambrogio Lorenzetti et le Bon Gouvernement*. Paris, France: Éditions Raisons d'Agir.
Starn, R. (1994). *The Palazzo Pubblico, Siena*. New York, NY: George Braziller. (Italian trans.: *Ambrogio Lorenzetti: Palazzo Pubblico a Siena*. Torino, Italy: Società Editrice Internazionale, 1996).
Strati, A. (1999). *Organization and aesthetics*. London, UK: Sage.
Strati, A. (2009). 'Do you do beautiful things?': Aesthetics and art in qualitative methods of organization studies. In D. Buchanan & A. Bryman (Eds.), *The Sage handbook of organizational research methods* (pp. 230–245). London, UK: Sage. Reprinted in S. Gherardi & Strati, A. (2012). *Learning and knowing in practice-based Studies*. Cheltenham, UK: Edward Elgar, pp. 194–209.
Strati, A. (2019). *Organizational theory and aesthetic philosophies*. New York, NY: Routledge.
Strati, A. (2020). Beauty of responsible management: The lens and methodology of organizational aesthetics. In O. Laasch, D. Jamali, E. Freeman, & R. Suddaby (Eds.), *The research handbook of responsible management* (pp. 410–419). Cheltenham, UK and Northampton, MA: Edward Elgar Publishing.
Strati, A., & Guillet de Monthoux, P. (2002). Introduction: Organizing aesthetics. *Human Relations, 55*(7), 755–766.
Strinati, C. (2009). *Il mestiere dell'artista. Da Raffaello a Caravaggio*. Palermo, Italy: Sellerio.
Taylor, S. S., & Ladkin, D. (2009). Understanding arts-based methods in managerial development. *Academy of Management Learning & Education, 8*(1), 55–69.
Yuedi, L., & Carter, C. L. (Eds.). (2014). *Aesthetics of everyday life: East and west*. Newcastle upon Tyne, England: Cambridge Scholars Publishing.

3 The Incompleteness Theorem

The Importance of Reinterpretation in Management Studies

Jerzy Kociatkiewicz

Abraham Maslow was a psychologist whose most significant texts focused on motivation understood as a psychological phenomenon. However, he, and his concept of the hierarchy of needs, commonly described and visualized as Maslow's Pyramid, found enduring fame within the field of management studies, in which scholars and students try to understand motivation as an organizational issue that needs to be addressed through managerial means. The idea of hierarchical ordering of needs is easy to understand: basic necessities such as safety and food have to be addressed before an individual can even begin to worry about social relations or self-fulfilment. It is similarly easy to visualize: levels of a pyramid, starting from its very broad foundations, represent the consecutively fulfilled needs; even such a stout and solid building would collapse if we attempted to build it out of order. Moreover, the concept is also easy to critique (which is always useful for textbook presentations), from its flimsy theoretical or empirical foundations to dubious claims of universality spanning cultural and individual differences. However, as Bridgman, Cummings, and Ballard. (2019) demonstrate, such recasting involves considerable drift in the use of Maslow's ideas: to start with, the very notion of a pyramid (or a triangle, if one were to take the most common visual representation literally) cannot be found anywhere in Maslow's writings, nor could the authors find any recollection of Maslow ever employing this metaphor verbally. Similarly, individual variation becomes much more of an issue when we try to apply the concept to groups of people, such as organizations, rather than to specific human beings.

Nor is the drift of meaning restricted to the thought of Abraham Maslow, or even to interpretations crossing academic domains. Thus, for example, rereading the writings of Henry Ford and Frederick Taylor, both known as the "founding fathers" of the mechanistic and dehumanizing approach of Scientific Management (or Taylorism), reveals surprising levels of concern for the common good and the well-being of workers (Kociatkiewicz & Kostera, 2019).

There are many ways we could react to rereadings (own or other readers') contradicting the established interpretations. Dismay at the distortions present in previous readings is perhaps the simplest one, but also the most reductive. It assumes our current reading as the definitive one, free from the biases accumulated from previous interpretations. This is not an unproblematic assumption, as it not only conflates interpretation with distortion, but also ignores any biases and blinkers we bring into the text. A subtler position is the one taken by Bridgman et al. (2019), who conclude their rereading of Maslow's texts by inviting the readers to recognize that the field of management studies is full of

> ideas filtered through our field's long-standing commitments to free-market capitalism, managerialism, organizational hierarchies, and the primacy of the individual.
>
> (p. 94)

As a response, they propose reflection and a rethinking of our academic domain, culminating in the creation of new readings that are "based on different events, times, people and places than have dominated to date" (ibid.). Such reinterpretations would, necessarily, reflect our own political and rhetorical positions, but could open up the possibilities for making the repertoire of management studies knowledge available for a wider array of organizational endeavours, including ones openly critical of the dominant capitalist discourse. This is certainly an important and timely endeavour: as Martin Parker (2018) has convincingly argued, contemporary schools of business and management serve largely as ideologically laden schools of capitalism, and as the contributory (or even leading) role of capitalist power and property relations in fostering social end ecological crisis becomes ever more apparent (Cederström & Fleming, 2012; Klein, 2014), the imperative of developing new discourses and new ways of working becomes ever more urgent.

The wish to engage with contemporary societal problems chimes well with the common justification for the existence of management and organization studies (and even social science in general): they promise to provide "implications for practice" (most commonly and rather shallowly interpreted as advice given to managers, but possible to understand as providing tools for solving organizational problems in ways beneficial to wide social groups). Unfortunately, our discipline's track record in this regard is not particularly heartening: managerial advice offered by academic publications is neither read by managers (e.g., only 2% of marketing managers of large computing enterprises surveyed by Bennett, 2007, reported reading academic texts). Methods for examining the quality of such advice are practically non-existent, and popularizing management bestsellers, from Peters and Waterman's (1982) *In Search of Excellence* to Kim and Mauborgne's (2005) *Blue Ocean Strategy* and beyond, have largely failed to create organizational success (Piazza & Abrahamson, 2020) beyond providing a steady income stream for their authors and undeniable reading pleasure for their readers. There is little reason to expect that widening the addressed audience from managers to all organizational participants and changing focus from financial success to achieving societal goals is likely to improve the actual impact considerably. I should note here that the same criticism could be applied to most social sciences: development of psychology has not resulted in a happier society, nor has the growth of sociology solved the multitude of observable social malaises. Political science has done little to help us build a particularly fair or fair-sighted society. All the aforementioned disciplines, including management studies, have of course found numerous solutions to various particular problems in areas ranging from decision making (Nightingale, 2008) to office design (Pitchforth, Nelson-White, van den Helder & Oosting, 2020) to promoting diversity (Daugherty, Wilson & Chowdhury, 2019); yet, our workplaces continue to be just as alienating (Kalekin-Fishman & Langman, 2015) and infused with bullying (Wright, 2020), time wasting (Graeber, 2018), and form filling (Graeber, 2015) as any in recorded history of work.

This leads us to the other justification for social sciences: providing explanation of social phenomena, promoting understanding that is not necessarily linked to any active ability to change the world. But even here, the situation is not overly rosy: the published explanatory research is largely ignored and quickly forgotten (for most publications) or taken up and then hotly disputed. Thus, while creating a list of the most significant organization and management studies publications might seem a daunting and contentious task (though various literature reviews routinely point out key works and theories), creating a list of significant findings in our discipline appears impossible (and very few texts endeavour to do so).

Yet, my aim is not to condemn social science, or management studies, as a failed project. The aforementioned criticisms of common justifications for management as an academic discipline are valid, but only because of the weakness of offered justifications. The vocational (teaching good management) and scientistic (explaining organizations) models of management studies create expectations that are impossible to meet and irrelevant in identifying research of lasting (or, indeed, any) value. And yet, the field of management is clearly successful in attracting the attention of both scholars and students and provides a rich vocabulary for identifying and discussing organizational goals, problems, and solutions. Such vocabulary is both rooted in various empirical studies and continually contested (from within as well from outside our discipline). But to understand its value we need to reconsider the expectation that social science will create large amounts of knowledge of lasting value. What management studies scholars create, instead, is a vast repertoire of field material and theories which can be reinterpreted and recontextualized, providing tools for making sense (rather than providing ready-made sense) of the incredibly complex world of organizations we live in.

Such recontextualization can involve quite radical reinterpretations of original material. Alf Rehn (2001) conducted an ethnographic study of computer pirates:[1] groups of enthusiasts involved in the illegal practice of distributing (for free and to a wide audience) of copyrighted software. To describe these porous and largely informal organizations, he needed a model that could be used to explain the curious combination of altruism and competitiveness, generosity and status consciousness which he observed in his research. He found the needed model in Marcel Mauss's anthropological theory of the gift economy, devised to explain gift exchanges observed in North American and Polynesian tribes at the turn of the twentieth century (though also, admittedly, proposed as a blueprint for a more general explanation of gift giving). Societies described by Mauss and his predecessors were quite different from the contemporary software pirates – rigid in their structures and largely governed by tradition, expecting lifelong participation from their members, geographically localized, and having access only to relatively simple technologies. Alf Rehn's pirates share none of these characteristics and, consequently, their gift economy is quite different from that described by Mauss. Nevertheless, I believe the analogy largely holds, and it is clear that Mauss's studies have made it easier to understand and explain the relationships binding software pirates.

Similarly, the same field material (sometimes augmented by new research) can be used to support a variety of different, and often conflicting, theoretical explanations. The story of the unexpected success of Honda Cub in the United States provides a good example. The rapidly expanding Japanese motorcycle manufacturer Honda decided, in the late 1950s, to expand its business into the potentially lucrative American market. After some initial difficulties, it achieved considerable success by selling Honda Cub, a small scooter-like motorcycle, serving a niche not catered for by existing manufacturers. The reasons for the success were probed by Boston Consulting Group (1975), with the resultant report highlighting economies of scale and learning curve effect: Honda was able to create a new market for its products, scale up production quickly, and continue to improve its manufacturing processes. Almost a decade later, and following additional interviews with the company's managers involved in setting up the American dealerships, Richard Pascale (1984) offered a competing explanation: the success could be attributed to luck, serendipity, and ability to learn from organizational and managerial mistakes. Later scholars provided other interpretations, showcasing explanations ranging from core competency in engine design and manufacturing (Hamel & Prahalad, 1996) to effective marketing campaign (Benjamin, 1993). Years later, the competing interpretations were themselves reinterpreted as empirical material for a study of how differing causal explanations are shaped by research interests and dissemination aims (Runde & de Rond, 2010).

Neither of the above examples supports the notion of management studies as a discipline producing stable knowledge, but both show the possibility of rereading, reuse, and reinterpretation of previously produced academic knowledge. And to help us make sense of the usefulness of such unstable material, I believe it can be helpful to turn outside – to the world of arts and art criticism where the possibility of constant reinterpretation and recontextualization of already evaluated and theorized works does not appear overly problematic. In its simplest form, this possibility is realized through continued appreciation of new stagings of old plays, of changing evaluation of the work of artists of bygone ages, or of new critical treatments of classic (as well as neglected) works as they continue to find new relevance to new generations of audiences. More specific arguments showcase the role of a specific reader or of the polyvocality of works of arts interpreted in different contexts.

Numerous literary scholars writing in the 1960s made a compelling case for reading as an active instance of meaning-making that cannot be reduced to a more or less successful reception of authorial intent. Umberto Eco (1989), in a text originally published in 1962, posits openness to multiple interpretations, never completely determined by the author, as a desirable characteristic in any artistic endeavour. He also imagines closed works, which do not allow such freedom, but deems them as less worthy of appreciation. Most contemporary manuals of academic style, in contrast, promote closedness by stressing clarity and single possible readings. Thus, LaPlaca, Lindgreen, and Vanhamme (2018) suggest that wannabes should actually check for such singularity:

> Authors could send just the introduction to six people not connected with the research and ask them to describe
>
> 1 The research question or the manuscript's contribution.
> 2 The underlying framework of the research.
> 3 The gap that the research will fill and the importance of doing so.
>
> If the responses to the above three questions vary among the people, the writing is not clear and needs improvement (p. 204).

I might note that the standards of unequivocal writings are clearly slipping: Septuagint, the earliest extant translation of the Hebrew Bible into Greek, derives its name from the claim that the entire text was translated independently by seventy different scholars, each arriving at the exact same text. It should be obvious by now that, even in the case of academic texts, I side with Eco rather than with LaPlaca et al. Most academic texts are read for a purpose (rather than for pleasure) and that purpose rarely coincides completely with authorial expectations. To pluck an example almost at random, I do not expect LaPlaca et al. conceived their text's contribution as showcasing an attempt to limit readerly freedom among academics.

And, Septuagint notwithstanding, translation is always a problematic act of reinterpretation. George Steiner (1975) uses the vicissitudes of translation to examine the issue of changing context: accurate translation requires not only finding word or sentence equivalents in the target language, but also the ability to evoke similar reactions (emotive and cognitive) and associations in readers of the translated text as the effect that the original text has on native readers. To do so, the translator needs to understand the context of both the original and the target language, including usage patterns, common and clichéd phrases, and audience expectations. But all of these change over time in both languages, in different directions and at different speeds. Other factors, such as appreciation for fluidity versus accuracy, change as well. Consequently, every act of translation is tied to the date of its creation and ages differently than the original text. And the problem is not confined to reading translated works: both Shakespeare and Chaucer employed contemporary (and often cutting-edge) idiom; yet, when read hundreds of years later, their writing styles (as well as the spelling) strike the reader as distinctly archaic. Which audiences require updating (and what form this updating should take) remains a perennial question.

Good academic texts (of which, admittedly, there are not that many) are similarly read by various audiences in different circumstances, bringing in not only their own aims, but also their own theoretical frameworks and corpus of significant texts. One of the great contributions of collated internet databases of academic texts has been the increased ease of searching for and accessing texts from across disciplinary boundaries, and diverse audiences inevitably lead to diverse interpretations (this insight constitutes, to me, one of the most important general contributions of feminist and postcolonial scholarship). Moreover, texts are not only read by different readers, they are also reread by the same reader in varying circumstances. As academics, we often return to significant works, in search of deeper understanding, to refresh our memories before lectures, or just to find quotes for use in our own writing. Christopher Cannon (2013) shows how the same text can be read by the same person in different ways, how rereading can take multiple forms, and how deeply it can change our understanding or appreciation of the reencountered work.

One of the most famous works dealing with the inevitable multiplicity of interpretations is Roland Barthes's (1977) essay "The Death of the Author." The proclaimed death is that of the genericized, demiurgic figure of the text-controlling author, supplanted by the active reader able to freely reinterpret the work according to his or her own perspective.

Is this an apt metaphor for the possibility of (re)reading academic texts? There is certainly a case to be made that Abraham Maslow of management textbooks and of Bridgman et al.'s rereading cannot be reintegrated into a single authorial figure.

All of the above ruminations have been based on an appreciation of management studies writing as a literary genre (Czarniawska-Joerges, 1995), a specific practice of producing texts holding many similarities to other literary practices and subject to similar readerly treatments as works usually classified as fiction or *belles-lettres.* And it is this need for engagement by the reader which constitutes the incompleteness theorem of the title: because new readers (and new readings) are always possible, no text, academic or otherwise, is ever fully complete. But it is also an exhortation for us as academic authors to invite readers' participation – by making academic texts engrossing and beautiful rather than just informative.

But if, as I claim, the role of management studies is to provide tools for interpreting and discussing the world of organization, it is easy to object that other forms of art also provide such tools, often much more interestingly or beautifully presented: films, novels, paintings, and videogames all offer us new possibilities of exploring and interpreting the social world. Good art offers new ways of seeing our life and our surroundings (Berger, 1973). Which, of course, leaves us with the nagging question of whether the tools provided by management studies, in the form of books, journal articles, study reports, models, and theories, are the most useful ones for making sense of the domain claimed by the academic discipline: the world of organizations. Unfortunately (or fortunately, depending on one's attitude towards ambiguity and doubt), it is not a question that lends itself to an easy answer. But there is no need to advocate for exclusivity. Management scholars should, as this very book strongly demonstrates, be able to use art to help build compelling interpretations of the organizational world. But they should also take care to write in ways which provide tools for readers, both academic and from outside academia, for use in their own quests of sense-making and pattern building.

Note

1 In the book, Alf Rehn insists on distinguishing between profit-driven pirates who sell illegally acquired software, and warezonians, the apparently altruistic subjects of his study. For the sake of simplicity, and because in other studies the term "pirate" is often also applied to the latter group, I chose to stick to the more common term here.

References

Barthes, R. (1977). The death of the author. In: R. Barthes (Ed.), *Image music text* (pp. 142–148). London, UK: Fontana Press.

Benjamin, C. (1993). Honda and the art of competitive manoeuvre. *Long Range Planning, 26*(4), 22–31.

Bennett, R. (2007). Sources and use of marketing information by marketing managers. *Journal of Documentation, 63*(5), 702–726.

Berger, J. (1973). *Ways of seeing.* London, UK: Penguin.

Boston Consulting Group (1975). *Strategy alternatives for the British motorcycle industry.* London, UK: H.M. Stationery Office.

Bridgman, T., Cummings, S., & Ballard, J. (2019). Who built Maslow's Pyramid? A history of the creation of management studies' most famous symbol and its implications for management education. *Academy of Management Learning & Education, 18*(1) 81–98.

Cannon, C. (2013). The art of rereading. *ELH, 80*(2), 401–425.

Cederström, C., & Fleming, P. (2012). *Dead man working.* Winchester, England: Zero Books.

Czarniawska-Joerges, B. (1995). Narration or science? Collapsing the division in organization studies. *Organization, 2*(1), 11–33.

Daugherty, P. P., Wilson, H. J., & Chowdhury, R. (2019). Using artificial intelligence to promote diversity. *MIT Sloan Management Review, 60*(2), 10.

Eco, U. (1989). *The open work.* Cambridge, MA: Harvard University Press.

Graeber, D. (2015). *The utopia of rules: On technology, stupidity, and the secret joys of bureaucracy.* Brooklyn, NY: Melville House.

Graeber, D. (2018). *Bullshit jobs: A theory.* New York, NY: Simon & Schuster.

Hamel, G., & Prahalad, C.K. (1996). *Competing for the future.* Boston, MA: Harvard Business School Press.

Kalekin-Fishman, D., & Langman, L. (2015). Alienation: The critique that refuses to disappear. *Current Sociology Review, 63*(6), 916–933.

Kim, W. Chan, & Mauborgne, R. (2005). *Blue Ocean strategy. How to create uncontested market space and make the competition irrelevant.* Boston, MA: Harvard Business School Press.

Klein, N. (2014). *This changes everything. Capitalism vs. the climate.* New York, NY: Simon & Schuster.

Kociatkiewicz, J., & Kostera, M. (2019). Textual *Flâneurie*: Writing management with Walter Benjamin. *Ephemera, 19*(1), 163–178.

LaPlaca, P., Lindgreen, A., & Vanhamme, J. (2018). How to write really good articles for premier academic journals. *Industrial Marketing Management, 68*, 202–209.

Nightingale, J. (2008) *Think smart, act smart: Avoiding the business mistakes that even intelligent people make.* Hoboken, NJ: John Wiley & Sons.

Parker, M. (2018). *Shut down the business school.* London, UK: Pluto Press.

Pascale, R. (1984). Perspectives on strategy: The real story behind Honda's success. *California Management Review, 26*, 47–72.

Peters, T., & Waterman, R. H. Jr. (1982). *In search of excellence. Lessons from America's best-run companies.* New York, NY: Harper & Row.

Piazza, A., & Abrahamson, E. (2020). Fads and fashions in management practices: Taking stock and looking forward. *International Journal of Management Reviews, 22*(3), 264–286.

Pitchforth, J., Nelson-White, E., van den Helder, M., & Oosting, W. (2020). The work environment pilot: An experiment to determine the optimal office design of a technology company. *PLoS One, 15*(5), e0232943.

Rehn, A. (2001). *Electronic Potlatch.* Stockholm, Sweden: Royal Institute of Technology.

Runde, J., & de Rond, M. (2010). Evaluating causal explanations of specific events. *Organization, 31*(4), 431–450.

Steiner, G. (1975). *After Babel: Aspects of language and translation.* Oxford, UK: Oxford University Press.

Wright, S. (2020). Hierarchies and bullying. An examination into the drivers for workplace harassment within organization. *Transnational Corporations Review, 12*(2), 162–172.

4 Hula Hoops and Cigars, Hiccups and Stutters

Thinking with Film about Organizational Control

Luc Peters and Anke Strauß

A city. We follow a camera slowly moving between its skyscrapers before focusing on the tallest one, which we learn is the headquarters of Hudsucker Industries. We enter the top floor where the board is gathered, old men in grey suits. A voice informs us that it is the end of the year and time has come to check the annual results. They are excellent and the financial director concludes, "Gentlemen, we are loaded" (Coen, Coen, & Raimi, 1994, p. 10). We then become aware of the CEO, Warren Hudsucker. He coughs and everything falls silent. Along with the board members, we observe him putting down his cigar and hear the ticking of his watch, which he takes off and places on the table. He then climbs onto the long board table, starts running, and jumps out of the window of the top floor of the Hudsucker building to make "abstract art on Madison Avenue" (Coen, Coen, & Raimi, 1994, p. 18).

This first scene of the film *The Hudsucker Proxy* (Coen & Coen, 1994) left us as puzzled as the board members in the movie, and although it was one of many movies we watched together in the course of an ongoing conversation about how to engage film for organization theory beyond representational or illustrational purposes, we have been musing about *The Hudsucker Proxy* for over eight years. Watching it over and over again on numerous occasions and in all kind of places, we noticed that this film, like other art films, has many entrances and can thus produce many shapes of knowledge that otherwise might remain hidden from our curious eyes and ears.

For this contribution we go back to our puzzlement that the film's beginning evoked, to think about the mystery, or even better, the paradox of control that is basis for but also haunts management and organization theory and practice since its modernist beginnings, as the notion of non-control clings on to it like sibling in some sort of Siamese entanglement.

In this chapter we elaborate on this entanglement from a visual aesthetic perspective as we consider the twenty-first-century subject to be visually literate. Yet, we argue, the discourse of the eye and thus what can and what cannot be known of the world and how goes beyond straightforward representation. Visual knowing also reigns in the forms we use to order space and time and thus operates much more subtly on the ways we perceive, think, and imagine the world as controllable or not.

In Western societies people used to believe in an order of a higher kind – an order that comprised both nature and societies, an order one should not mess about with. The disintegration of this order in the French and consecutive revolutions, however, led to "the [shocking] discovery that human order is vulnerable, contingent and devoid of reliable foundation" (Bauman, 1992, p. xi). A response to that shock, Bauman says, "was a dream and an effort to make order solid, obligatory and reliably founded" (Bauman, 1992, p. xi). Order, now, was not recognized but made, and this modernist production of artificial order necessitates some form of control. One means of producing such order is practices and technologies of organizing. In the interior milieu of organizations one can operate on the assumption of order.

> The struggle for order, is a fight of determination against ambiguity, of semantic precision against ambivalence, of transparency against obscurity, clarity against fuzziness. The other of order is not another order: chaos is its only alternative. The other of order is the miasma of the indeterminate and unpredictable. The other is the uncertainty, that source and archetype of all fear.
>
> (Bauman, 1993, p. 7)

Thus, organizations are obsessed with control, and to steer the "ship" in the "right" direction, managers have developed numerous technologies of control that boil down reality into abstract figures to feed the desire for managing their interior and environment. Yet, holding on to the modernist will to order does not only imply investing considerable energy and effort in developing ever more sophisticated technologies of control to exclude, devalue, and keep at bay all the messy aspects of life that refuse to be brought into order. Current discussions, for instance, on climate change or precarization suggest that technologies of ordering themselves produce mess – and increasingly so. Having said that, we sense that mess and order are not binary positions; they are like Siamese twins drenched in chiaroscuro, the melting of black and white and in this case of control and non-control.

Abstractions do not only involve numbers or business models. They are also expressed – as we show in the following – in spatio-aesthetic figures such as straight lines or perfect circles, which shape how we perceive and operate in this world. Especially these spatio-aesthetic figures are not always deliberate abstractions geared to fulfill a specific task, such as corporate reporting. Instead, they are part of the basic pillars that constitute Western ways of thinking and are thus more sensed than made sense of. Thus, this subliminal tendency makes these spatio-aesthetic abstractions all the more powerful as secret agents of control. Their peculiar capacity of hiding, thus, constitutes a considerable challenge for gaining insight into the zone of tension between control and non-control.

When trying to make sense of the world, it is a common habit to translate perception into some sort of language. This language can assume a plethora of shapes and forms. Within organizations, written words or numbers are ways of translating that seem to be more solid and reliable than translations like gestures, chattering, chanting, screaming, or exhaling. At the same time, however, the seemingly precise character of numbers or linguistic expressions within organizations – and organization studies – fails to register that which is more sensed than made sense of. In contrast to that – we argue – art is a form of poetic expression that touches upon what is powerful because it cannot be directly boiled down to a singular concept, interpretation, or logic (Otto & Strauß, 2019; Linstead, 2018). Engaging with art, thus, has the potential to open up a world that is normally hidden from our perception in everyday life. In other words, art can kick us awake and make us wonder about what goes on before our eyes, what penetrates our ears or excites us in any other sensory way. Art's way of translating experiences of the world into certain forms and shapes using a wide variety of substances or materials does not only inform us of the way disruptions collide with the regular, the familiar, the ordinary. We believe that it thereby also increases our ability to diversify the ways in which we make sense of the world and therefore nurtures our capabilities of thinking difference, of imagining and inventing.

That is the reason why we decided to use *The Hudsucker Proxy* to engage with the relationship between control and non-control, between order and mess on the level of spatio-aesthetic figurations such as the obsession with straight lines and perfect circles and the way these are disrupted by uninvited guests.

We did so not only because we love film. We also did so because film combines sound and sight, can involve literature, painting, sculpting, or music and thus produces meaning on a multitude of levels. This doesn't mean that every film uses this potency. Popular films are geared towards reproducing what is known. Watching does not surprise but meets expectations. Relating to Deleuze (1986, 1989, in Peters (2016)), these films can be considered entertainment, in contrast to films as art. The difference between art and entertainment is that while the latter is killing time and putting us to sleep, the former is revealing time and kicking us awake. Being curious what and how film would kick us awake, we thus took seriously Deleuze's idea of film's potency – to make us think and engaged – with *The Hudsucker Proxy* (Coen & Coen, 1994).

The crucial role of (business) organizations in contemporary Western societies is mirrored in the number of films that deal with organizational life, such as *Modern Times* (Chaplin, 1936), *L'Eclisse* (Antonioni, 1962),

High & Low (Kurosawa, 1963), *Brazil* (Gilliam, 1985), *Office Space* (Judge, 1999), *The Naked* (Swiêtnicki, 2002), and *The Wolf of Wall Street* (Scorsese, 2013). One can find a similar variety in the approaches for sourcing film to generate insights on organizational life. With several exceptions (Earhart 2019; Peters 2016, 2019; Peters and Yue, 2018), most of the writings on film in organization studies seem to engage popular films with a specific focus on plot, genre, or representation of subjectivities. In contrast, we draw upon the musings of Deleuze's take on film as art. This does not make the plot fully irrelevant. But instead of reigning the centre of attention, the plot is only one element of a cinematic assemblage that displays many more entrances than just the plot. Therefore, we first give a short summary of the plot together with musings about how we watched *The Hudsucker Proxy*, before we delve into the spatio-aesthetic forms that are constitutive of it.

Watching *The Hudsucker Proxy*

The Hudsucker Proxy is a movie about organizational life in the aftermath of the death of the founder and CEO – Warren Hudsucker – involving employees at all levels, from the basement all the way up to the top floor of the board of directors, who try to steer the ship in a preferred direction. The movie starts with the aforementioned scene at the top floor of Hudsucker Industries' headquarters. The loss of their CEO and majority stockholder left the board of director speechless, also because Warren Hudsucker's childlessness meant that his shares of the company would be automatically sold to the public over the stock market, making the board accountable to external shareholders. Due to their tremendous annual results, Hudsucker Industries' market value was so high that the board could not afford buying the majority of the shares over the stock market, and so Sidney Mussburger (SM), the "second" man of the company, immediately takes charge with a plan to maintain control over the company: choosing a "schmuck" or an "imbecile" as their new CEO they would ruin Hudsucker Industries' market value so that the board would be in a position to buy stock cheap and thus maintain its majority of shares.

The possibility for executing this cunning plan becomes realistic when Norville Barnes – a graduate of the Muncie School of Business – enters the Hudsucker building just when Warren Hudsucker hits the pavement. Norville is looking for a job, and more importantly, a chance of realizing his invention. He happily shares his idea in a rather idiosyncratic manner with everyone who wants and does not want to know, that is, by showing them a red circle drawn on a piece of paper, accompanied by his words "You know, for kids," which people usually respond to with a bewildered look. Norville gets hired in the mailroom located in the basement and one of his first tasks is to deliver a letter to Sidney at the top floor.

When seizing his chance to show Sidney his exciting invention, Sidney is convinced that this is the imbecile he needs to execute his plan. Norville is appointed CEO and allowed to materialize the circle drawn on the paper to which the board responds with bewildered looks and the question "What the hell is it?" (Coen, Coen, & Raimi, 1994, p. 101). Nevertheless, he is allowed to proceed, and the company brands Norville's invention as the Hula Hoop. It seems like Sidney's plan works out perfectly as no one buys the hoops and Norville's dream turns out to be disastrous for the company's market value. However, due to a strange twist of fate, the Hula Hoop takes control of the situation and moves itself to success. Sidney's plan goes sour, and Norville solidifies his position as CEO while losing his naive excitement over the chorus of praise making him businessman of the year. Sidney tries to get rid of Norville as CEO by declaring him insane with the help of a German scientist. Unfortunately, his plan goes wrong again when former CEO Warren Hudsucker reappears – this time as an angel – demanding Norville to read out the letter he had to but did not deliver to Sidney:

> The new president must be free to fail – and learn; to fall – and rise again, by applying what he has learned. Such is business. Such is life. Accordingly, I hereby bequeath all of my shares in Hudsucker Industries to whomever [...] the board shall elect to succeed me as president.
>
> (Coen, Coen, & Raimi 1994, 153–154)

This means that Norville is the legitimate CEO and holder of the majority of shares, which closes the circle and brings the film to an end. While Sidney is devastated and ready to jump off the Hudsucker building, Norville, excited as ever, is presenting to the board of directors the prototype of his new invention (a circle that he sketched on a piece of paper): a Frisbee – "You know, for kids!"

How Do We Look at (Art) Films

As mentioned, this chapter on *The Hudsucker Proxy* wasn't written in one swift session behind a typewriter with the windows closed. No, it started long time ago after discovering our common fascination with the movie, which eventually left us only one option: watching it together. Watching it once was however not enough. The movie seduced or even demanded us to watch it again. We watched in while on a train from Berlin to Istanbul where we were to present our findings on this specific film at the 2011 Standing Conference of Organizational Symbolism (SCOS) conference. The insights gathered during this journey are to be found, largely, in this chapter. Being aware that watching it on a large screen with proper sound, just the way the Coen brothers must have intended it, is a very different experience than watching it on a computer screen – an experience that makes full use of its power of artistic expression – we also included it in the programme of the *CORPORATE BODIES Film Fest 2016* that we organized at the Filmhuis at The Hague.

But given that there are so many ways to watch a film, we feel bound to say some words on how we approached it. As we consider *The Hudsucker Proxy* a work of art, we suggest that the film does not operate independently of the intentions of the directors, Joel and Ethan Coen. This does not reduce the film to only one reading, quite the contrary. As a work of art, this film has a certain kind of openness that offers different entrances and can be read in various ways. This openness invites the viewer to engage with the film, interpret it in different ways, but at the same time, these readings cannot be made arbitrarily. The Coen brothers offer an aesthetic frame within which the viewer is asked to interpret the images they have created. Engaging with and thus meeting in this aesthetic frame, authors and audiences co-create the artwork.

Hence, the idea of using film as art goes beyond the idea of entertainment, although it can be entertaining. It goes beyond just the story or the representation. This implies that just like a painting or a book you can or should watch it over and over again, because it is not a static object, but a living and breathing concept that challenges the experiences and knowledge of the viewer. American director Robert Altman describes it as follows:

> The worst statement to my ears is when somebody asks, "Do you want to see this movie?" And someone else says, "Oh, I've seen it." If you see a film once, and it has any quality whatsoever, you haven't really seen it. Because the first time you watch a film, no matter how savvy you are to movies and techniques, you're playing "Whodunnit?" You're playing a guessing game: "Oh, she's going to leave him. No she didn't. Well she's probably a lesbian. Oh no she's not." And you're going through the film and finding out how all these suppositions are wrong. Well, now you know and you go and see it a second time: you're not faked out by the plot, you're able to deal with corners of the frame, with the nuances – which is what I feel the film is really about.
>
> (Altman in Thompson (2006, 153)

So we approached this project by watching *The Hudsucker Proxy* over and over again. We did not limit ourselves to always_watching it from beginning to end, but also engaged with parts of it or jumped through it, watched it without sound. As such, we did not chose a systematic approach but chose a more poetic method – as, for example, suggested by Maya Deren (2005) – to constantly discover new meanings or get excited for the repetition of ludicrous actions, events, or verbal expressions, looking at camera movements, the way in which frames are composed, what we can see in these frames, the way the various scenes are welded together as montage, and so on.

Doing so we noticed two design features as rather prominent in the whole aesthetic of the movie: the circle and the straight line. Only later we learnt that the Coen brothers intentionally built their film around these. They were "the design element which drives the movie. The tensions between straight lines and circles; you have these tall buildings, and then these circles everywhere which are echoed in the plot... in the structure of the movie itself" (Joel Coen in Woods, 2003). We thus decided to make these spatio-aesthetic figurations – the circle and the straight line – the analytical lens through which we engage with the notions of control/non-control in organizations.

Perfect Circles and Straight Lines

On the level of content, this movie explicitly engages with managerial notions of rationality and control but also with stock markets, inventions, production circles and shows how these get constantly disrupted. As mentioned, discipline and loss of control consume a pretty problematic but intense relationship. But it is especially on the level of form that this film is a rich resource for new knowledge creation on organizational life and management practices.

In the following we will therefore look at the aesthetic composition of three scenes that allow us to engage with the strange world of straight lines and perfect circles, the movements they enable, and the ways these intersect with other kinds of forms, dynamics, and movements. This informs us on how control becomes uncontrollable and how organization is not taking place despite disruption but how disruption and organization are entangled in complex and ambiguous relationships and how this challenges our notion of managing in organizations.

Scene 1: Circles and Cigars

The first scene starts when Norville Barnes is requested to deliver a "blue" letter to Sidney Mussburger. Sidney is on the phone doing "business" when Norville clumsily enters the huge, bombastic office, something exemplified by its sheer size and the massive horizontal lines that communicate the position of power that Sidney inhabits. On close examination, we see that the whole office consists exclusively of lines. It is structured in a rectangular way, an order that suggests transparency and control. The crosses of the huge windows seem to frame the world that lies behind them. They cut the world into little pieces that are assumed to be more manageable and therefore also more controllable than the complexity of the whole. This also suggests that adding up the small pieces allows one to "get the whole picture" – never mind the parts that vanish behind the frames or lie outside of them. The perfect circle of the company's clock can only be seen to a quarter, so that it seems as if it is on the way to a straight line. The lines, however, do not only seem to control current events, they also point beyond the immediate present, suggesting that the future, too, is manageable, foreseeable if approached in a certain way. Control is all encompassing.

Sidney is seated behind his huge desk, talking busy on the phone, dressed in a three piece, armed with a cigar and his deep, raspy, and "bossy" voice. During this scene, we can hear a constant and regular clicking sound, which we discover stems from a Newton's Cradle Click, a pendulum that cuts through the flow of time through straight movements back and forth. Smoking his cigar, Sidney Mussburger – whose initials match the initials of scientific management, a management style that aims at full control – is at the centre of the scene and it seems that he is not only "spinning the wheel" but also in full control of the world and the processes that are going on. This impression is further supported when later in the scene Sidney shouts, "Wait a minute!" which makes the clicking of the Cradle Click stop.

When Norville enters Sidney's office, Sidney is living and thinking in his own world of perfect circles and straight lines and how these can steer the stock market and thus the company in Sidney's direction. Norville, on the other hand, has a totally different focus and driven through his excitement wants to present his great new idea, the perfect circle of the Hula Hoop.

Thus, Sidney identifies Norville as suitable means to carry out his plan to beat down the stock price of Hudsucker Industries. He invites Norville to sit on the boss's chair and offers him the straight line of a cigar, to see "how it looks." In contrast to Sidney, however, who has taken over control with the cigar that Warren Hudsucker had left when he jumped out of the window, handing over a cigar to Norville triggers a rupture. With the cigar, Norville accidentally sets a bin on fire, which he tries to extinguish by pulling a heavy water tank out of its unit and carrying it across Sidney's office. Due to the weight of the water tank, Norville is not able to walk straight to the source of the fire and therefore introduces an irregular line on the office floor by means of the leaking water – the first time we see something else than straight lines and perfect circles.

Norville thus introduces chaos into the otherwise controlled world of Sidney Mussburger, who, turning his back to it, manages to be blind to everything that does not fit into his frame. He remains blind to the sudden appearance of other forms – forms that are non-symmetrical and generated by uncontrollable and irregular movements linked to the potentially life-threatening event of fire in his office. He seems to be locked up by the perfection of straight lines. Norville struggles to extinguish the fire, while Sidney perceives these efforts to mitigate the threatening potential of the fire as a mere annoyance. It is only at the moment when Norville throws the burning bin through the frosted glass of one of the office windows that Sidney leaves the routine of managing the world of Hudsucker Industries. This is the window at the long end of the office, which, so far, has been blind to the world but now displays the outside world with its skyscrapers. One could almost perceive it as a scenery in a painting – similarly framed as the world that is safely tucked away in the multiple small window frames in Sidney Mussburger's back. One could hold on to this frame if the glass wasn't broken and if the wind – this irregular, this uncontrollable force – was not blowing through the office, lifting up the Bumstead contracts that Sidney has been working on for the last four years. Not looking at the world but with the eyes on the sheets of paper that swirl up and out of the window nearly costs Sidney's life. Moving in a rather uncontrolled manner when chasing after what he considers the "most sensitive deal of my career" (Coen, Coen, & Raimi, 1994, p. 39), he falls out of the window.

It is a brief moment of losing control – of leaving the controllability of straight lines – that makes him end up dangling upside down outside of his office window on the 44th floor. It is not only due to Norville, who "got [him] on [his] pants" (Coen, Coen, & Raimi, 1994, p. 43), but also because these trousers were tailored by a man who ignored Sidney's order to sew with a single stitch to make it cheaper, that he survives. The movie makes a cut to the situation of the tailor working on Sidney's trousers. One can see the tailor on his sewing machine, hesitating for a second, asking himself whether he should obey or disobey Sidney's demand and eventually deciding for the latter. This hesitance is a stutter in the apparently seamless system of control within which Sidney moves, believes in, and uses as a basis to "operate" the world. Although this impossibility of ubiquitous control – expressed by the stutters in the straight line – seems to be unthinkable for Sidney, it is individuals defying this control that enables him to eventually regain control in this rather vulnerable position – taking another cigar out of his pocket. Stutters in a running system – as undesirable as they might seem to the Sidney Mussburgers of this world – can produce the possibilities of survival when straight lines become irregular.

Scene 2: Fixing the Price

The second scene happens after Norville has been appointed CEO of Hudsucker Industries, which offers him the chance to exploit his excitement and materialize his dream represented by a circle on a piece of paper: "You know for kids." A puzzled board of directors approves

Norville's "dingus" (which eventually becomes the Hula Hoop), although they have no clue what it is after their question, "What the hell is it?" is answered by Sidney stating, "It's brilliant" (Coen, Coen, & Raimi, 1994, p. 101). It is then that we witness how the machine of Hudsucker Industries is set in motion. We see the camera moves fast, zooming in and out, following tubes and shifts to different departments involved in the production, such as R&D, Marketing, Production, and Finance, all of them doing their work in a predetermined order. The tempo of the camera has increased considerably and is further emphasized by the fast-paced music by Aram Khachaturian. Next to the production of multi-coloured plastic hoops, one sees people brainstorming on the name of this new product, testing its safety, and, most importantly, Finance dealing with the question what it will cost. Seemingly endless lines of men in grey suits whose desks are arranged in straight lines are hammering away on their calculating machines. They all move in unison, implying that it is the same goal they're working on, namely, the fixing of the price of the Hula Hoop. This seems a logical, straightforward process where any deviation from the norm is ruled out. We get the impression that the application of the correct formula reveals the correct price of the product, while the amount of people doing it suggests the formula to be highly complex. At the end of the calculating activity, the camera pans to the line manager, who is seated on a podium overlooking his staff. He is the one who has to approve the results. An assistant places the extremely thick book, with all the calculations, upon his desk and opens it. The outcome is $ 0.79. The line manager raises his eyebrows in a disapproving look as if it doesn't look good. His assistant takes a pen and changes it to $ 1.79. His approving smile makes us realize that beauty is in the eye of the beholder.

Despite all calculations, the line manager's personal aesthetic feelings more than doubles the price, but this deviant behaviour – behaviour that is linked to gut feeling rather than rational decision making – does not bring the calculative process(ing) of the machine to a halt. Just like in the brief moment when Sidney Mussburger loses control over the situation in his office, this micro-moment of deviance does not produce a breakdown. It produces merely a hiccup. In contrast to the stutter, hiccups do not change the overall trajectory but only slightly distort the process, which carries on seemingly untouched. The line manager's raised eyebrows do not halt or change the overall product development process, which smoothly progresses after the manager's assistant immediately changes the number. Hiccups are apparently not only integrated but also leading in straightforward business. Not despite but because people deviate – so the impression – the system really functions and vitalizes itself. A hiccup or stutter doesn't imply a breakdown, but a survival, or rather, success. The straight line has to be curbed in order to function.

Scene3: Hula-hooping

The third scene starts with a Hula Hoop poster in a shop window and on it the suggested retail price of $ 1.79. We see a shopkeeper waiting for customers. As these do not show up, the price is decreased until they are even given away for free. When this doesn't work, we see the shopkeeper throwing the Hula Hoops out into his trash in a back alleyway. The logical and predetermined process has ended in a way Sidney had predicted. His plan performs the linear movement of a straight line.

Then, however, something unforeseen happens. Something goes not according to plan. One Hula Hoop, a red one, takes matters in its own hand. It rolls out of the alleyway and slowly across the street. The camera is still, just watching the moving Hula Hoop circling its way through the streets until it meets a kid, who looks at it. The Hula Hoop starts circling around him and finally lays itself on the sidewalk in front of him. The kid looks at it, steps into the Hula Hoop, picks it up and immediately starts Hula-hooping like mad. Other kids look at him in amazement and they all run to the store to get their own Hula Hoop. The Hula Hoop becomes a massive success, and we see that its retail price is raised to $ 3.99. A hype is born, and Norville is a success. Hudsucker Industries is saved but not in the way as intended by Sidney.

In contrast to the first two scenes, in which humans deviate, in this scene it is an object – the Hula Hoop – that takes matters into its own hands and deviates from Sidney Mussburger's straightforward plan. The element of chance now clearly has disturbed the perfect circle – or any notion of it (ignoring stutters and hiccups). Control has become uncontrollable. Sid couldn't foresee this event, and Norville could only hope for it. It is not Sid managing and controlling the circle, but vice versa. The circle decides not because it operates on an alternative perfect circle but through the irregular movements it carries out in order to spin. Looking at the film we get the impression that the Hula Hoop has traded in the prefect circle for a new, uncontrollable movement – back and forth and up and down, irregular and unpredictable. Instead of operating a straight line, it carries out hula hoop movements.

Merry-go-Round or the Ashtray

Now that we have made a visual reading of three scenes, we can wonder how this results in new knowledge on organization.

It has become clear that circles and lines are ubiquitously present in this movie on various levels: the perfect circle of the clock, the annual cycle of a corporation that ends with an annual statement of accounts, Norville entering the ground floor to go all the way up the minute Warren hits the ground, creating "abstract art on Madison Avenue"

(Coen, Coen, & Raimi, 1994, p. 18). We have witnessed that lines can be detected in the verticality of the skyscrapers, the horizontal lines of the desk of the board of directors turning into a runway, the cigars but also in the camera movement that alternates between zooming in and zooming out.

The description of the first scene, which we named circles and cigars, points to how the two aesthetic features of the straight line and the perfect circle are constitutively entangled with the way the board members around Sidney perceive the world and the way they do business. It is no coincidence that Sidney Mussburger's initials, SM, correspond to the abbreviation for scientific management (Taylor, 1911/2011). Scientific management, here, is not only characterized by a belief in logical sequences, teleology, or the distinctive leader who makes the difference or the happy end. It is also exemplary for a cognitive frame dominating the way the (business) world is organized since modernity (e.g. Bauman, 2000). This modernist cognitive frame and its resulting ways of approaching and acting upon the world are constitutively linked to a particular notion of time.

Expressed in Hudsucker Industries' claim "The Future is Now," this notion of time considers the past insignificant and the future a result of present activities and planning. It is closely linked to the notion of man-made progress that does not know any past. Or so Henry Ford (1916 in Bauman, 2000, p. 131) stated, "[H]istory is more or less bunk. We don't want tradition. We want to live in the present and the only history that is worth a tinker's damn is the history we make today." Hence, within a modernist worldview, the "sole history that counts is one not-yet-made-but-being-made at the moment and bound-to-be-made: that is *the* future" (Bauman, 2000, p. 131). The form of the annual cycle of the corporate year is closely connected to the clock as a perfect circle. Here time has a beginning and an end – the beginning and end of a minute, hour, day, year. It is a regular sequence, without interruptions or disturbances. A perfect circle ends; a new circle begins – unhinged by what has been before – with the board of directors formally approving the company's affairs for the business year. The past is forgotten the second another cycle is completed. "We are loaded!" (Coen, Coen, & Raimi, 1994, p. 10).

Such a perfect circle of a clock representing time creates a similar understanding of the world as lines do. Cut up, a perfect circle and a line are the same. A clock becomes a cigar. Moving in a world of straight lines or perfect circles that cut through the multiple flows of reality and generate order that can be managed allows believing in a world of causes and effects; it allows believing in control. In the world of perfect circles and straight lines, taking over a cigar means taking over control. But is there really such a thing as taking over control? Taking over by incorporating the aesthetics of control? As we have, seen control gets disrupted.

We argue that SM gets into trouble because of HH – irregular movements (of the Hula Hoop or of Norville).

During the movie we witness multiple moments of non-control or loss of control but Sidney and his board of directors, together with most of the employees, seem to be blind to these instances until they are defeated by it. This blindness is so puzzling that it poses the question how they actually do this.

Sidney and his followers use straight lines and perfect circles to cut through the multiple flows of reality and generate order that can be managed, for instance, the (perfect) annual circle. The perfect circle of the annual year always promises a fresh start, a new beginning, a clean cut. Only then can the desire for ordered perfection be actualized over and over again: A fresh start, a new day, a new business circle, eliminating and excluding all the rough objects, all the messiness of politics, all wrong decisions and allowing a fresh start. The perfect circle of the business year allows him to believe in and act upon a world of cause and effect and this controlled environment holds the promise of safety. The linear managerial instruments, however, seem to be less means of control than means of camouflaging non-control or the (temporary) loss of control so that the general sense of control can be maintained. Instruments like the annual report (or the notion of stock markets going up and down) thus are apparatuses that carry out camouflage operations necessary for maintaining the fantasy of managerial control. Using camouflage apparatuses, despite the comfort and legitimacy they provide for managers and other members of organizations, is also dangerous. As we have seen with Sidney, he is unable to transgress the notion of the controllability of the world that the apparatuses produce. He is trapped in and blinded by straight lines. Using too many times these apparatuses against mess, chaos, disorganization – in short, the Other of order that is the "source and archetype of all fear" (Bauman, 1993, p. 7) – makes us forget that the world is a flux of genuinely uncontrollable events.

This also means that the urge of the organization to function according to a perfect circle or straight line doesn't work. The organization is basically uncontrollable and functions under the influence of Hula Hoop movements. Knowing this might cause trouble for any board of directors or management. Steering or managing or even controlling an organization is hardly possible with a message of uncontrollability. But what does this mean for engaging with or even deciding and leading in organizations? When watching the Hudsucker we realize that it is not just Norville or the Hula Hoop that disrupts the order of a seemingly perfect circle. Next to various actors producing hiccups or stutters, it is also the jumping out of the window of Warren Hudsucker at the beginning that can be read as part of his management style. He knows that when there is no life left in the perfect circle – no surprises, no chance, nothing unexpected –, when the straight line rules, the perfect circle should be disrupted. As soon as he hears the result from his financial director, "Gentlemen we're loaded," he knows swift action is required in order to keep the company viable and successful. He decides that jumping out of the window is necessary. This management by jumping out of the window seems absurd, but nevertheless it happened and was successful. It points to a way of managing that embraces the notion of organizational life as being constituted by rhythms of organizing and non-organizing, of control and non-control that invites not suppresses chance.

After this event, Sidney had plexiglass installed in the boardroom as a precaution for anyone trying to step into Warren Hudsucker's shoes and imitating his management style by jumping out of the window. A board member who tries, lamenting, "I'm getting off this merry-go-round" (Coen, Coen, & Raimi, 1994, p. 116), ends up against the plexiglass window that doesn't give in. It gives the impression that Sidney doesn't underestimate the power of management by jumping out of the window, but instead of embracing it, he does everything possible to exclude unforeseeable events in order to hold on to his managerial fantasies.

Some Concluding Remarks on Blindness

So what is the conclusion of this? While for some, it might be tempting to try management by jumping out of the window, we refrain from using this conclusion as a camouflage apparatus pretending to know what is going on. Instead, we insist on the principal inaccessibility of the world for any (ultimate) means of understanding and control. Seeking understanding of phenomena, we go around in circles from parts to context and back again but we are never able to close, to complete a (perfect) circle, for life keeps on happening in the meantime and turns circles into spiraling movements. This, however, does not mean that we do not learn – quite the opposite. The fundamental openness of the world allows us to never stop learning, never stop thinking, never stop making sense and we need art – such as film – to make us aware of and engage with the enigma of the world.

Film does not "unblind" us but it allows us to open up to our internal blindness, which, according to Peretz (2008), allows us to become visionary. This becoming visionary is a different kind of perceiving and a different kind of blindness. It is not fueled by the desire to foresee, to anticipate, to prepare for, and to control that what is coming, supported by all the camouflage apparatuses we discussed. Instead, it is driven by the desire for new experiences.

Derrida (2002/2017) muses on humans' predisposition for anticipation that is rooted in the way our eyes are situated at the front our heads and that, as a consequence, produce a horizon. This line of the horizon, this ability of seeing what is coming protects us. That's why we are so crazy about forecasting. It makes us feel we are in control, and we tend to strip reality from that which we cannot control. *The Hudsucker Proxy* shows that this can backfire as it does not allow experiencing events, for an event cannot be anticipated.

"An event that one anticipates, that one [...] foresees is not an event," writes Derrida (2002/2017, p. 45), and furthers, "events only exist without horizon" (p. 46). Acknowledging that we are blind and tapping into this blindness bestows us with the gift of wonder, of being able to be surprised by what is happening to oneself.

This is a mode of opening that Peretz (2008) refers to as futurity: "[N] ot the fact that the future that will happen as something we can predict, but the fact that the world is transformable in essence and open to unpredictable change, an openness that is part of what the world is" (p. 14). So organization might have a function after all, although it is difficult to predict which function it might be in the presence of transformation. But then wonders should remain wonders and have this allergy for control.

It is not about solving the questions. The scientific approach to organization, scientific management, isn't enough for it runs on the line of the horizon and the perfect circle to anticipate, to usurp that which is coming before it has arrived. Instead, we need to become sensitive again to the flux of organizational life, by opening the world with our blindness and exploring it: exploring the irregular and illogical movements, experimenting with hula hoop movements, inventing irregular patterns, experiencing events. It's not about SM, but HH.

Life might run in circles – what goes around, comes around – but we never know how as it never moves on a perfect line. It is the inventive, exciting, weird irregular movements that make it spin.

References

Antonioni, M. (1962). *L'Eclisse.*

Bauman, Z. (1992). *Intimations of postmodernity.* London, UK: Routledge.

Bauman, Z. (1993). *Modernity and ambivalence.* Cambridge, UK: Polity.

Bauman, Z. (2000). *Liquid modernity.* Cambridge, UK: Polity.

Chaplin, C. (1936). *Modern Times.*

Coen, E., & Coen, J. (1994). *The Hudsucker Proxy.*

Coen, J., Coen, E., & Raimi, S. (1994). *The Hudsucker Proxy.* London, UK: Faber & Faber.

Deleuze, G. (1986). *Cinema 1,the movement-image.* Minneapolis: University of Minnesota Press.

Deleuze, G. (1989). *Cinema 2, the time-image.* London, UK: Athlone Press.

Deren, M. (2005). *Essential Deren: Collected writings on film.* Edited by B.R. McPherson. Kingston, NY: Documentext.

Derrida, J. (2002/2017). *Denken, nicht zu sehen. Schriften zu den Künsten des Sichtbaren. 1979–2004.* Berlin, Germany: Brinkmann & Bose.

Earhart, R. S. (2019). The future is now! Cure your students of the disease of images in Wim Wenders' film 'Until the end of the world'. In H. Letiche & J. L. Moriceau (Eds.), *Turn to film – Film in the Business School* (pp. 3–18). Amsterdam, Netherlands: Brill.
Gilliam, T. (1985). *Brazil.*
Judge, M. (1999). *Office Space.*
Kurosawa, A. (1963). *High & Low.*
Linstead, S. A. (2018). Feeling the reel of the real: Framing the play of critically affective organizational research between art and the everyday. *Organization Studies*, *39*(2–3), 319–344.
Otto, B., & Strauß, A. (2019). The novel as affective site: uncertain work as impasse in Wait Until Spring, Bandini!. *Organization Studies*, *40*(12), 1805–1822.
Peretz, E. (2008). *Becoming visionary, Brian de Palma's cinematic education of the senses.* Stanford, CA: Stanford University Press.
Peters, L. (2016). *Cliché & organization, thinking with Deleuze & Film.* Newcastle upon Tyne, England: Cambridge Scholars Publishers.
Peters, L., & Yue, A. (2018). *On mirrors! Philosophy, art, organization.* Newcastle upon Tyne, England: Cambridge Scholars Publishers.
Scorsese, M. (2013). *The Wolf of Wall Street.*
Swiêtnicki, W. (2002) *The Naked.*
Taylor, F. W. (1911/2001). *The principles of scientific management.* Mineola, NY: Dover.
Thompson, D. (Ed.). (2006). *Altman on Altman.* London, UK: Faber & Faber.
Woods, P. (Ed.). (2003). *Joel & Ethan Coen – Blood siblings.* London, UK: Plexus.

5 Writing, Dreams, and Imagination

Matilda Dahl, Pierre Guillet de Monthoux, and Jenny Helin

Prologue

How can we write about the power of daydreaming? We are searching for ways of writing that resonate with the act of dreaming, and what that act can offer us. We are trying, in particular, to write in such a pictorial way that, in reading, it can enable poetic images to unfold, fully conscious that texts are not only a matter of information but also making images by painting in words (Jakobson, 1985). Is it even possible to create an ekphrastic effect (Krieger, 1992)?

Studies of philosophy have shown that daydreaming is essential for our imagination and the formation of new ideas where "[i]magination is a laboratory of the possible inviting us – through reverie and poetry – to give a future to the past" (Kearney, 2014, p. xxi). Through daydreaming, the present reality can be expanded as new life worlds take shape. How this happens and how the dreamt realities play a role in today's organizations we, however, know little about. But taking the word "imagination" seriously, namely, as generating images, put us on the track of art when embarking on our quest.

The background to this focus on dreaming is a research project that was initiated a couple of years ago with local farm owners. At that time, the dairy farm crisis with falling milk prices hit farmers on an almost global scale and many farmers were driven out of business. We wanted to learn from those who survived: how did they go on? During the interviews they told us about their life and how they make a living often under tough conditions. Importantly, they talked about a life different from the here and now and we heard stories about better days that are still to come. In explaining their ordinary work with their dairy cows, beef cattle, and the soil, they touched upon how they could daydream about other things as they went on doing what they had to do for the time being. At first we did not know how to make sense of what we heard and we talked about it in terms of "life." Eventually we sensed that it was something less total that was of significance to them. Actually, the farmers themselves helped us narrow down our attention to "dreaming."

That farmers working under tough conditions emphasized the role of activities such as dreaming was unexpected and we thought it worth exploring. In parallel with our fieldwork we read the philosopher Gaston Bachelard's (1884–1962) extensive work on imagination and daydreaming. Bachelard was a French philosopher known for finding it impossible to account for any human action in science, everyday existence, and working life without taking dreaming seriously. Over a number of publications, he developed a phenomenology of dreaming and what he teaches us, broadly speaking, is that dreaming is an important, difficult, and vulnerable act that needs poetic circumstances to unfold. Dreaming in the Bachelardian sense can be seen as a special kind of act: an aesthetic process that creates newness and a multiplicity of previously non-existing images. Further, dreaming can be seen as a fundamental human right –all human beings should have *The Right to Dream*, to quote the title of one of his books (Bachelard, 1990). To account for the process of dreaming, Bachelard positioned "reverie" as the most dynamic form of an act, a phenomenological fusion between an imaging consciousness and the world. Bachelard's approach offered a take on "dreaming" as "daydreaming," which was very different from views tainted by the Freudian tradition.

Through his elaboration on "reverie" as the action of daydreaming, Bachelard articulated that a poetic image "can be the seed of a world, the seed of a universe imagined out of a poet's reverie" (Bachelard, 1969, p. 1). We can all be poets and "dream well" if only we have the right poetic circumstances. Here, poetry is not referred to in a literal sense, but rather should be understood from a wider perspective drawing on the etymological meaning of *poiesis* – meaning to make with our full body – since it "is about hearing and feeling as well as crafting and shaping" (Kearney, 2014, p. xix). The beauty of poetry is that it rejects principles, systems, and proofs. Partly this has to do with the rupture, the breach with prose and narration, created when we engage with poetry, which enables a break from chronological timing because time no longer flows in continuity – "it shoots up" (Bachelard, 1988, p. 175). When time shoots up through a rupture, we can start to explore the verticality of the present moment. A sentence, a poem, a meeting, a special moment can all be understood as pieces of art that can make us "take off" vertically in dreaming.

The nature of this process seems material and therefore the phenomenological body is seen to be at the core of reverie and it is in the flesh that images are born (Kotowicz, 2018). For our dreaming body, our eyes are significant since through looking we can invent new life. In so doing, the eye has the capacity not only to see but also to deform that which is clear and distinct; that is, these poetic images are not based on what we see, as in a sensory activity, rather what we see is shaped by our imagination. Thus, the imagination of the images enters before thought, which is why "poetry, rather than being a phenomenology of the mind, is a phenomenology of the soul" (Bachelard, 2014, p. 4). The important challenge of an image is to awaken deeper engagement that goes beyond visual cultivation and awareness of the social meaning of signs, styles, or symbols. It is not a question of observing images but of experiencing them in the moment of now (Kearney, 2008), where images enable the emergence of "newness," something that emerges in the interconnections between the image and imagination:

> We always think of the imagination as the faculty that *forms* images. On the contrary, it *deforms* what we perceive; it is, above all, the faculty that frees us from immediate images and changes them. If there is no change, or unexpected fusion of images, there is no imagination; there is no imaginative act. If the image that is *present* does not make us think of one that is *absent*, if an image does not determine an abundance – an explosion – of unusual images, then there is no imagination. There is only perception, the memory of a perception, a familiar memory, a habitual way of viewing form and color.
>
> (Bachelard, 1988, p. vii, emphasis in original)

Following this line of thinking, dreaming starts in imagination. Without imagination we would not be able to experience images – images that enable us to reach out for that which is not yet. Existence needs images and imagination is fundamental to being (Kearney, 1991). Bachelard valued imagination because "he recognizes that understanding without imagination is doctrine without growth. And without growth, what chance is there to engage the complexity that bounds us?" (Danielewski, 2014, p. xv). As noted by Kearney (1991, p. 4, emphasis in original), in his treatise on different philosophies of imagination, "*yetser, phantasia, eikasia, Einbildungskraft, fantasy, imagination* – have at least one basic trait in common: they all refer, in their diverse ways, to the human power to convert absence into presence, actuality to possibility, what-is into something-other-than-it-is." In other words, imagination has the fundamental possibility to transform our present moment so that it reaches out beyond our current concerns.

Having been engaged in research about daydreaming among farm owners for a couple of years (Helin, Dahl & Guillet de Monthoux, 2019), we are working on how to make sense of all our research material and trying out different ways of how to write about reverie. In these attempts we face a fundamental question: is it a dream in itself that an academic text, in the context of a woman who works on her farm, can give rise to poetic images?

In what follows, we are experimenting with how to write about Birgitta du Rietz,[1] one of the farm owners, and how she is "working with daydreaming," as she describes it herself. As we read, write, and rewrite poems and stories and look at photos and listen to recordings from interviews, we get close to the material and new understandings emerge. In this way of using writing as a form of inquiry in itself (Richardson, 1997), different forms of written images take shape.

Birgitta du Rietz is the owner–manager of Stora Gåsemora, a farm located on the peninsula of Fårö, north of the island of Gotland, in Sweden. Fårö is the place where the famous writer and director Ingmar Bergman chose to build his house and have as his primary place for creation. Birgitta lives just a few kilometres north of the Bergmans' house, overlooking the Baltic Sea. Except for a couple of months in summer, the island of Fårö is a scarcely populated and quiet place with 500 inhabitants on a yearly basis. Birgitta is one of those who live there all year round. Over the years she has turned her old milk farm into a business within the hospitality industry: there is a hotel and a restaurant, the place caters concerts, conferences, weddings, and yoga to riding retreats. The aesthetic quality of the place and the buildings is of key importance to Birgitta. She has transformed Gåsemora Farm from a crumbling milk farm into a popular and unique hotel, conference center, concert hall, and restaurant made up of 15 different buildings that are a combination of old, restored farm buildings and contemporary architecture dwellings – a development few would have imagined as possible a decade ago. She has been responsible for this development, after inheriting the farm from her late husband, who died from cancer, leaving her with a newborn baby and milk cows.

Can we find the seed for a poetic image in writing about her work? This is our attempt, in the form of a triptych: a photo album (Figures 5.1–5.3), a poem, and a portrait.

Photo-album

Figure 5.1 Gåsemora, Gotland, by Matilda Dahl.

Figure 5.2 Gåsemora, Gotland, by Matilda Dahl.

Figure 5.3 Gåsemora, Gotland, by Matilda Dahl.

Poem

Two Lives

"It's not good, you cleaning and all that.
You are the boss here,
It's not good, making beds and all that,"
my ex used to say
But it's damn good I think
Sometimes I just want to do that
Dream myself away
To those projects that I dream away with
How I do things

It is as if I had two lives.
The ordinary life and my dreaming-life.

***

The Accusation

"Oh you lie like hell" my ex used to tell me
"You lie and make things up"
No I don't
But it is so difficult to know where I am sometimes

***

The Chain

I was daydreaming a lot when Anders was sick
when he passed away in cancer
Then I dreamt a lot, about that he would get well
About what we would do
how one would
Then when he passed away...
Then I also had to...
Not that I pretended he was alive...
But I know that all the people who have lived on this farm...
Even though it is so improbable
It makes me feel safe
because I am one of those who will have lived here
on the farm
I am part of a team now, I am part of this link
It is like a long chain
I can't break

***

Broken Order

I was bouncing [ideas] back and forth
I was bouncing with myself
I could see it
Would I have other actors here?
Yuk yuk I don't like that
It was a bit like a bad dream
It has always been only us here, in charge
And then suddenly other people would come
take care of the fields, the restaurant
I'm not leasing out the farm, no way

I'm not losing control
I do not want to see
how they place bales randomly
and make a mess
Plastic all over the place
I could see it wobbling in the wind
No order whatsoever
No
They would put their wagons and all that shit
Higgledy-piggledy and broken machines
It was impossible to get used to that thought

***

Alone

No I want to be alone
No I don't want to
Be Disrupted
I go crazy when the phone rings

***

Portrait

Birgitta of Gåsemora Farm

Silence. The only audible sound is the creak from the wide floorboards when Birgitta moves around the room. The sheets have been stripped off, to be replaced by new, white, ironed ones. Outside, all is still, and across Gåsemora Farm, the mist is beginning to rise on this slightly bleak November morning.

We are on Fårö Island. A short time ago, the last weekend guests left the farm to return to the mainland, back from the rustling of the solitary junipers to the clamor of the city. Another working weekend is over. The guests have been riding, conferring, and practicing yoga.

This is the best time for Birgitta, who owns and runs the large facility. During her mute domestic toil, with nothing to disturb her, her thoughts can take her very far away. She gazes into the distance.

"People think I look crazy," she says. "I kind of stare emptily into space. I'm not there."

Making the beds, cleaning, and forever painting – skirting boards and mouldings, doors and window frames... there is no end to her diligence as a painter. When she is left in peace, free from other people and phone calls, life is at its best. Her visions can then transport her, letting her escape from reality's monsters - death and betrayal. Ideas for converting the property then also take shape. How many panes should the windows of the new house have – four, six, or eight? What really looks best? Then, too, fantasies about what happened on the farm several centuries ago can come to life. She speculates about the builder of the stone wall that surrounds the farm, wondering whether he was in love and happy.

These things happen when nothing else is going on.

Birgitta has always daydreamed a great deal. During her first few years of life, she lived alone with her maternal grandmother on a small farm. Life was dull – boring in the extreme. There were no other children. That was when the dreaming started. Since then, it has been her strategy for transcending reality and creating new realities. Later in life it served to comfort a despairing daughter whose parents had separated. It enabled her to build a new enterprise on an old agricultural estate. It inspired a brilliant gift for her neighbour. But, most of all, it has been her way of coping with life – living and surviving.

What worked fine to pass the time was sometimes a problem in school.

"Are you sitting there daydreaming again, Birgitta? Stop it!"

Her daydreaming is constantly interrupted. But she dislikes interruptions.

"I go crazy when the phone rings while I'm doing the housework, because sometimes my daydream is so darn good," Birgitta explained.

How can that be, then? What is so good about it? Well, she explained, it is like watching a good movie in which she herself decides on the action.

Or, as Birgitta expressed it, "In my head I read, think, ponder... I play movies in my head."

Inside her mind, no outsider can come in and mess things up. There, she has control. It is Birgitta who decides what her inner movies are about, how they start, and how they end. And there are only happy endings. Nothing boring or horrifying gets a look-in: "Only good things."

Using the daydreams, it is even possible to hide the unpleasantness. The man who betrayed her is shut into a cold room, with the door locked. There is no way he can get out and into her dreams. If he intrudes, he is shooed away: so there – so much for you! Now I'm locking you in.

In the vision, the invalid recovers. The husband – the eldest daughter's father, heir to the farm – never died of cancer. In the inner daydream that took place at the same time as the nightmare out there, he would recover and all would be well. In her mind's eye, everyone who once lived on the farm is still around, and she is not alone there.

"I know everyone who has lived on this farm in the past is with me," Birgitta said.

This gives her strength to move on, especially when the grim reality is unbearable: the invalid stopped being part of it and disappeared from the reality she lives in. He left Birgitta alone with an eight-month-old daughter, on a huge hereditary estate that she came close to losing in a foreclosure.

Where the dairy used to be, there is now a farm complex of a partially modern design, used for conferences, concerts, and weddings. Birgitta has prioritized a focus on developing the farm's aesthetics, with new buildings and extensions to the old ones. Nothing has been left to chance. Everything is handsome and in harmony with the landscape – the colour scheme and the siting of the various buildings. Here, Birgitta works hard all year round and makes sure that she is left in peace to daydream.

"You shouldn't be doing the domestic chores. You're the boss here. That's no good at all," people say to her. But she disagrees.

"It's terrific, I think. I just want to do it. Then my dreams can carry me away [...]. It's like living two lives, more or less: the usual and a dream life."

The dreamt reality can confuse the reality she lives in. The two easily become conflated. What happened where? Did it happen out there or in here?

"Sometimes I don't know if I'm dreaming, or have been. I usually say, 'I've been dreaming again.' I can also get comments about it: 'Oh, you're such a flipping liar,' my ex used to say. 'You tell lies and make things up.' No, I don't, but sometimes it's really hard to know where I am."

Still, dreaming is something that solves problems rather than creates them. When Birgitta moved back into her family home, she related her fantasies instead of reading to her siblings.

"I told them stories I'd made up – ones I'd daydreamed about. There were lots of crazy things in them. My siblings thought it was totally awesome. They just longed to go to bed so I'd tell them stories."

In there, the sun shines; out there, it is dark and cold. But the dreadful reality must not get in. It must stay out there because Birgitta has "no filter," as she describes it.

"I can't take it. Everything gets to me. It goes straight in. When the hurt goes straight in and has its destructive effect – well, something else has to take its place. Then your own creation of reality, through dreaming, becomes the way to keep the rest away. Creating something new, that's possible to control and steer in a direction that you yourself want."

The stuff of her visions often relates to building projects and colours. Should there be a sliding door? What shade of yellow? How many windowpanes? What would be good, or beautiful? Imagine if the big manure pit that is no longer used weren't there any longer, in the middle of the barnyard. What might be there instead? A spa? A restaurant? No... no.

"Yes, and I always wanted to do something [about the manure pit]. I stuck to that. But then I thought, no, that would cost a heck of a lot of money. I'm not sure it'll be OK. Then I see it in front of me. Darn, it smells of manure down here. Oh no, it won't work. It'll never be possible to get rid of the manure that's in the walls." But what about just leaving it there, then?

"No, that wasn't an option. Once a project has started in your mind, it has to be finished. I just have to see it through, so that I can let go of the thing. Otherwise it will keep on popping up in my head," Birgitta explained.

In the event, the big round concrete block became neither a spa nor a restaurant. It suffered a harsher fate: being removed altogether.

"I thought and thought. Heck, should I do it or not? I'll regret it... I'll think... maybe I'll be disappointed... it may not turn out well at all. I have to think about whether I'll be sad... because, after all, I put it there. We worked hard to install it. It's part of the farm. Should I get rid of something so wonderful? I remember when I got it, and I was so keen to have it, so that the manure didn't get out and spoil our groundwater. I remember what it cost and what a slog it was to set it up."

Getting away from farming meant a complete upheaval, from working in the barn to doing completely different things. When Birgitta's husband fell ill three months after their youngest daughter was born, she milked the cows herself and simultaneously breastfed her baby.

"I had to milk them all the time [...], and for a year and a half I did the milking myself and breastfed at the same time. I had 52 cows."

Later, when she faced the big decision to sell the cows and leave the farming behind her, she imagined a bovine existence.

"Sure, I thought about that before selling the cows. I'd visualize life as a cow or some other animal. I could fantasize about that as I walked around there: How I'd want things to be if I were an animal, and what should be done."

What drives Birgitta lies outside herself, in her self-image as a link in something bigger – the chain of generations. The people in this chain are also her "team." She feels a kinship and a connection across time with people who lived before her and those who are to come after her. What binds them all – predecessors, herself, and her successors – together are matter, space, and the estate. The sense of fellowship is a real presence in her thoughts. Her link in the chain must not be broken, she feels, even if things have not gone to plan, and although she has been left alone. But there is more to it than that.

Her children ask: "Mom, if you sold up you could live in luxury and travel round the world. Why do you keep going?"

The response comes quickly: "Put your Mom in an apartment and she'd die."

Epilogue

We find it striking that we have a tradition in organization studies of developing different research methods depending on the research question at hand, but when it comes to writing we are less elaborate. As a critique, Kostera already wrote in 1997 that different forms of writing, in particular subversive ways of writing through poetry, can enable us to reach out in ways other than we usually do. Maybe it is time to ask ourselves: "What forms of writing does the research question demand?" (Bränström Öhman & Livholts, 2007, p. 9). Or, in the words of Rhodes (2019, p. 31), do we need different forms of "scriptologies"? "just as methods and methodologies are many," each one suitable for different problems and questions, should that plurality not naturally extend to writing?

As we search for ways of writing that can give rise to poetic images, we have here experimented with a triptych in the form of photos, poetry, and a portrait. In hindsight, we seemed to approach the poetic image by a kind of triangulation among the pictures we see through the lenses of our cameras, the impressionistic biography, and a rendering of what we hear when we listen to a farmer – as if the poetic image would emerge from these impressions offered by our studied organization.

These are different ways of writing that suggest different images. But they are not "Images of Organization" in the Gareth Morgan sense (1986). Rather, we have attempted to open up to a multitude of ways of writing where different images can be born to evoke poetic aspects of the material at hand rather than merely represent its factual "evidence."

Bachelard (1969) emphasized the need for rupture in order to see new images. Working with the triptych, and hopefully in reading it, the different texts create this kind of stop in the flow of reading, enabling us to pause. However, for the triptych to work, it needs to be created as an invitation for movement and as an invitation to a journey: "Through this invitation, our inner being gets a gentle push which throws us off balance and sets in motion a healthy, really dynamic reverie" (Bachelard, 1988, p. 3). The question is: are we as organization and management scholars capable of making those invitations ourselves or do we need to cooperate with artists to make this happen?

Ekphrastic Energy

Phrases, photos
Complex words, simple pictures
Moving in between, moving beyond
Moving is the thing
How to write reverie?
Boil it down to words?
Writing the inner life of the other
Manager, woman, human being
A piece of art?
A triptych we did
To create a movement
From what is
To what can become
To take us somewhere else
But where?

Note

1 We publish the name of Birgitta du Rietz and the name of her farm, Stora Gåsemora, with her consent. That consent was given after we read the story about her aloud in Swedish and after which she said, "Yes that is exactly how it is."

References

Bachelard, G. (1969). *The poetics of reverie. Childhood, language, and the cosmos.* Boston, MA: Beacon Press.

Bachelard, G. (1988). *Air and dreams, an essay on the imagination of movement.* Dallas, TX: The Dallas Institute Publication.

Bachelard, G. 1990. *The Right to Dream.* Robert S. Dupree and Joanne H. Stroud (Eds), Dallas: Dallas Institute of Humanities & Culture.

Bachelard, G. (2014). *The poetics of space.* New York, NY: Penguin Classics.

Bränström Öhman, A., & Livholts, M. (Eds.). (2007). *Genus och det akademiska skrivandets former.* Lund, Sweden: Studentlitteratur.

Danielewski, M. (2014). Foreword. In G. Bachelard (Ed.), *The poetics of space* (pp. vii–xvi). New York, NY: Penguin Classics.

Helin, J., Dahl, M., & Guillet de Monthoux, P. (2019). Caravan poetry: An inquiry on four wheels. *Qualitative Inquiry*, doi:10.1177/1077800419843949.

Jakobson, R. (1985). *Verbal art, verbal sign, verbal time.* Minneapolis: University of Minnesota Press.

Kearney, R. (1991). *Poetics of imagining from Husserl to Lyotard.* London, UK: Harper Collins.

Kearney, R. (2008). Bachelard and the epiphanic instant. *Philosophy Today, 52* (Supplement), 38–45.

Kearney, R. (2014). Introduction. In G. Bachelard (Ed.), *The poetics of space* (pp. xvii–xxv). New York, NY: Penguin Classics.

Kostera, M. (1997). Personal performatives: Collecting poetical definitions of management. *Organization, 4*(3), 345–353.

Kotowicz, Z. (2018). *Gaston Bachelard: A philosophy of the surreal.* Edinburgh, UK: Edinburgh University Press.

Krieger, M. (1992). *Ekphrasis the illusion of the natural sign.* Baltimore, MD: Johns Hopkins University Press.

Morgan, G. (1986). *Images of organization.* Beverly Hills, CA: Sage.

Rhodes, C. (2019). Sense-ational organization theory! Practices of democratic scriptology. *Management Learning, 50*(1), 24–37.

Richardson, L. (1997). *Fields of play. Constructing and academic life.* New Brunswick, NJ: Rutgers University Press.

6 Conformity and the Need for Roots

Two Anarchist Utopias and a Christian Politeia

Piotr Graczyk

Language and Politics

My starting point is the hypothesis of the fundamentally political nature of language. One can assume that human tongues have antecedents in animal signaling systems. Their origin can be derived from an ability – typical for some higher species of living creatures – to treat physical facts as signals. These signals are a type of signs that an individual must be able to read under the threat of death ("there is water here," "there comes a predator"). Animals seem to be much more locked up in their environment of signs than humans, though. For them, there is virtually only one correct, acceptable interpretation of signs in every single case. Failing to comply with it causes death. The ways of reading are changing slowly and this change involves the species as a whole. That is to say, every type of interpretation is related to a distinct species; the rise and fall of species depends on right or wrong interpretations on a massive scale and over long periods of time.

Human being can be seen as a moment of discontinuity in this natural process. Humans read and write signs on their own behalf. Furthermore, the human species uses numerous paradigms of reading signs, and changes within these paradigms may occur much quicker than it is the case in the animal world. Despite this, death in case of a "wrong" interpretation of signs may be a free choice (just as Socrates says in Phaedo), not only a mistake. We can define human being as an animal with the open paradigm of reading signs. That is to say, human languages differ from animal languages by its political character. The political aspect of human languages can be identified as a quest for cultural hegemony (Gramsci, 1971; Mouffe & Laclau 1985) – a struggle that is at least not directly dependent on any external higher level system (Schmitt, 2007).

From this point of view, one can see the language as a phenomenon (or rather, a process) consubstantial with the division of labour/power. My notion of labour/power division refers to Foucault's term of "power/knowledge" (Foucault, 1977). By proposing this notion I try to give a more economic and materialistic character to Foucault's notion. The labour/power division is the power over the division of labour and, consequently, over the functioning of institutions. It is the power that establishes social organization. The human language is thus a phenomenon (or a process) that was established as the tool serving to conduct the division of labour and of power. Its occurrence means the origin of humanity, as a species that exceeds the previous logic of evolution and transforms consciously its own conditions of existence, its own ways of reading signs.

The conscious character of this transformation is based on its linguistic tools – the changes in paradigms of sign reading occur through the medium of language. The key assumption of my chapter is that this medium, from the very start, develops as a tool for the domination of some social groups over others. This is how I understand the thesis of *The Communist Manifesto*: "The history of all hitherto existing society is the history of class struggles" (Marx & Engels 2004, p. 14), and this is why I consider it to be true – I reckon that the thesis speaks about the origin of human society, or of the species being, as young Marx puts it (Marx, 1844). Humanity – open species, a free molecule in the process of evolution – employs this new, unprecedented political tool of the language in the very moment of its birth. By this anthropogonic event, which cannot be historically located (it's the genesis of history, not a fact within history), the political character of a language is revealed. The task of this tool is to establish a certain kind of collective inequality. Furthermore, the human language is a tool that establishes social inequality as an *objective* trait of the world, that is, as a fixed and invariable way of reading signs within the world. At the same time, the very possibility of such an operation – namely, the *political objectivization* of the human world by the means of a language – indicates its arbitrariness. Thanks to the medium of language, the world becomes this being that it is linguistically declared to be – and this way of expressing the reality contains inequality: it is marked by the dominance of a group or a constellation of groups controlling the language (i.e. *culture* or rather a paradigmatic and institutionalized way of reading signs) over the rest of society. On the other hand, the language, by its very claim of objectivity and truth, undermines the dominant group's claim of power. It's a double-edged sword – it can always be used by the dispossessed and humiliated to reclaim their powers. It contains the notion of a state free of any inequality – and it contains means to express such a state. This is the utopian aspect present in the political function of the language.

The political character of the language – the fact that it decides, by way of its very organization (already in its grammatical layer), who the master is and who the servant – is thus identical with the power of establishing institutions. Contemporary philosophy was often referring to this power of language by raising the question of its "non-natural" (i.e. conventional, artificial) character. This is the nominalist trait of modern philosophy. It was an important topic for both the merely Anglophone, analytical philosophy following the trail of the later Wittgenstein (like John Austin and his pupils) and the so-called continental philosophy, especially the part of it that has been influenced by Friedrich Nietzsche. Nietzsche can be interpreted not only as a competitor of Marxism (as Georg Lukacs, 1980, claims in his late dogmatic writings) but rather as someone who enriches the Marxist intuition of class struggle, adding a linguistic–literary dimension to it. So, to the Nietzscehan heritage belongs the Frankfurt School (especially Walter Benjamin and Theodor Adorno) and French thinkers like Michel Foucault and Gilles Deleuze. In this respect, not to be missed is also Martin Heidegger, who was philosophizing accordingly to Holderlin's slogan: "Was bleibt aber stiften die Dichter" (Heidegger, 2018) – what remains the poets provide.

Three Layers of Literature

In the latter formula the relationship of literature and social institutions is openly expressed. For the sake of this chapter I would like to go one step further. Can't we understand institutions that regulate the relations of power and the division of labour as specific works of literature? In this chapter, literature is interpreted as the totality of human institutions and human relations, in a shape that was elaborated by human societies. Stanisław Brzozowski said (in his Diary): "Whatever we can say about the world is always a product of a certain history expressed in terms of a certain literature" (Brzozowski, 1913, p. 98). I agree with this but the expression "terms of literature" I will understand in a broader sense than he did, that is, not only as "every linguistic creativity" (Brzozowski, ibid.), but also as every material social creativity. Along with things, people always created words, concepts. In this sense, I include not just the usefulness of art for management but rather the identity of literature and management: management produces a certain kind of social literature, and the literature itself ("the linguistic creativity," Brzozowski, ibid.) is an extreme case of management: the most flexible and open to utopia.

Literature in this sense has, so to say, various degrees of density. So, first, we have the ontological level of linguistic density. It's a space of decisions about the very existence of things. What exists and how does it exist? How about gods, angels, souls of ancestors, Confucian heaven, Taoistic equilibrium, neurons, black holes, discourses? The ontological level of language gives the answer. This "ontological literature" is not a continuous text to be found in a special kind of books. It's rather an unevenly dispersed – like ozone in the atmosphere – historically changing set of relatively fixed rules of reading. Perhaps it can be understood as the remains of the animal paradigm of reading signs – one and only for each species – which still exists in a partial form within the state of factual multitude of interpretation. The ontological layer of literature is rather a "implicit text" as Nicolás Gómez-Dávila puts it (Graczyk, 2016, pp. 871–879) than a explicit text. The Foucaultian notion of discourse and the discursive formation may be another similar concept but it's too broad, and contains also a layer that I would like to call *nomothetic* in the further part of the chapter.

There is one thing I want to stress: the ontological layer of literature not only decides about the being, it is the being itself. One cannot distinguish between this layer of literature and reality itself. Being is literature – seen from a certain angle, at a certain level. But this level evolves over time – and this is what the historicity of being means. There is no point in thinking about being beyond the thinking about being – and literature, in its ontological layer, is the Thinking of Being. Each time anybody does it, it is like the implementation of Parmenides's formula – "thinking and being are the same." It is the implementation that falsifies itself because it passes with time – but, simultaneously, it is the horizon of times, beyond which, in a given time, one is not able to look (or it is very hard to look beyond it, at least). That makes this layer so thick.

The consecutive, softer layer of literature is the law, broadly understood: it is nomos as the general principle of space organization (this is how Carl Schmitt, 2006, interprets it). This juridical and moral level of literature is definitely the *explicit text*. It must not be legal text in a narrow sense – for example, in ancient Greece lawyers used to quote poets as legal authorities. Furthermore, it must not even be a "text" in the literal sense! It can be, for that matter, a road sign. What I mean by *nomos* is a publicly visible material structure demanding to be understood in some or another way – like a lock that can be opened or closed; like a button that can be pushed or not. What this level of language is about is the overt necessity of choice. And the necessity of choice (a necessity to choose an interpretation and react) is a trait of any scripture. Every kind of door is a sort of scripture. It divides the space into the inside and the outside. It's a well-known theme in Jacques Derrida (1976) but it's also a favourite figure in Giorgio Agamben, namely, a threshold (Agamben, 1998).

This nomothetic layer of literature (literature as a door, literature as architecture) includes in my view the explicit structures of all public institutions. Countries, monasteries, corporations – all of them have structures, and these structure have a linguistic shape. This layer of literature also includes linguistic machines, all kind of abacus and computers. Any machines of control (in the Deleuzian sense, 1995) – automatic sensors, walls with guarded gates, frontiers – may be also understood as a specific kind of institutional literature. Thus, the novel by Ursula Le Guin, *The Dispossessed* (1974) (one of the anarchist utopias mentioned in the title of this chapter) begins with a description of the one and only border wall on the planet of Annares. It is a wall built around the spaceport; it separates the anarchist society of Annares from the rest of the world – the world divided into countries and submitted to written laws, and, more importantly, to a monetary economy, not present in Annares. This wall and, moreover, the city planning in Annares or the design in Urras are examples of the nomothetic layer of literature (for the visitor from Annares – Le Guin says – the design in Urras seems to be saturated with eroticism. It's the lack of gender equality and the existence of repressive sexual norms that creates tension that can be seen even in the shapes of furniture). It's softer than the ontological layer, because one can intentionally shape and reshape it, whereas the ontological layer is predominantly not even noticed by its users.

This nomothetic layer is also this very level of literature that forces conformism – the necessary aspect of socialization. Thus, socialization must be seen as the internalization of language forced from outside. Only if the language is internalized, the possibility of resistance occurs. I can tear the wall down with an axe, but to be able to do it, I must adapt to this tool – submit the body to a certain rigour. Every answer to the question *who am I* is a report of a taming I have undergone. I am the one to whom I was tamed to be. I am a specimen of a social training type.

On the other hand, the fact that it was just me (and nobody else) who was the subject of a social training is hard to explain – it's a phenomenon beyond the language, maybe even beyond ontology. Maybe it's a fact that occurs at the intersection of two levels: the ontological and the artistic.

Hence, there is the third, lowest layer of literature's thickness – the artistic level. One can also call it the level of fiction. The origin of literature as literature – the birth of literary fiction – was a complex process. Its outline is similar to the scheme sketched by Walter Benjamin (1969) in *The Work of Art in the Age of Mechanical Reproduction* in regard to the visual arts. The loss of the nomothetic (i.e. auratic as Benjamin puts it) element of art was accompanied by the loosening of rigours binding the artist. Thus, links between the interpretation of the art's forms and the functioning of power can become visible. Thanks to this process the artist can become a creator of political art consciously, according to Benjamin. This consciousness doesn't compensate the loss of sacral and magical authority, though.

In relation to the topic of this chapter, Benjamin's thesis can be put as follows: the literature, leaving the nomothetic level, gains more freedom of expression but loses importance and social strength. It can be easily reduced to the role of entertainment, a product of the cultural industry that petrifies the status quo. A possible solution for an artist may be to stick to common conventions in order to bend them, and so to inspire the reader with a thought that the social convention is flexible, too.

This can be done by means of literature popular in its form and radical in the message. The element of fiction doesn't only entertain here (providing the participation in Lust zu Fabulieren – the desire to storytelling); it is also a kind of trick allowing to make the nomothetic structures of social life more loose. It allows to think of a different division of labour/power than the historically existing one. Thus, it allows to think about alternative history.

From this point of view, the fiction is at least equivalent to the theory, or even has its advantage over theory, namely, because fiction can create so called "unreliable narrators" (Booth, 1961). In fact, every narrator, every subject in the work of fiction speaks under the clause of unreliability. According to Bakhtin's book on Dostoyevsky (Bakhtin, 1984), an author must not, or even cannot, suggest which voice of his novel is *ontologically reliable* or at least *nomothetically reliable*, that is, which opinion expressed in his work should be read "seriously" or "without brackets." The very convention of fictionality makes the voices appear in a novel within some kind of quotation marks, within fictional brackets, or in invisible italic. Fiction confronts only the voices within brackets – and so it experiments with reality, showing how the language could function in fictional conditions. Thus, the task of literature is to create fictional conditions and to confront fictional narrators and fictional narrations (narrations of invented characters and of invented institutions) in these fictional language conditions.

To sum up, there are three levels of literary density. The first, ontological, is hard – it contains stones, angels (supernatural beings), and quarks. We don't notice it but we live within it constantly. The second, nomothetic, is softer – it contains codexes, walls, and computers. The third, artistic, is the most flexible one – it involves the literary fictions and other works of art.

Ursula Le Guin and Simone Weil

From this point of view I am going to discuss three texts. Two of them are novels, that is, fiction – *Dispossessed* (1974) and *Always Coming Home* (1985) – by Ursula Le Guin (the plot pattern of the latter novel is reduced in favour of a fictional anthropological documentation). The third text is *The Need for Roots* by Simone Weil (1952). At first glance the essay looks like an academic treatise, even if Weil avoids technical expressions and the text can be read by an unprepared, "naive" reader from the lower classes (or at least she wished it could be). In fact, Weil's book has the traditional form of utopia, though. It remains in a tradition of Plato's discourse on the ideal state, among such authors like Thomas More and Tomasso Campanella. On the other hand, some of its content makes it similar to dystopian work of literature by authors like Herbert George Wells, Aldous Huxley, George Orwell, Philip K. Dick, and, last but not least, Stanislaw Lem. It's a form situated between treatise, utopia, and dystopia, a form that testifies the affinity of theory and fiction.

What seems to be common to all three of the texts is the awareness that the utopia – representation of equality – must be written in a language formatted for the sake of inequality. Because we have no other linguistic tools, all we have comes from internalization of linguistic tools of inequality and from conformity resulting from this socialization. Thus, to express the utopia, one has to use the language against the language. The necessity to use the language that is the machine of social regulation and control makes every utopia an ambiguous one. Every liberation can have only a partial character, and the tools it uses – which always have a linguistic and thus political character – are ambiguous and may be used to establish new types of social oppression. Claiming this is not necessarily a sign of a conservative and passive type of pessimism, nor an attempt to avoid any change, since every change can lead to a new type of evil. It rather resembles the active pessimism praised by Nietzsche. One could call it also ambiguous optimism: change is always possible but all changes come with costs.

The Dispossessed

The first of the three mentioned books, *The Dispossessed* (some editions bear the subtitle *An Ambiguous Utopia*), deals explicitly with the question of these costs. Le Guin, the daughter of American anthropologists studying the life of Californian Indians, is one of the best-known authors of twentieth-century popular literature. She wrote fantasy and science fiction but her writing could be also called anthropological fiction or even organizational fiction because above all she was interested in inventing fictional types of social organization and sketching relations between institutions, language, and power.

Within these institutionalized and culturally rooted relations of power, Le Guin paid special attention to sexual and gender institutions and relations. Thus, her whole writing can be seen as series of fictional cultural or gender studies. These "gender fictions" can be seen as an equivalent of gender theories.

Questions concerning technologies or fictional laws of physics – typical concerns of "hard science fiction" – play in Le Guin the role of general settings for social themes, which are her main point of interest. Physics is like a formal framework: "Let's suppose that." For example, let's suppose there is a planet where one season of the year lasts decades according to the earthy measures (*Planet of Exile*, 1966). Or let's suppose there is a species very similar to the human, but completely intersexual: each time it comes to a kind of rut – every month – an individual becomes a male or a female for a few days, and nobody is normally able to control this process; thus, motherhood and fatherhood can be an experience of all (*The Left Hand of Darkness*, 1969). How would such a society work? Questions of technology and science are not the main point of interest in these books; they are rather an excuse to deal with organizational questions. If we compare Le Guin's attitude in this respect to Stanislaw Lem's inquiries, we can see of lot of similarities (by the way, Lem was a great admirer of Le Guin and he made a lot to popularize her books in Poland; in Le Guin we can also find enthusiastic remarks on Lem). Lem, like Le Guin, made his name as an author of popular literature (their career shows, by the way, the general pointlessness of the distinction between popular and avant-garde literature; they managed to exceed this distinction on many levels). Yet, Lem was much more interested in ontological questions than Le Guin was (though their interest in nomothetical questions was the same). On the other hand, Lem was rather deaf to the gender issues, whereas the gender question is key to Le Guin's writing.

In *The Dispossessed*, the Annares, a desert planet, which is a satellite of a bigger and much more fertile sister planet, Urras, becomes an area of an anarcho-communist experiment. Annares is populated by the society of emigrants from Urras; its inhabitants have abandoned the traditional forms of authority, economy, and family. There is no state, law, monetary system, and private property on Annares. The society is a confederation of autonomous collectives – syndicates of work that can be joined by everybody. This system is the implementation of ideas created by a revolutionary theorist from Urras, Odo. The ideas of Odonism, Le Guin took from Kropotkin and Bookchin. But even more similarities with Odonism can be found in Edward Abramowski, a writer probably unknown to Le Guin. His ideas of "cooperative republic" and "associations of friends" (Abramowski, 2012) as the molecular structures of society might be helpful in describing the institutional order of Annares. There is no legal form of family in Annares (well, it's no wonder, since there is no written law in Annares – which does not however mean that there is no nomothetical layer of literature there; on the contrary, it is present everywhere, written in shapes of cities and houses – lovely shapes, as Le Guin claims – as well as in the gestures and habits of people). Thus, there is a widespread informal institution of civil partnerships – people who love each other and raise children together. But children grow up very fast in Annares – very early they achieve maturity in the sense of ability (and necessity) to manage their lives. The school is also a voluntary institution (to a certain extent, like every institution in Annares, it seems that, when you are young, the only collective that is willing to accept you is school – and it's hard, though not impossible, to live without a collective on a desert planet). All educational process is fulfilled with voluntary collectives, and all they teach is autonomy, help by decision making and respecting the autonomy of others. But even the formation towards independence is still a formation and must adopt the tool of conformism.

The main character of the novel is a prodigy physicist, Shevek. He resembles Einstein but his thoughts on time, which is the main topic of his inquiries, have a merely poetical shape in the novel (albeit we learn, he uses mathematics to write it down). His inquiries are all about the simultaneity of time, eternity hidden in time and accessible for human beings. The novel shows the formation of his ideas and his personality; thus, it's a kind of bildungsroman. Shevek's constant inclination to question the obvious forms and to reject the usual solutions that make up the life of the community is seen by his fellow citizen as "egoizing."

> Speech is sharing – a cooperative art. You're not sharing, merely egoizing.
>
> (Le Guin, 1974, p. 37)

He hears this already as a small boy in an educational circle when he tries to utter the logical paradox he discovered. The only support he finds is in a love relationship, in his relation with his wife and son, and with his friends who merely chose the life of artists. There was no censorship in Annares, of course, but the dominant artistic taste was rather bourgeois, while Shevek's friends were looking for new forms in art, just like he was looking for new solutions in physics. The scientific syndicates – just like artistic ones – turn out to be based on a certain type of conformism. It's the only way that opens the possibility of career – something that should theoretically not exist in a society without authority. And yet, as we can observe, even the anarcho-communist life is based on routine, and this is a factor that enables the establishment of informal elites, that is, groups that monopolize decision making in important issues. In the case in question, there was a group of influential scientists who monopolized the scientific exchange with the external world. In response to this blockade of their initiatives by the social routine and an informal system of authority, Shevek and his friends established their own syndicate – "the syndicate of innovations." It was a commune proposing new solutions in various spheres of social life. The very existence of this syndicate was seen by many citizens of Annares as a fundamental danger for anarchists principles. A group of "egoizing" arrogant people want to teach others what is good or wrong, questioning the very principle of equality. Le Guin can offer only a plot-related (and not a structural) solution to this conflict. Shevek goes to the sister planet, Urras, where he gets in contact with a sui generis comic syndicate, a league of all planets inhabited by humanlike creatures. This Ekumen is in many Le Guin books an exemplary model of non-violent coexistence of all possible cultures and political organizations. But this emplotted solution is not a conceptual one; it's more like an expression of hope that there is a solution that can be found one day. It resembles the myths that appear in some key parts of Plato dialogues, like Phoedo or The Republic. These myths have a similar function: they signal aporia as well as hope that the truth is to be found – not in the text but in philosophical life, perhaps.

Always Coming Home

Shevek's theory of time makes it possible to communicate for civilizations lying many light years from each other – in Le Guin information can be faster than light; the word wins over the time, so to say. In contrast to this techno-optimism, in *Always Coming Home* we find a vision of a future society that takes a deliberate step backward from the achieved level of technology. It is perhaps a good text for the times of the climate crisis. The society depicted by Le Guin – not only in the story, but also in various fictional anthropological documents, like interviews, poems, maps – lives in the California of the future, after a huge ecological disaster caused by capitalist greed and imperialist expansionism. People who survived, after thousands years of trials and errors, decided consciously to maintain their civilization in neolithic-like forms. Independently from human institution, there is a nest of artificial intelligence (AI) on earth – a completely unpolitical bunch of autonomous computers, interested not in power but in information. The "new savages" sometimes use autonomous computers to obtain information or know-how – but it happens quite rarely. Their society, according to Levi-Strauss's terminology, is a "cold" one (Levi-Strauss, 1966). Thus, its main effort is to keep away the influence of time – to remain timeless. This can be achieved through participation in natural cycles, by means of rituals like collective and individual performing of dances and songs. The whole nature dances its dance of the equilibrium; people must learn to do it from nature. Their especially admired teachers of being in the world are thus animals (it makes me think of a certain notion in Deleuze, namely, becoming-animal, one of the key concepts in *A Thousand Plateaus*, 1987). The life of these people seems harmonious and free of violence; their thinking, full of common sense. All energy of an individual human being is focused on the task to live one's life in harmony with nature – to dance one's own dance as a particular dance figure of the universe. That is the terminology these people are using: the dance of nature, the songs of animals – and human dances and songs among them. There is no juxtaposition of human being and nature; no contrast between culture and nature.

The story of the novel is built around the unsuccessful journey undertaken by a female character raised in the stable tribe of "new savages" to the tribe of her father. Instead of harmony (or rather the controlled stagnation) the father's tribe chooses military aggression with the support of technological innovations. Yet, the territorial expansion fails, and militarist tendencies in the daughter's tribe are happily nipped in the bud. "The warriors" have to go. The society of tolerant individuals is able to fight in defence of its sovereignly chosen inertia (which they do not consider a bad thing, of course). What gets lost in this fight is perhaps the Faustian element in human society. The eradication of violence and expansionism is achieved through the abolition of every critical institution that could put in question the once established "natural" lifestyle. Or, to be more exact: this lifestyle is not "natural" but it tries to imitate natural life, and, in fact, it only produces the notion of "nature" as the accordance with tradition – which is forgotten to be a tradition at all.

The Need for Roots

The third book is *The Need for Roots* by Simone Weil. It's a kind of political treatise written in 1943 for the Free French in order to guide discussion on the subject of the future political order in France. One should notice that Weil's suggestions were completely inacceptable to both the left wing and the right wing – even if Weil's spiritual evolution, leading her from heterodox communism to mystical Christianity, could be interesting for the Christian democratic wing of Gaullists.

It think it is possible to describe this book in contrast to both Le Guin's novels as a conditional praise of tradition. While the society of Annares formally rejects tradition (in fact it sinks in bad kind of tradition – in social routine), and the future Californians are traditional to such an extent that they confuse tradition with nature, Weil suggests a certain playful attitude towards tradition. Instead of talking about human rights (which she finds too abstract), she proposed a narration focused on the "needs of the soul." They enable people to take root in tradition, which is the foundation of every community. "Taking root" in tradition does not require blind obedience but a critical and free choice of forms that can be called one's own. This choice enables the community to change the tradition, since it makes the tradition a part of the community.

> The degree of respect owing to human collectivities is a very high one, for several reasons. To start with, each is unique, and, if destroyed, cannot be replaced. One sack of corn can always be substituted for another sack of corn. The food which a collectivity supplies for the souls of those who form part of it has no equivalent in the entire universE.
>
> (Weil, 1952, p. 7)

Thus, the community is something unique, irreplaceable for Weil. But loyalty to the community is in no way the highest or autotelic value. An individual requires a community in order to be able to fulfill, as Weil calls it, "the eternal destiny" of the soul. This expression can be read in a religious as well as in a secular sense – as a pursuit of redemption or a pursuit of the truth in existential meaning. That is to say, a meaningful life. This pursuit – an individual way towards a goal that is yet indefinite, but guides all the life efforts like Plato's *epekeina tēs ousias (ideas)* (R. 509b) – is more important than any external commitment. And yet this ride towards the sun – in another Weil's text we can find a metaphor of "taking root in the sun" – is impossible without taking roots in the earth, that is to say, without a discovery of an individual, unique destination in one's own, unique – shaped by the history and tradition – political community. The road towards heaven leads always through the earth.

What Weil calls "taking roots" is the possibility of sustainable satisfaction of needs of the soul. The sustainability comes from the tradition that can be understood as a consciously, patiently trained *hexis* – a constant disposition, a virtue of a community. This community training – construction of the collective disposition – is labour to harmonize the opposite "need of the soul," namely, order and liberty, obedience (the need to be guided) and responsibility (the need to guide), hierarchy and equality, security and risk – and some others. All this should not lead to the conclusion that Weil, towards the end of her short life, became a conservative, or that she rejected the notion of radical social change. First, tyranny never satisfies the needs of the soul. The fact that an order is old or stable does not mean it is good. Tyranny must be fought by any means. The thing is, the resistance has its own tradition and creates its own communities, and these communities may be tyrannical as well if they don't satisfy the needs of the soul. That is the eternally returning experience of the twentieth century. Second, Weil's interpretation of hierarchy and equality confirms the non-conservative character of her politeia.

She writes:

> Equality is all the greater in proportion as different human conditions are regarded as being, not more nor less than one another, but simply as other. Let us look on the professions of miner and minister simply as two different vocations, like those of poet and mathematician.
>
> (ibid., p. 17)

Hence, she wants a society where the hierarchy of power is not identical with the hierarchy of prestige. How to achieve this? By the constant control of those in power. The juridical authority must be strengthened – Weil claims. This advice may be not be sufficient.

The society in Weil's politeia resembles the community of monks or nuns, who are less interested in the earthly business of monastery management than in the spiritual treasures they expect from contemplation – even if the notion of contemplation is extremely exended here and contains every manifestation of sensual life. Every bodily action is what Weil wants to interpret as a kind of prayer – a way of praising and admiring the very fact of existence and the possibility of participating in it. It may seem highly unrealistic to expect that such an attitude could prevail in society as a whole. On the other hand, is not the climate crisis the right moment to question the old social engines like greed, ambition? If we want to survive, must we not reorganize the society around the praise of existence as such?

Conclusions

What is, in the end, the relation between conformity and the need for the roots? It is a complex dialectical relation. Conformity is the hierarchizing side of the language: it introduces the inequality. But the nonconformity goes in trail of the same conformist socialization; it just heads to the opposite direction. Nonconformity is rebelling against the conformity in the name of an "ego" that is a result of conformity. This is why nonconformity is never sufficient; it needs orientation towards utopia. The utopia must not be an empty signifier speaking about something "what no eye has seen, nor ear heard." It may be a way of taking root in the tradition, namely, in the tradition of the resistance. We can construct this tradition by balancing the needs of the soul. In order to achieve this, we can reshape the existing traditions and communities, trying to built just institutions for the individual meaningful life – because the "eternal destiny" of the individual soul can be achieved only when based on really existing, earthly means available in each unique cultural environment.

References

Abramowski, E. (2012). *Braterstwo, solidarność, współdziałanie*. Łódź, Poland: Biblioteka Obywatela.

Agamben, G. (1998). *Homo Sacer*. Trans. D. Heller-Roazen. Stanford, CA: Stanford University Press.

Bakhtin, M. (1984), Problems of Dostoevski's poetics. Trans. C. Emersen. Minneapolis, London, UK: University of Minnesota Press.

Benjamin, W. (1999). *Illuminations* (pp. 217–252). Trans. H. Zohn. New York, NY: Schocken Books.

Brzozowski, S. (1913). *Pamiętnik*. Lwów, Europe: Księgarnia Polska B. Połonieckiego.

Booth, W. C. (1961). *The rhetoric of fiction*. Chicago, IL: The University of Chicago Press.

Deleuze, G. (1995). Postscript on control societies. In *Negotiations 1972–1990* (pp. 177–182). Trans. Martin Joughin, New York, NY: Columbia University Press.

Deleuze, G., & Guattari, F. (1987). *A Thousand Plateaus*. Trans. B. Massumi. Minneapolis: University of Minnesota Press.

Derrida, J. (1976). *Of grammatology*. Transl. G. C. Spivak. Baltimore, MD and London, UK: Johns Hopkins University Press.

Foucault, M. (1977). *Discipline and punish: The birth of the prison*. Trans. A. Sheridan. London, UK: Allen Lane, Penguin.

Graczyk, P. (2016). Nicolas Gomez Davila. In P. Nowak (Ed.), *Historia filozofii politycznej* (pp. 870–879). Warszawa, Poland: Kronos.

Gramsci, A. (1971). *Selections from the prison notebooks*. London, UK: Lawrence & Wishart.
Heidegger, M. (2018). *Hölderlin's hymn "Remembrance"*. Trans. W. McNeill and J. Ireland. Bloomington: Indiana University Press.
Le Guin, U. (1966). *Planet of exile*. New York, NY: Ace Books.
Le Guin, U. (1969). *The left hand of darkness*. New York, NY: Ace Books.
Le Guin, U. (1974). *The dispossessed*. New York, NY: Harper & Row.
Le Guin, U. (1985). *Always coming home*. New York, NY: Harper & Row.
Levi-Strauss, C. (1966). *The savage mind*. London, UK: Weinfeld and Nicolson.
Lukacs, G. (1980). *The destruction of the reason*. Trans. P. R. Palmer. Talgarth, Wales: Merlin Press.
Marx, K. (1959) [1844]. *Economic and philosophic manuscripts of 1844*. Trans. M. Miligan. Moscow, Russia: Progress Publishers.
Marx, K., & Engels, F. (2004) [1848]. *Manifesto of the communist party*. Marxists Internet Archive. https://www.marxists.org/ Retrieved on 14 March 2015.
Mouffe, C., & Laclau, E. (1985). *Hegemony and socialist strategy. Towards a radical democratic politics*. London, UK: Verso.
Schmitt, C. (2006). *The Nomos of the earth in the international law of the Jus Publicum Europaeum*. Trans. by G. L. Ulmen. New York, NY: Telos Press Publishing.
Schmitt, C. (2007). *The concept of the political*. Trans. G. Schwabb. Chicago, IL: The University of Chicago Press.
Weil, S. (1952). *The need for roots*. Trans. A. Wills. London, UK: Routledge & Kegan Paul.

7 The Alchemical Life of Ernesta Thot – A Romantic Heroine of Art

Marta Kudelska

What do we mean when we describe a curator's ways of acting or trying to determine who he actually is? Curating itself is mostly associated with organizing exhibitions – not only dedicated to contemporary art, but also to early art. However, it is the field of contemporary art that we should look at for the starting point of curating history. Curating is a modern practice that dates back to the late decades of the twentieth century. It combines various, often quite different, skills, ranging from specialist knowledge on culture and art through competences related to art management and art criticism to the ability to work with artists to create an exhibition (Brenson, 1998).

Curating contemporary art is a profession strongly dominated by the conviction that the work is rather special, which has often led to the fact that curators are considered to be extremely strong, independent entities operating in the field of contemporary art. Similar to many other "unusual" characters, representatives of this profession are strongly convinced of the individualization of their narratives, but also about the impossibility of creating obvious rules creating the success of a given art curator. This certain enigmatic nature is also associated with what Lucy Lippard mentions in an interview with Hans Ulrich Obrist: a certain amnesia regarding the beginning of curating (Obrist, 2016). Lippard herself admitted that, in her own archive, she did not even have photos from her first exhibitions and artistic shows. Therefore, when we examine the history of curating, we are often doomed to rely on memories, enigmatic notes, or stories about exhibitions that were once carried out.

This openness to interpretations became the starting point for Arthur Danto to create the concept of "artworld," under which a certain community of people, who voluntarily participate in its construction, are hidden, working behind the scene. They have some common sensitivity, aesthetic preferences, but also if they want to exist in this world, they must become its active members. It is this particular group that has the power to define and name what art is and what it is not.

Danto even goes so far as "elevating" this world and comparing it to the divine world:

> The artworld stands to the real world in something like the relationship in which the City of God stands to the Earthly City. Certain objects, like certain individuals, enjoy a double citizenship...
>
> (Danto, 1964, p. 582)

Can we therefore compare the art world to a secret, closed group of people who have gained the knowledge of transforming ordinary objects into art? Following this line of thought, could you compare art curators to alchemists? And what about the characters from this world who, due to the lack of material traces of their activity, were lost in the depths of history? The following text is an attempt to answer these questions by restoring the memory of a forgotten curator – Ernesta Thot. An extraordinary figure who, in her curatorial practice, sought to equalize two worlds – the world of alchemy and the world of art. Thot believed that modern art was governed by rules similar to the alchemical and magical world. This perspective seems extremely interesting for us today, as we are increasingly leaning on exploring the past and searching for answers to describe our present. The story of Ernesta Thot can therefore shed a new light on the development of the profession of a curator of modern art.

For over a century, the figure of Ernesta Thot – a Styrian–Polish art curator – has been one of the many greats of contemporary art lost in the depths of history. Aside from fringe characters and personalities like charlatans, or misfits, schizophrenics, and mystics, no one considered, referred to, or explored her ideas, or similar ideas. In this way, she came to be forgotten, lost and adrift in time, on the tides of history for so long.

Miss Ernesta's Bitterness

Miss Ernesta (a Miss, as she is said to have never been married), contrary to the contemporary mores of the time, delighted in oneiric, mystical, phantasmatic, surreal, and avant-garde forms of art (Figure 7.1). She advocated cabarets, alchemy, and occultism. Long before the arrival of the postmodernists, she was of the opinion that modernist beliefs about the neutrality of the "White Cube" (art gallery space) were just another myth, and nothing more than a camouflaged element of ideology. In other words, a white, ideal, modernist art space – originating from the Vienna Secession (exhibition pavilion in Vienna) – seemed highly suspicious to her, because she felt that it could be used for ideological warfare, exclusion, and advocating symbolic, political, and economic violence.

Unfortunately, Ernesta never fully developed her idea that the space of the institution of art did not mean anything objective, because it was

Figure 7.1 Miss Ernesta's bitterness. Jakub Woynarowski (2012) "Iconoclastia," "Novus Ordo Seclorum" cycle.

only a mirror in which the problems of modern times were reflected. However, it also depicted the growing problem of the instrumentalization of the artistic object.[1] A growing bitterness towards this instrumentalization led her to turn to a completely different approach in her curatorial research, compared with that of her contemporaries.

Death Did Not Come Quickly

Ernesta Thot died on 12 August 1936, having fallen into a coma on 20 May earlier that year. As has been the case for other exceptional characters, it all started following an unfortunate – completely unexpected – incident: Ernesta had collapsed while strolling through the garden, having choked on the smell of a strange golden flower.[2] What makes this story more extraordinary is that these dates coincided with the alleged illness and death of Michał Sędziwój, the "Prince of Polish Alchemy."

Like many other visionaries, Ernesta was labelled as crazy during her life, and after her death. For many years, she was overcome by feelings that Roland Barthes would later describe as a "feeling of sickening boredom" (Bartnes, 2006, pp. 200–201). Anthony Gidens described it as "an individual sense of nonsense" (Gidens, 2002, p. 13). For Ernesta Thot, Weber's "iron cage of modernity" in the art of the avant-garde was too constricting. This affliction, characteristic of modern society, led her to become the first romantic heroine in the history of art curation. Until the end of her days, she believed that art has the power to transform. Like Paul Celan, Ernesta believed that "the artist fulfills the role of a modern alchemist, both in relation to forms and to the meanings that make up a whole culture" (Guzek, 2007, p. 101).

Ernesta the Bad Ghost

It is difficult to pick out the moment when she decided to weave this conviction into her area of interest. One day, however, Ernesta was ready "to enter into a sinful relationship with the Evil Spirit" (Beneveni, 1863, p. 458). The catalyst may have been Ernesta's fascination with Barbarogenius (Czaplik-Lityńska, 2005), one of the more unusual fictional characters of the first avant-garde. Barbarogenius had the power to transform beings. For Ernesta, the Expressionists, and the Surrealists, whom he inspired, he became an extraordinary figure from whom they took the belief that "properly used symbolic signs have the power to process and even produce things in the world" (Wierciński, 2010, p. 136), which perfectly fits in with ancient magical thinking.

Magical word had the power to reach an extradimensional world, and many magical practices themselves were "based on the assumption that a name and its object are (intrinsically) connected (…); hence verbal actions are simultaneously actions 'within' objects" (Szczęsna, 2002, p. 167). It was only after her death that similar demiurgic features would be attributed to the curator of art, and conceptual art as a whole. This idea, this concept – or at least, this belief – just somehow never bloomed: it didn't achieve full expression or articulation. Looking at it now, this lack or prevention from reaching a resolution may have been a factor that (along with others) pushed Ernesta over the edge of sanity.

In an alchemical sense, this mortal breakdown became her point of rebirth, a little like the Phoenix, which hatches from the ashes of its last incarnation. She became a heroine of contemporary art, whose ambitions exceeded her, as did the expectations placed on her by herself and others. The theory she wanted to demonstrate did not evolve to become a sphere for summoning or transporting creations from the realm of dreams and imagination to the realm of reality.

It Takes a Revolution

Ernesta was convinced that modern art needs a guide, a translator. Appearing in the second half of the twentieth century, the figure of a curator as a master, a ruler, and creator of modern art brings to the mind of some the archetypal hero Barbarogenius: a Messiah, a Saviour, a Destroyer of the Old Order. His causative powers partially correspond with those of a Saviour and partially with those of a Shaman: the curator is partially a channel for the power and authority of a "God," while at the same time preparing for changes, moving balances, and rhythms that only the perspective and experience of a Shaman could reveal. This power cannot be rationally explained, but it is the curator, and no one else, who has the power to possibly cause the expected or unexpected changes. Artists and art theorists contemporary to Ernesta had been seeking and looking out for this kind of breakthrough, but they did not completely know the "shape" of the thing they were reaching out for. It is very possible that, for this reason, all their revolutionary ideas and proposals took the form of manifestoes and crazy postulates, whose effects and impact were expected to manifest at some point in recent near-history.

It is without a doubt that Ernesta (as an enlightened and curious person) came across the "Manifesto of Expressionism" by Stanislav Vinaver in 1920. In the manifesto, he writes:

> Today we are entering *the Spirit of Change*, the Spirit of Flow, the Dynamics of Chaos, the revolution of Expression, and what is expressed. And once the revolution is finished, everything will grow, even without much effort on our part. The forces of nature will serve us and revive our revolution. Anyone who desires will not make a revolution/One needs to know how to start the release of words, concepts, imagination – from their limitations and trenches. We, Expressionists, we start a revolution, we enter into chaos, into *the endless release of everything from everything.*
>
> (Vinaver, 1980, p. 82)

Such a perspective for us today – with the experience of postmodernism just behind us – is not at all that strange. Jameson (2011) mentions that in a "sense that since everything we say is only part of a larger chain or context, all impressions that seem primal are really just links in some larger text" (ibid., p. 402). This mindset can serve as the key to unraveling the enigmatic commentary that Ernesta left in her navy-blue notebook with heavy, hard covers: the sole testament of her life, theories, and thought. Beside the aforementioned section from Vinaver's manifesto, she hurriedly wrote the word "V.I.T.R.I.O.L" in her slightly crooked script, under which (clearly annoyed) she wrote, "Everything is the fault of the Fish!"[3]

The Alchemist's Manifesto

Ernesta prepared a manuscript titled "The Alchemist's Manifesto," but in a moment of clumsy misfortune, it "fell into a pool of small, swimming creatures." These creatures had their way with the manuscript, and this unfortunate event, without a shadow of a doubt, redirected the future of the history of art and curating, while also laying the foundations for an unconscious narrative to evolve and surround the manuscript – a narrative that never resonated out loud. Ernesta wrote out her grief surrounding this unfortunate event. These writings at once close the incident, and – by strange paradox – open up the way for us to interpret her concept of the art curator as a Guardian, Alchemist, and romantic Hero.

In the end, the incidents that surrounded and followed her may be the best indicators of what she meant.

Ernesta's Diary

To future generations of art and curation researchers, Ernesta Thot became a hidden object of desire and the purest form. In the theories, art descriptions, and exhibitions that these generations of researchers have compiled, presented, and exhibited in the years since Ernesta's death, you can easily find fragments and echoes of Ernesta's thoughts. "Deciphering" these writings is like "taking a walk through a forest of fiction" (Eco, 2007), because Ernesta did not really leave behind an organized text, a complete diary, or something that would allow us to clearly understand her character today. What she did leave us are hurried notes made in the margins of the navy-blue notebook. One such key note is the inscription "V.I.T.R.I.O.L" in the margin of the aforementioned fragment of the "Manifesto of Expressionism." Thanks to this mysterious inscription (and ticket stubs that, by some miracle, simply did not fall out from between the notebook's pages over the course of the ages), we can be very confident of the fact that Ernesta Thot – at a point in her mature life – set out on her own grand tour, during which she came to Greece. Perhaps she spent a few days in Delphi so that (in accordance with the ancient Oracle's maxim) she could "get to know herself." This seemingly familiar maxim was, however, one of the central axioms of alchemists, for whom we know Ernesta had a special respect and affection. The term "V.I.T.R.I.O.L" also refers to the Oracle's maxim: "V.I.T.R.I.O.L" encourages the symbolic descent of "man" to the depths of themselves. "Visita Interiora Terrae Recitificando Invenis Occultum Lapida," meaning "Visit the Interior of the Earth, and by Rectifying, You Will Discover the Hidden Stone."[4]

Plato's Cave

During one of her last outings while in Greece, Ernesta was around the island with some friends when they got caught in a rainstorm in one of the many grottos that are scattered in the area (Figure 7.2). To pass the time, this cheerful group performed a shadow theatre on one of the walls of the cave, and told the stories of their – as yet – unrealized artistic ideas. Ernesta eventually became bored with this and went for a solitary wander to explore the depths of the rock labyrinths. Going up along a stony path, she reached the mouth of a cave, where she found strange objects basking in the light of the sun. Wanting to tell her companions about what she had discovered, Ernesta hurried back down the path, but she slipped during this rocky descent. Adding an insult to the injury, not only did she pick up a large bruise, but she was knocked unconscious for

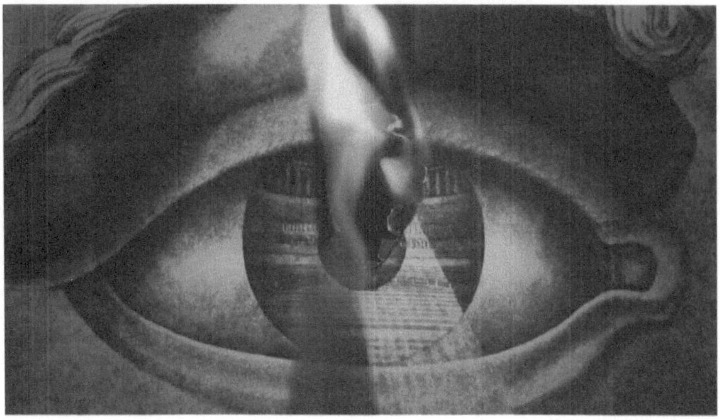

Figure 7.2 Plato's Cave. Jakub Woynarowski (2013), "Nigredo," frame from the video.

a few moments. Her companions were unsympathetic upon hearing her story and decided that it was evidence of her peculiar madness, attributing this "episode" to the pessimism that was commonly believed to manifest in old maids beyond a certain age. The resulting disputes led to social exclusion for Ernesta, sadly not for the first time. Ernesta herself, however, was inspired by her discovery of – and encounter with – the mysterious objects in the mouth of the cave, and her thoughts crystalized into a concept we now recognize as "the Ready-Made." This concept and approach was popularized a few years later by Marcel Duchamp.

André Rouillé and Ernesta Thot

An attempt was made many years after Ernesta's death to reconstruct the alchemical source and pedigree of conceptual art and – by logical extension – of contemporary art. This work was undertaken by André Rouillé. Duchamp's shift towards creating art using various common, even mundane objects caused a significant change in the perceptions of the role of the artist, in both the public sphere and the sphere of academics/theorists. The activities of artists were no longer solely concerned with "producing" work, because there was now room (both actual and theoretical) for encountering, noticing, and turning the attention of others to (already) created objects. The modern artist – more than his historical counterpart – had become like a magician, elevating mere things from the mundane and drab, into Works, of massive cultural significance. In order for this to even take place, however, it was necessary to help other magicians – these being critics, curators, and theorists – who place these Works at the centre of art institutions and make them visible to all (Rouillé, 2007).

An enigmatic reference to Ernesta by Rouillé appears in the following sentences:

> Not everything is art, but everything can become it, or rather, every "thing" can become "matter"[5] for art, provided it becomes a part of the artistic process. Thus, art "appears" as a (result of) procedure and as a faith.
>
> (ibid., pp. 341–342)

The full breadth of Ernesta's influence is revealed elsewhere in Rouillé's work. Opening the section that considers the relationship between *ready-mades* and Photography, Rouillé uses the statement "symbolic alchemy is equivalent to (an appropriate) ready-made " (ibid., p. 342), a phrasing that could well have been uttered by Ernesta as she was gripped by a delirium or trance while visiting a vernissage.[6]

Granddaughter of Ladies of Alchemy

Ernesta's fascination with alchemy and its processes grew over time, moving on to fixation and onto obsession (Figure 7.3). Associating herself with the Surrealists, Cubists, and Expressionists, Ernesta became convinced that she was the heiress of the old masters of alchemy: Philadelphos, Komanos, Zosimos, Jabra Ibna Hajjan, Rhazes, Avicenna, Albert the Great, Georg Bauer (who authored the tome *De re metallica*), Paracelsus, Michał Sędziwój, John Dee, Edward Kelley, and Nicolas Flamel. She felt that her greatest spiritual relationships were with the legendary alchemists who supposedly had possessed the skill and understanding to create a "Philosopher's Stone": Maria Prophetissa – also called Mary the Jewess– Cleopatra the Alchemist, Medera and Taphnutia, and

Figure 7.3 Granddaughter of Ladies of Alchemy. Jakub Woynarowski (2013), "Damaged object," "Corpus Delicti" cycle.

also Paphnutia the Virgin. Based on Cleopatra's story, Ernesta began her own version of the sketch *Chrysopoeia of Cleopatra* – a mysterious document with an icon of Ouroboros: the symbol of oneness with the cosmos, and eternal return. This document was found close by her, after that fateful stroll through the garden where she encountered the Golden Flower and greeted unconsciousness. Like the alchemists she admired and connected with, Ernesta needs the words of others to tell her story.[7]

The Need for Immortality

Perhaps Ernesta imagined that she was a visionary who would wake up and overcome her own death one day, and be reborn. Like the "Great Daughters of Alchemy," she cultivated a conviction of her own agency and believed that, like them, she dealt with energy, with what was natural, material, and spiritual at the same time. She tried to combine what was "low," "common" with what was "high" and "noble."[8] What some artists dilated, blurred, or hid in the crevices of the studio, she merged and transformed into new and different forms. Nobody else but Ernesta Thot had the power to transform what is earthly into something spiritual and extraordinary. She looked for reflections and echoes of the ideas she worked with and in the art that surrounded her.

The Operation of the Sun

In conversations – both real and imagined – about building and creating art exhibitions, Ernesta spotted several similarities with a hermetic tradition called *The Operation of the Sun*, a tradition alchemists were known to practice (Figure 7.4). There were four stages, each one

Figure 7.4 The Operation of the Sun. Jakub Woynarowski (2013), "Albedo," "Novus Ordo Seclorum" cycle.

corresponding with a particular stage of the alchemist's search for perfection and the continuation of their quest.

The expected transformations would be initiated by heating the correct elements over a fire. The resulting hot, bubbling mass would be black in colour – *nigredo* – was identified with the primordial state of matter, and was the symbol of "the internal death." This *massa confusia* (mixed mass) was – despite appearances – a harbinger of future glory and rebirth. The second stage was the process by which the *massa confusia* returned to its initial form, only now it would be white in colour, having been purified by the fire of the first stage. Due to the white colour, this stage was called *albedo*. The third stage was called *rubedo*, during which the white mass would become red in colour. This stage identified with elevation. The fourth stage identified with a rebirth at the highest possible levels and obtaining the Philosopher's Stone. Intuition told Ernesta that her instinctive grasp regarding these processes, and their intrinsic connection to the space in which she could arrange exhibitions, was no haphazard coincidence.

White Cube and Death Mole

> The "ideal" gallery strips away from a given artwork all of the clues and markers that would interfere with the "clear" fact that the artwork is an Artwork. It (the Artwork) is isolated from anything that could diminish its intrinsic (of itself) value. This endows the gallery with the "remit" to possess spaces with the attributes of other places, in which conventions are maintained by creating a system of closed values. By combining the feeling of sanctity from a church with the formal structure of a courtroom, and the mystique of an experimental laboratory with a chic layout, a unique aesthetic "chamber" is created.
>
> (O'Dohery, 2005, pp. 452–453)

The focus of the perceptive fields within such a space are so strong that outside of this space, art objects seem to "'shrink" and slip down to the order of the mundane and everyday. The opposite is also true, in that "things" become art in a space that is able to focus artistic ideas around them (Figure 7.5).

> In reality, the (art) object often becomes a "medium" (or a catalyst) around which particular ideas crystalise and, in turn, become the subjects of conversation and debate; this is a popular form of academic late-Modernism (...the ideas are more interesting than the actual art ...).
>
> The sacramental aspect of the space becomes clear, as does one of the Great Immutable Laws of Modernism: as Modernism ages,

Figure 7.5 White cube and death mole. Jakub Woynarowski (2013), "Nigredo," "Novus Ordo Seclorum" cycle.

> its Context becomes its Content. By some strange twist, the objects within the gallery "frame" the gallery, and define its jurisdiction.
> (O'Dohery, 2005, pp. 452–453)

Brian O'Dohery writes about this extraordinary space for the presentation of art. In this "aesthetic chamber," Ernesta enacted the second stage of the alchemical process – *albedo*. To Ernesta, this strange and seemingly irrational place was like the abyss: "in order to get there, you must be already dead" (ibid., p. 453). The art objects Ernesta saw there filled her with fear, but still she looked at them with child-like fascination. It was akin to the time when she was five, and she buried a dead mole she had found and covered it with a piece of glass. Over the following days, she returned to this place and would clear the earth back from the glass with her fingers, revealing the cold, transparent border that divided her from death and decay. Art in galleries was dead in just the same way, but that was a price that had to be paid for the next step of its existence.

Night Butterfly

The first stage in the process of transmutation in preparation for an art exhibition, according to Ernesta, was the symbolic immobilization of the artistic object. Circling like a night butterfly, she set about searching artists' workshops for eye-catching objects: paintings, sculptures, notebooks, posters, mugs, cutlery, sketches, installations, pens, toothbrushes, beads, knick-knacks, including also books, albums, and photographs. Sometimes she had to take great pains in order to get the object of her desire. Artists did not willingly give her their works or souvenirs,

Figure 7.6 Night butterfly. Jakub Woynarowski (2013), "Rubedo," "Novus Ordo Seclorum" cycle.

but seeing her slightly demonic look thought the better of it than refusing her. Ernesta – satisfied – would then disappear from those dark, dusty places hidden between the alleyways of shabby neighbourhoods, leaving behind only the rustling sound of her long, black cloak. She hid her treasures, like many other exhibition creators, away from prying eyes – in storage units, safes, caskets, and lockers (Figure 7.6). Every now and then, she took her notebook, and staying alone with the object, wrote down its characteristics, applicability, history, and curiosities. Like the mythological Moirai,[9] she cut off the threads connecting the object with reality and let it have one, only one, function: being an object to look at (O'Dohery, 2005). Once the last thread was broken, the object was "torn out of life practice" (Bürger, 2006, p. 61). It became "nothing" and therefore potentially "Everything." Thus, the next stage of sublimation could take place – *albedo*.

Filius Philosophorum

In her mad raptures, gigglingly nervously, Ernesta had no doubt that she had discovered one of the many mysteries of the world. How could she be wrong, since even the walls of the gallery were white and it was right there: on the pedestal, in the glass case, behind the windows, on the platforms, that the "art" was regaining its value and meaning? Ernesta did not believe in the randomness of those clues. The last stage of these transformations, the final effect of her hard work, the Opus Magnum, was *rubedo* – the final elevation, involving the manifestation and revelation of Art by its Follower (Kudelska, 2019). The researcher Carol

Duncan wrote about places that could reveal this alchemical process, repeating after Victor Turner:

> [T]hey can open a space in which the individual can distance himself from practical issues and social relations of everyday life and look at himself and his world – or certain its aspects – in a different way.
> (Duncan, 2005, p. 285)

In today's world, museums and places for the presentation of art are supposed to be special places, marked out with an unusual aura, where the supernatural transformation of the well-known world was to take place. When the anticipated changes had run their course, *Filius Philosophorum* (philosopher's stone) started to materialize. And what of it, that it did not look like stone? Well, Ernesta was of the opinion – like many of her significant (legendary) predecessors – that it did not have to be limited to one final form and shape, but that it most surely granted immortality. Although this did not play out for Ernesta Thot, she – on opening nights, while drinking red wine – believed that the art was gaining immortality with every passing moment.

Emerald Array

While looking through Ernesta's navy-blue notebook (Figure 7.7), next to a ticket from a trip to Greece, you can find another clue revealing yet another plank of her art theory, which was about to manifest and appear in the pages of "The Alchemist's Manifesto," the one that sank and was nibbled by the fish. This time, her hand is less hurried, and it appears that Ernesta has had the time to lay out every word carefully:

> What is lower is like what is higher, and what is above is like what is below, for miracles penetrate/pass through only "One" thing.
> (Bugaj, 1991, p. 120)

It seems that her bizarre adventure in the grotto – which does evoke associations with Plato's cave – was not a fabrication of some hysterical old lady, but an actual extraordinary, revelatory event. The quote itself presented by Ernesta comes from the text *Corpus Hermeticum* (written between the third century BC and the third century AD), and named after its legendary author, Hermes Trismegistos. One of the most important texts of this collection was the so-called Emerald Array, which was considered a crucial key to the creation of a Philosopher's Stone. The sentence Ernesta so carefully wrote indicates clearly that she had stumbled onto the next element of this amazing puzzle, which she might have created herself. However, we can reasonably

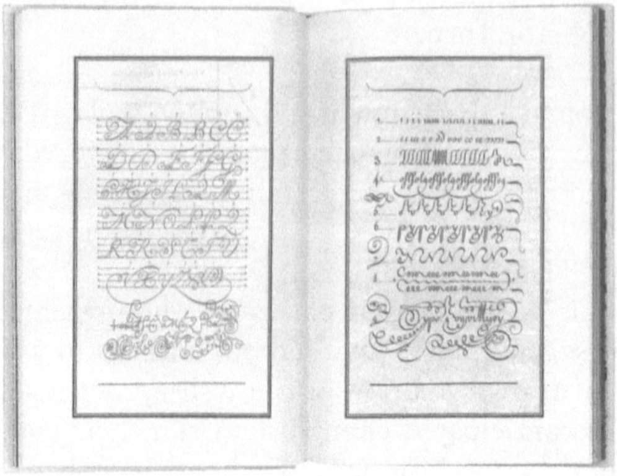

Figure 7.7 Emerald Array. Jakub Woynarowski (2013), "Signifying object," "Corpus Delicti" cycle.

speculate that, once again, she sensed "something" coming. Looking carefully at the yellowed sheet, under the visibly rough section of the paper, you can see an arrow directing our eyes towards the slogan "Fountain." No doubt about it, Ernesta's directing us to Marcel Duchamp's "Fountain."

Plato, Aristotle, and Duchamp

The philosophers who inspired Ernesta in her alchemical search were Plato and Aristotle. The Platonic Science-of-Ideas as the hierarchy of perfect beings was one of the foundations for alchemists who strove for perfection. Like the ancient philosophers, the alchemists and Ernesta were convinced that by perfecting their knowledge, they perfected themselves. Hence – probably – her compulsive need to collect various (now lost) objects and books, in which she saw the order for ruling the world. For her, these strange collections became a mirror reflecting and indicating the rules that governed human culture (Clifford, 2010). Guided by the old alchemical principle of *solve et coagula* (dissolve and coagulate), she built and connected her objects' most diverse stories to each other. Like Plato in "The Feast," she believed that first she should know material things (Platon, 1984), but her real purpose was to reach the essence of things, the so-called fifth disclosure, which she found out about while looking through "Letter VII" (Platon, 1987, p. 341). In this way in ages past, alchemical thought and recognition had been arranged and ordered, and Ernesta internalized this order too. She examined and investigated the world and art around her, attempting to discern their laws and mechanisms, all of which would help her capture that which was invisible, and rise above everyday life. Unlike Plato, she was not so critical of art, and did not think that she should get rid of it. Looking at the achievements of her contemporaries, she became convinced that they had accomplished something

> that – even though it was a deep desire and intention of Plato – could not be realised in that time: Art, as a result of internal change evolved into a philosophy, which resulted in a cascade of multiple serious changes.
>
> (Sosnowski, 2007, p. 138)

In her opinion, the alchemical transformation of things into art, which Duchamp had achieved, was nothing more than a question about the cause of the creation of art (ibid., p. 138). *Ready-Mades* were nothing more than the fulfillment of the sentence from the Emerald Tablet, and thus conceptual art ceased to use objects and focused on ideas.

The Aristotelian *quinta essentia* (fifth essence), which alongside the four basic elements made up the world, was something volatile, elusive, immaterial, and invisible; it became for Thot a new quality in art, which only a few years after her death would manifest in the form of land art, ephemeral art, and performance,[10] but also appeared in the form of a curator of art, who "should always be open to surprise, so that the unexpected may happen" (Obrist 2010 cited in Krawczyk, 2016, p. 79). Ernesta Thot's crazy ideas came from the fact that she was always ready for a surprise.

An Ending That Is Also a Beginning

The Alchemical Life (…) is the first text in the form of a verbal and artistic collage devoted to the alchemical heritage of Ernesta Thot (…– 1936). Over eighty years after her death, Thot is an extremely forgotten figure, and her intellectual achievements remain one of the most dispersed and obscure perspectives of twentieth-century art and curatorship. Though forgotten, and so very on the fringes, this proto-curator and researcher appears marginally as a recurring echo of the magical, surreal, and alchemical narratives present in art. None of Ernesta Thot's texts have survived to our times and no photographs of her are available. The navy-blue notebook with its hard covers, that is mentioned here, does not exist either. The author's aim is not to fill this gap, but to reflect on the potentiality, possibility, and vitality of the ideas of this extraordinary woman. Her biography is full of gaps and ambiguities. We do not know when she was really born or that she really died. Looking at the traces she left, one can point out that her character bears the typical hallmarks of a romantic hero. Undoubtedly, Ernesta, like all future curators, was characterized by individualism, a premonition that individual happiness is not dependent on the general public, and was also convinced of its uniqueness and charisma. Her thoughts were directed towards great ideas and she felt torn between what was here and what was there. That is why, like all romantics, she dreamed she was where she was not (Janion, 2010). She also had a conviction of her own prometheanism, characteristic of the romantics, and a certain dark fatality, which manifested itself in inexplicable events whose aim was to cover up all the traces she had left behind (ibid.). This dark fatalism is revealed in the story of a cave expedition, and when Thot destroys her "Alchemist Manifesto" through her own apparent momentary clumsiness. What was in it really? Was it really all the fish's fault...? It is unlikely we will ever find out.

Focusing on contemporary texts, appropriating certain theories, events and thoughts, I created a fiction – a potentially possible story (Figure 7.8). Potentially, because Ernesta Thot never really existed...

Except on these pages...

However...

The figure of a mysterious woman in a black coat appeared in my head thanks to the many conversations I've had with the visual artist Jakub Woynarowski. He is a lover of conspiracy theories in art, and he explores potentially possible narratives at the junctions of modern art and secret teachings such as alchemy, as well as mysterious groups like the Freemasons. After these many years of conversations, particular strands, strange clues, and premonitions began to appear before me, which (after "heating," purifying, and crystallizing) took the form of Ernesta and her "peculiarities." When I read books about art, I started to stumble across strange, resonant passages, and by chance, I found historical female alchemists. In my curatorial activity, I have begun to turn ever more towards the amazing and the magical, but also towards terror and mystery.

To sum up, everything indicated that Ernesta Thot was crazy? A lunatic? A romantic? Although she has never existed, she had to be "born" in

Figure 7.8 An Ending That is also a Beginning. Jakub Woynarowski (2012), "Geometria et Perspectiva," "Novus-Ordo-Seclorum" cycle.

order to present her never-created theory. As her creator, I accepted this fact with joy and undisguised relief that the figure who appeared in my head during a certain sunset by the sea (of all places!) finally said who "she" was.

A few clarifications are due here for the Honorable Reader. The first is undoubtedly the heroine's surname and its two-part origin. Let us start with the first one. *Thot* is not a random name. In the beliefs of ancient Egypt, Thot (or Thoth) was the god of the moon, but also a patron of wisdom. It was believed that he invented writing, and also the calendar, music, and numbers. Ancient Egyptians considered him the Patron of Writers, people of Science and Art. Thot was also the one who invented magical and sorcerous formulas. It was he who escorted souls to the Kingdom of the Dead and acted as an intermediary between the two worlds. His Greek counterpart was none other than Hermes – a winged, cunning youth who was also called a god with two faces. Like his Egyptian counterpart, he mediated between the World of the Living and the World of the Dead; only he could travel between two worlds with impunity. Both Thot and Hermes were Gods of Magic, because they knew all the mysteries of the Heavens, all the secrets of the Earth, and all those secrets still hidden deep within the Earth. Ancient Greece and Egypt are considered to be the cradle of alchemy, so it is not surprising that as a result of a confrontation between these two cultures in the second century, the archetypes of Hermes and Toth began to cross-identify. The result was the aforementioned legendary figure of Hermes Trismegistos, whose persona inspired alchemists right up to the seventeenth century (Nawrot, 1999)!

The function of the intermediary between the two worlds immediately evoked in me the idea – or even the recognition of the core concept – that the role of the curator is to be that one who is the bridge between the world of Art and the world of the Public. It was mentioned, for instance, by Michael Brenson (1998) or Aurelia Nowak (2019) for whom the curator's function is indispensable, even as its scope (and list of required qualifications) expands with time. French researcher André Rouillé, quoted in the text, also pointed to the dependence between particular figures in the art world, but unlike Pierre Bourdieu, he did not see this dependence in the field as a struggle for authority (or "among authorities") (Bourdieu, 2007), but as some magical skill. This magical metaphor illustrates perfectly the way of thinking of people unrelated to art, for whom the processes occurring in art are not of a completely clear nature, and result from some strange, mysterious practices. By assembling all these elements together, I could not call Miss Ernesta differently, as she was supposed to be a subtle precursor to curating, a person who was discovering the alchemical and unusual side of modern and contemporary art.

Ernesta Thot has a double "Styrian–Polish" origin. The latter because of what Maria Janion faced in the "Amazing Slavdom" (Janion,

2006) – a great, inarticulate phantasm of Polish culture, which – due to its rapid baptism in 966 – was supplanted, becoming an "unconscious core" (Freud, 1982), which re-emerges every now and then in the form of ghosts and phantoms harassing Polish culture, art, and also politics (Sowa, 2011). This perspective seemed to me extremely tempting, especially from the perspective of Central and Eastern Europe as the "Orient of Europe" (Wolff, 1996) – a place that is wild, inaccessible, torn by strange forces so different from the law and order of Western Europe. To heighten this feeling of strangeness as Ernesta Thot's second homeland, I pointed to Styria – a land in the eastern Alps located in the basin of the Drawa, Mura, and Raba.

This strange land, like the whole of Central Europe, has been known for centuries as a land full of dark tales. The Herberstein family, which settled in Gorzanów in the seventeenth century and lived there until the twentieth century, also came from there. One of the members of this mysterious family who put the sculpture of a vampire on the gate to his palace was named Ernest. I could not determine if he had ever been in the castle in Gorzanów. Nevertheless, he was a priest, so contact with mystics, God's madmen, or bards undoubtedly occurred in his life story. Hence, Miss Thot had to have a name coming from this strange land that figured in her ancestry.

Ernesta Thot liked to play with a mysterious and dreamlike art and tracked its relationships with alchemy. The history of the latter is still full of gaps, insinuations, and ambiguities for us today. That is why I decided on a "jolting" narrative, reminiscent of Walter Benjamin's way of telling a story in *Pasaże* (*The Passagenwerk*). It was the best way to present this mysterious story. I could not imagine talking about this character and the dependencies discovered by her using "scientific cosiness" (Benjamin, 2005, p. 914), and a narrative full of gaps was closer to the aesthetics of automatic surrealist poetry, which no doubt Ernesta Thot would read and engage with. Anyway, the "literary" perspective in the visual arts is not a new phenomenon. It is enough to mention a significant part of Sebastian Cichocki's texts, the literary experiments of Norman Leto, Łukasz Ronduda, or Roberth Smithson. However, the main inspiration for me was Agnieszka Taborska's prose about Leonora de la Cruz and Phoebe Hicks.

By presenting this text to the Honorable Reader, a text full of alchemical echoes that from time to time reverberate in contemporary art, I wanted Ernesta Thot to become an incarnation of the many phantasms and strange contents present at the crossroads of art and alchemy. This phantom heroine was supposed to be a pretext to tell a hidden chapter in the history of art, the history of exhibitions, and the curator's profession. The story of Ernesta Thot, although fictitious, seems to be dangerously real, and the echoes of magical thinking every now and then are discussed by various researchers, including those mentioned in the text.

It remains to be hoped that Ernesta Thot can become more realistic and may eventually announce her "Alchemist Manifesto."

Notes

1 Almost 30 years after her death, this thought will develop under such researchers as Peter Vergo and Carol Duncan. Artists also initiate and engage with a phenomenon called "institutional criticism," involving the disclosure of hidden sub-texts in the museum and exhibition message.
2 The motif of a golden flower is one of the symbols of initiation in eastern alchemy.
3 In alchemy itself, the fish symbolizes the secret substance of the arcanum; as a result of its transformation, a philosopher's stone is created. The fish is also a symbol of the unconscious, something small floating in a great sea full of undiscovered contents. For Jungian psychoanalysis, the fish was a sign of the Self – the unconscious, something hidden beneath the surface of the psyche. Sometimes this impossibility of discovering these contents, their unawareness, could be Jung's reason for multiple neuroses and psychiatric diseases. It is likely that such neuroses eventually led Thot to madness.
4 Acrostic poem created by the alchemist Basil Valentina.
5 Matter, as in "material." A raw material that can be utilized in the production of/generation of/evolution of/elevation of art.
6 Vernissage – French – before the varnish (is applied), a term to describe a private opening of an exhibition before it was opened to the general public.
7 Thot was not alone here. During her conversation in 2007 with Hans Ulrich Obrist about the origins of her curatorial practice, Lucy Lippard stated that she did not even have documentation of her first activities. This peculiar "amnesia," concerning not only Lippard but other founders of modern curation, became the starting point for "a protest against forgetting" and the creation of something like a patchwork about curating (Obrist, 2008/2016, pp. 205–206).
8 A similar way of working can be seen in the curatorial action of Harald Szeemann, or in the project of the "Museum of the Eagle" by Marcel Broodthaers, "Mnemosyne Atlas" by Aby Warburg, or essays "Ways of Seeing" by John Berger.
9 Greek myths – Moirai ~ the Three Sisters of Fate, who wove out the Threads of Life, Destiny, and Fortune for Mortals and Gods alike.
10 Once again, the premonitions of Ernesta Thot turned out to be accurate, see P. Możdżyński, *Inicjacje i transgresje. Antystrukuralność sztuki XX i XXI wieku w oczach socjologa,* Warszawa 2011, pp. 97–106.

References

Bartnes, R. (1980/2006). *Światło obrazu. Uwagi o fotografiach (La chambre claire. Note sur la photographie).* Warszawa, Poland: Wydawnictwo Aletheia.

Beneveni, F. (1863). Dzieje alchemii, czyli nauki o kamieniu filozoficznym. *Przegląd Europejski, II*(4), 403–483.

Benjamin, W. (1982/2005). *Pasaże (Passagen – Werk 1927–1940).* Kraków, Poland: Wydawnictwo Literackie.

Bourdieu, P. (1992/2007). *Reguły sztuki: geneza i struktura pola literackiego (Les Règles de l'art. Genèse et structure du champ littéraire).* Kraków, Poland: Wydawnictwo Universitas.

Brenson, M. (1998). The curator's moment. *Art Journal, 57*(4), 16–27.

Bugaj, R. (1991). *Hermetyzm*. Wrocław, Warszawa, and Kraków, Poland: Wydawnictwo Orion.

Bürger, P. (2006). *Teoria awangardy oraz Burkhardt Lindner Zniesienie sztuki w praktyce życiowej? O aktualności dyskusji na temat historycznych prądów awangardowych*. Kraków, Poland: Universitas.

Clifford, J. (2000/2010). *Kłopoty z kulturą (The predicament of culture. Twentieth-century etnography, literature and art)*. Warszawa, Poland: Wydawnictwo Aletheia.

Czaplik-Lityńska, B. (2005). *Chorwacka i serbska awangarda w perspektywie badań porównawczych*. Katowice, Poland: Wydawnictwo Uniwersytetu Śląskiego.

Danto, A. C. (1964). The artworld. *Journal Philosophy, 61*(19), 571–584.

Duncan, C. (2005). Muzeum sztuki jako rytuał. In M. Popczyk (Ed.) *Muzeum sztuki. Antologia* (pp. 279–299). Kraków, Poland: Universitas.

Eco, U. (1994/2007). *Sześć przechadzek po lesie fikcji (Six walks in the fictional woods)*. Kraków, Poland: Wydawnictwo Znak.

Freud, Z. (1916/1982). *Wstęp do psychoanlizy (Vorlesungen zur Einfuhrung in die Psychoanalyse)*. Warszawa, Poland: PWN.

Gidens, A. (1991/2002). *Nowoczesność i tożsamość. „Ja" i społeczeństwo w epoce późnej nowoczesności (Modernity and self-identity. Self and society in the late modern age)*. Warszawa, Poland: Wydawnictwo Naukowe PWN.

Guzek, Ł. (2007). *Sztuka instalacji. Zagadnienie związku przestrzeni i obecności w sztuce współczesnej*. Warszawa, Poland: Nerition.

Jameson, F. (1989/2011). *Postmodernizm, czyli logika późnego kapitalizmu (Postmodernism, or, the cultural logic of late capitalism)*. Kraków, Poland: Wydawnictwo Uniwersytetu Jagiellońskiego.

Janion, M. (2006). *Niesamowita Słowiańszczyzna*. Kraków, Poland: Wydawnictwo Literackie.

Janion, M. (2010). *Prace wybrane. Zło i fantazmaty Tom 3*. Kraków, Poland: Wydawnictwo Universitas.

Krawczyk, L. (2016). Co dzisiaj znaczy być organizatorem wystaw?. In *Zeszyt realizatora / realizatorki wystaw*. Kraków, Poland: Galeria Sztuki Współczesnej Bunkier Sztuki.

Kudelska, M. (2019). *Novus Ordo Seclorum – z Kubą Woynarowskim rozmawia Marta Kudelska*. Retrieved on 21-06-2019 from www.punktmag.com/punkt-10/

Możdżyński, P. (2011). *Inicjacje i transgresje. Antystrukuralność sztuki XX i XXI wieku w oczach socjologa*. Warszawa, Poland: Wydawnictwo Uniwersytetu Warszawskiego.

Nawrot, L. (1999). Źródła hermetyzmu i alchemii. *Nowa Krytyka*, 10. Retrieved on 22-06-2019 from http://bazhum.muzhp.pl/media//files/Nowa_Krytyka/Nowa_Krytyka-r1999-t10/Nowa_Krytyka-r1999-t10-s179-199/Nowa_Krytyka-r1999-t10-s179-199.pdf

Nowak, A. (2019). *Curatorial ethics w Kunsthalle Wien*. Retrieved on 22-06-2019 from www.magazynsztuki.eu/teksty/curatorial-ethics-w-kunsthalle-wien/

Obrist, H. U. (2008/2016). *Krótka historia kuratorstwa (A brief history of curating)*. Kraków, Poland: Wydawnictwo Korporacja Ha! Art.

Obrist, H. U. (2010). Foreworld. In C. Thea (Ed.), *On curating. Interviews with ten international curators* (pp. 2–10). New York, NY: D.A.P. Distributed Art Publishersp.

O'Dohery, B. (2005). Uwagi o przestrzenii galerii. In M. Popczyk (Ed.), *Muzeum sztuki. Antologia* (pp. 451–467). Kraków, Poland: Universitas.

Platon. (1984). *Uczta*. Warszawa, Poland: PWN.

Platon. (1987). *Listy*. Warszawa, Poland: PWN.

Rouillé, A. (2005/2007). *Fotografia. Między dokumentem a sztuką współczesną (La photographie)*. Kraków, Poland: Wydawnictwo Universitas.

Sosnowski, L. (2007). *Sztuka. Historia. Teoria. Światy Arthura C. Danto*. Kraków, Poland: Collegium Columbinum.

Sowa, J. (2011). *Fantomowe ciało król*. Kraków, Poland: Wydawnictwo Universitas.

Szczęsna, E. (2002). *Słownik pojęć i tekstów kultury*. Warszawa, Poland: Wydawnictwo Akademickie i Profesjonalne.

Vinaver, S. (1980). Manifest szkoły ekspresjonistycznej. *Literatura na Świecie*, *9*(113), 75–82.

Wierciński, A. (2010). *Magia i religia. Szkice z antropologii religii*. Kraków, Poland: Wydawnictwo Nomos.

Wolff, L. (1996). *Inventing easter Europe. The map of civilization on the mind of the enlightenment*. Stanford, CA: Stanford University Press.

8 Rooted in Transitory Places of Gathering

Performing Spacing in Tino Sehgal's Performance "These Situations" at the Palais de Tokyo[1]

Jean-Luc Moriceau, Philippe Mairesse, and Yannick Fronda

Tino Sehgal is given carte blanche to work in the immense space of the Palais de Tokyo, a leading public contemporary art museum in Paris. He does not put any painting, sculpture, or installation there. He just puts moving bodies – three hundred bodies. These bodies, at the beginning indiscernible from spectators, walk, run, sing, or stand motionless; they enter into interactions forming a kind of choreography. These are performing bodies, and their moving presence is performative, that is, it has an effect on the participants. They generate "situations."[2] It is difficult to imagine a simpler configuration, and yet it communicates a powerful impression. Something gets moved in the sharing and in the constitution of space, in the performers, in the work/viewer bonds, in us who observe and experience. The artist affirms that what is thus performed is political.

As far back as forty years ago, K.E. Weick (1979) recommended the use of verbs in their gerund form, instead of nouns, to stimulate process thinking. Thinking and speaking of organizing, instead of organization, make us see it less as a constant and unchanging entity; rather, the intermingled processes of constant production, various dynamics that coalesce to make the organization emerge, take shape, work, and act. Even more unsettling, substituting spacing for space could orient "the understanding of organizational space toward its material, embodied, affective and minor configurations" (Beyes & Steyaert, 2011, p. 47). Space is no longer imaged just as a container, but

> as processual and performative, open-ended and multiple, practiced and of the everyday. Such a reframing of space as spacing implies exchanging a vocabulary of stasis, representation, reification and closure with one of intensities, capacities and forces; rhythms, cycles, encounters, events, movements and flows; instincts, affects, atmospheres and auras; relations, knots and assemblages.
>
> (idem, p. 45)

Tino Sehgal's performance allows us to feel and thus better understand how much organizing and spacing is production. As with a sculpture, all functionalist and symbolic purpose would have been removed; everything that prevents us from seeing this organizational and spatial production would have been carved out as clearly and sensitively as possible. In this neutral parallelepiped, we see the organization taking shape and dissolving; we see it emerging, asserting itself, as though only for itself, without having anything to function for. We witness social organization producing space: body positions and movements, human interactions, rhythms, noises, accelerations and decelerations, entries and exits, usages, appropriations, repetitions, habituations, what seem to be forbidden places, more intimidating regions, lighting… all this distorts and reforms space, curves it, fills it, loads it with affects and expectations, connects it to other places, other experiences.

What can such an artistic performance of spacing tell us about organizing? We will look at the paradox of trying to perform spacing; then some of the ways spacing is researched. We'll then wonder whether this allows some place for the minor (non-mainstream affects and becomings), and finally whether it might provide a place to dwell and flourish in our digital age.

Our approach belongs to the turn to affect and triangulates the spectator's and the performer's experiences. From the performance, no trace remains: no recordings or pictures were allowed. Our account of the piece is not based on recordings but on our personal ethnographic experience and memory as a participant or a spectator. One of the authors was hired as a participant and took part in the performances for two months, three times a week, four hours each run. He went through enthusiasm, exasperation, revolt, anger, exaltation, or contempt and had a privileged position to live, experiment, and learn from the inside. Otherwise the performance was observed as spectator. Our approach was not to judge or analyze the performance or to connect with it first through a research question or preselected concepts, but rather to open ourselves to the experience of being there (Letiche & Lightfoot, 2014; Moriceau, 2016), body and mind, to let ourselves be contaminated by the performativity (Stewart, 1996). We were not looking for data, but rather attending to affects, that is, to surges that throw themselves together in a moment as an event and a sensation, both animated and inhabitable (Stewart, 2007). A diary was written by the performer, and personal notes by the observers.

Our goal is not to prove or achieve a particular point. Rather, in the movement of non-representational theories (Lorimer, 2008; Thrift, 2007), thus in resonance with the calls of Beyes and Steyaert (2011), to set in motion and challenge our reflexivity on spacing on the occasion of Tino Sehgal's singular performance. The performativity of performance is described with a performative idiom (Pickering, 1994), that is, not only people have agency; spaces and places also act and give rise to affects.

Movements, Fish Shoals, and Rhythm

Let's start with the visitor's experience.

> I first see a set of performers starting to move in the basement space of the Palais de Tokyo sometimes running,[3] sometimes walking. Sometimes these bodies stop and sing words in chorus. Here they are running on the stairs. Their eyes meet our own. A smile. They breathe a thank you when I make room for them to climb a few steps, following what I guess being a trajectory, a line, a displacement. I feel sympathy with their effort, the exercise seems difficult, singular. They resemble a shoal of fish, an organic form that moves with accelerations and changes in direction. They seem to follow a "logic," a movement of their own of which we perceive a hidden code, not yet deciphered, or yet to be deciphered. I start to feel being one of them. Fascination! My body is caught in this machine, touches these movements and takes me into an aesthetic (body and feeling) experience.

This aesthetic experience makes us feel the generative production of space by bodies in motion, in their sometimes organized, sometimes disorganized mundane movements. The distribution of bodies whose face, cloth, shape matter far less than their geographical positions and gesture in relation to the others creates the naked space rather than take place within it. The various effects, impressions, sense experienced by the spectator are produced by the spacing produced by the distribution of bodies. This is what interests us: how the political rearrangement of bodies due to the application or questioning of rules creates the spacing, in turn creating the organizing of an ephemeral community. The space changes from being a symbolic cultural spot to an empty container, to a place where we meet, to a landscape with rows of bodies, to an aquarium with shoals of fish choreographing a fast dance, to something that we fully forget, to a maze where we look for toilets or the coffee place. At some moments, the space looks small, then big, void or full, strange or intimate, absent or present, indifferent or singular, cool or hot, pleasant or inconvenient. Sometimes it looks organized, ordered, functional, beautiful, and at other times, messy, uncanny, any old place.

Physically, or architecturally, the space has not changed, not moved, not done anything. But here space has already gained the three dimensions identified by Lefebvre (1991) in the production of space: conceived, perceived, and lived. The aesthetic gaze makes us oscillate between these three poles or gives us all three at the same time, in the same rich experience that surprises us by the way it affects us.

As researchers, Lefebvre's approach encourages us to enrich and complexify the issues of space for organizations. Researchers first considered these issues in terms of efficiency and production: to introduce a change in culture (van Marrewijk, 2009) or to foster collaboration (Fayard & Weeks, 2011).[4] Then symbolic aspects were taken into account: how spatial arrangements might communicate certain messages or come with specific connotations (Gagliardi, 1990; Yanow, 2006). But space was not spacing, being still relatively static, and the users' active role within it was incomplete (De Molli, 2019).

However, Lefebvre, especially in his later approach in terms of rhythmanalysis (2004), invites research to pay attention to rhythms that communicate and spread throughout the organization and are a key part of organizing. On the one hand, rhythms appear as regulated time, governed by rational laws, often imposed by managerial command, but on the other hand, they put researchers in contact with what is least rational in human beings: the lived, the carnal, the body. Rhythms communicate via affects more than with meaning or sense making. The rhythmanalyst thinks with his body, not in the abstract, but in lived temporality.

> Facing the performance, we get contaminated by a set of various pulsations that start from the performers' bodies and steps, invade the space, reverberate from wall to walls, take our bodies and make them move or incorporate the rhythm. Space is a territory, full of vibrations, pulsations, ritornellos. Our experience is bombarded by such rhythms that emanate from others, form groups and encounters, that will bounce and reverberate on the walls, differently according to the positions of each one. While observation preserves what is studied at a distance, the opening of the bodies to rhythms and reverberations allows the physical, human and social geography of the place to enter in us, to be experimented and be lived for a moment. And let us wonder how capitalism, organizations, social, space interpenetrate the carnal, the living, the more intimate, animal, or preconscious and preindividual parts of us.[5]

But this is not yet the "spacing" Beyes and Steyaert (2011) are after. For them, spacing is the material, embodied, affective, and minor (re-) configuration of space, as a way to bring space back into critical organization theory. By a minor configuration, they mean a diversion of space, a re-appropriation, a breath in the race for performance, and above all the possibility of creativity: the invention of other uses of space, outside the functional, organized, ordered, planned, policed, predefined, authorized, scripted use. Spacing entails other ways of living and using space, decorating it, frequenting it, placing other walls and openings, setting up other connections and routines. The organizational space is a space of performativity, where everything must be optimized, everything must be designed for management purposes. Spacing introduces a slowdown in the race for organizational efficacy, to invent other passages, other rhythms, other ways to be in space.

The paradox is that Tino Sehgal's performance has eliminated all the aspects of usual organizational scripting of space. He has done it to such an extent as to destroy and remove all physical additions to the naked architectural structure of the building, added year after year by the organizers–curators of the Palais de Tokyo, organizing exhibitions and reconstructing the spaces in relation to it. Tino Sehgal wants us to see the space that is ordinarily occulted. Moreover, he wants us to co-construct with his performers a new moving space of relations and physical co-existence. We could then interpret the performance as a production of spacing. But in this case, all the performance would have been organized for this production of spacing, spacing would be the production... and then no more spacing in Beyes and Steyaert's sense. Spacing would no longer be minor. The question is then if there is still some room for spacing, as a minoration of the usage of space, in the performance at the Palais de Tokyo.

Pace, Rules, and the Minor

It's time to see the same part of the performance, but this time from the performer's experience. This is part of the diary of the author who acted as a performer.

> I run. For ten, fifteen minutes, I run, quicker and quicker, slower and slower. I stop. I sit down, kneel or lie on the floor. I run, I follow the group, I manage my distance with the others, I calculate the mean direction of the group and try to follow it. But the direction that the group follows changes continuously, so I have to move, to change direction, thus contributing to the shift of the group in the space. We run, we run, we all stop, standing, sitting or lying down, and wait. We wait, looking in chosen directions and not moving a finger, or slowly. From time to time some of us move, from one position to another, carefully decided among the innumerous possibilities in the space. They stop, sit or stand. I wait, I think. I think of what I am doing here, why, for how long. I think of myself, my life, my love life, my professional life, my art, my research. One of us makes a step. One step, and stop. Then another step after a while, in another direction. Then another. Then another of us stands and steps too. Then a third one, then several others. One step at a time, all together, in different directions. Soon we are all stepping in rhythm,

step – stop – step – stop – step, slowly, less slowly, quicker, much quicker, very very quick now, running and crossing each other in complicated lines avoiding contacts. I run, faster and faster, attentively avoiding the others but running into them, the noise of our steps, breathing, the sweat, the brushing of bodies one against the other, of the feet on the floor. I choose someone, I choose a second one, I focus on the two, I carefully strive at staying equidistant from both. But they move, run, walk, never stop. The distance between them, between me and them, is continuously changing. I have to move continuously in order to stay at the same equidistant spot, we build a triangle. They don't know I build a triangle with them, they are focused on building triangles with others, who in their turn are focused on building triangles with others. Sometimes the person is chosen by several, close packs occur suddenly, then loosen across the whole space. The group is scattered or gathered, dispersed and united, one and multiple. Some start jogging in the same direction, a subgroup almost invisible among our dislocated triangles. I notice them, three or four, slightly embarking on a bifurcating trip across the space and the bodies. I follow them, I jog and swirl, sometimes following sometimes leading, others join us, soon we are all a school of fish, a cloud of starlings, a swarm of locusts. It is incomprehensible how or why we move in this or that direction, it is simple and mysterious. We are all jogging about one meter from one another, sometimes we're getting closer, our arms touch, a foot avoids a leg, I pass my fellows, I follow my own way. Alone suddenly. I return to the group as if returned by an elastic band. The group is now gathered in one end of the space, tightened, still jogging, trotting slowly, disordered and collected, hesitating. Then suddenly it starts. All of a sudden, the matt high beat of our eighty feet slamming the floor, legs as mill wings, bodies horizontal. The run. The quickest we can, on the two hundred meters across the whole space. A horde of horses. No words, strong breaths, frictions, hammering, wind of the speed of forty bodies running together the fastest they can. At the end of the room we hit the wall and bump back, we turn back and go on running, a little slower, to where we come from, avoiding the concrete pillars in the room. The wind of our speed, again, the hammering of the feet, again. The wall at the end. Then back again, slower, then again crossing the whole room, slower, again, slower, slower, again, slower, slower, walking now, walking slowly, slow motion walking, almost stopping but still moving. It takes hours to cross the room now. And come back. One of us stops and sits down, the others go on. A second one stops, she lies comfortably on her side. I pass her, make some slow steps more, stop. Turn on myself, looking around me slowly. I settle down and wait, immobile, one arm touching the other, my hand on my thigh. I look on things, people, space,

> time. I don't think, I look. My looking is a description. It is as if my look was building what it sees. We are all motionless now, looking, lying down, sitting, settled in a disordered organized setting across the whole space. Time passes by. Some of us move now and then. It's long, it lasts. Visitor stand around us, or walk slowly between our lying, standing, sitting bodies.[6]

Performers, and hence spectators, are invited to play and experiment with different paces, and this is an occasion of radical estrangement. No doubt, pace is part of our experience of space. Often overlooked or taken for granted, the importance of pace becomes striking when it suddenly slows down or accelerates beyond usual norms. Pace is social, regulated, and controlled. All you have to do is go to a country where pace is organized differently to realize how alien we feel, often irritated and embarrassed by what we feel is a weird pace. Nowadays, the pace of research seems to have accelerated, and we feel alien and perhaps alienated by this acceleration. Some call for slow research to regain righteousness and responsibility (Stengers, 2016; Ulmer, 2017). Accelerated research prevents us from taking the time to feel an atmosphere, to listen and give a voice to the participants, to experiment with different rhythms and different ways of producing space. Beyes and Steyaert (2011) urge researchers to experiment with slowness. Slow research seems necessary in order to live writing and research through locality, materiality, and artisan craft. It is a kind of return to an originary, to paying attention to sensory impressions, affects, materiality, milieus. A slow ontology promotes alternative rhythms of inquiry through participating and through writing, experimenting with varying degrees of intentionality and awareness. Here, humans are not the sole authors of space, and landscape could claim some authorship for the research.

Looking for the performer's point of view enables one to reach to the construction of the performance (Paes, 2019). Performers were hired for two months, trained, and had to exercise, and there was a long rehearsal period to make sure the rules were engraved in the brains and the bodies. However, the performance was mainly organized around a small set of rules that had to be followed. Organization and space were then produced according to a preset and purposive design.

> We had rules to follow. The triangle rule. The mean distance rule. The slow walk rule. The singing rules. The run rule. The configuration rule. The speech themes rule. We had to choose where and when to shift from one rule to another, collectively, without speaking. We were taught five ways of going through all the rules, five chains of rules, and we had to switch from one chain to another, spontaneously, collectively.[7]

Using a very restricted name of rules, we see the organization being formed. We are here as if in front of a kind of laboratory of organizing. Organizing is based on local rules: I want to get closer to one type of person, to move away from others, and in total, global organizational movements are being formed. Organizational movements are here to be seen as formed from individual decisions or local rules, without the actors being aware of the effects at the global level or even being able to predict the movement with certainty. Such organizing movements have been observed in cities, for example. Artists often gather in certain inexpensive neighbourhoods because of lack of resources. The neighbourhood often becomes more lively, vibrant, improving its reputation, attracting a trendy population. But this influx raises prices, which quickly become unaffordable for most artists, forced to migrate to other parts of the city (Vivant, 2009).

And yet, no global movement in the performance was foreseeable. Probably never, during all the exhibition period, were two performances identical. We see here another facet of the paradox. The shift from one set of rules to another had to be made "spontaneously, collectively." Each one has to know when a collective shift has to occur. And each one has to spontaneously feel and know when this collective shift has to happen. The shift is not ordered by the clock, by Tino Sehgal, or any outsider position. It is simultaneously and spontaneously acted by forty performers with no leader or discussion. And each one is calculating in his own head, which strategy to adopt, and in relation to whom the rules would be followed. There does not seem to remain any space for spacing.

Tino Sehgal thinks about groups – collective and individuals – modern and ancient societies, movements and bodies and wants his art to emphasize forgotten or dismissed ways of human social grouping and organizing. He claims liberalism has lost something, even though it has brought individual freedom, which he greatly favours. His issue is: how to be individually free from any constraint and nevertheless participating fully in a group? How to be a liberal and a socialist? How to bring in more ethics into liberalism, at the individual and collective level? He speaks of the other and caring for the other (Sehgal, 2016a, 2016b).

There were moments when individual performers could break the collective unity and address a visitor.

> We the performers always have the possibility and duty, at any moment (except during the singing), to extract ourselves from the performers' group, walk out to a visitor and start talking to her, abruptly telling a personal story from our own life (...) I hang on the look of a visitor, I stop running, I walk towards her. I stop, close to her, she is surprised, I start directly, speaking: I was maybe six, or seven...[8]

Then the performer told a very intimate remembrance of his youth, to a complete stranger, who had not asked for anything. For a short while the conversation went on about the political aspects of the situation. Initiatives and very personal happenings were authorized and were part of the intended performance, as if even deviations and encounters had to be organized, not qua content but qua forms.

And yet, in such moments, something seems to actually happen. The performer suddenly barges into the visitor's intimacy and vice versa the visitor is somehow entering the performer's universe. The visitor suddenly knows things about the performer that no one else knows – he has an access to her deep being. He can look at her running with a totally new look, knowing – perhaps – what she has in mind while running. Reciprocally, a part of each visitor she spoke to is running with her day after day. Tino Sehgal's situations are performances. A performance is not just a representation of social life. It is an important part of social life (Schechner, 1988; Turner, 1994). It is not through the effectuation of the right movements at the right place and time that something happens, but because something actually happens in the here and now. Performing is not imitating or faking. Performing is at the same time being, doing, and showing doing (Schechner, 2002). Much is prepared and rehearsed, but the mere representation would probably fail to produce the effect.

Performing is an activity that affects both the performer and the viewer. That is why not all the performance can probably be controlled.

Something quite fraudulently might happen in the well-organized and controlled performance. This is probably where spacing might happen. Spacing is performative. It has to be performed and not merely exhibited or represented. Here it is as if some spacing were organized, would even stand as a rule. That is where the paradox runs, and what needs to be further thought through.

Politics of Performing Space

Is there a place for the minor in the performance? Let's take another extract from the performer's diary.

> Disturbing as a way to participate in organizations which exclude me? In order to become kind of participants, when they don't see how to do anything else, some visitors would in fact try to disturb our mysteriously ruled Brownian agitation. Either ironically, they mimic our gestures and moves, some following our runs for a while and smiling at us (we never know if they smile at their satisfaction of being integrated and participating, or at their clever disruption of our secret organizational rule). Or more violently, intruding into the group and targeting one of us aggressively or seductively. One visitor physically interrupted the movements of Alice, embraced her with

insistence, pushed her outside her trajectory, until Henri walked up to him and started speaking to him eye to eye, forcing him to listen and pulling him to the side. The interruption stopped the disturber. Why did the visitor try to disturb to the point of aggressively accosting the woman? I had noticed him for some minutes, he was agitated, like feeling ignored, unseen, he was visibly looking for something to do and being seen, here, visible, an active participant not a ghost. I understand that he was playing the same strategy as I did [with my previous intimate confidence]: disrupting organizations which exclude us, is disturbing as a way to create participation. That is precisely what we are suggested to do with impolite groups of visitors who defy our walking or take up the space for their own personal affairs, chatting and laughing loudly without any attention to us. One of the rules advises us to disrupt their disturbing behavior by walking up to them, addressing them directly, separating them from one another, in order to get them to participate in our situations not theirs. In fact, this is what happens with the talk rule, which allows us to go and talk to any visitor at any moment, telling personal stories. Every time we walk up to someone and start speaking, we interrupt him. The visitor has her own pace, her own understanding of being there with us (which can be staying distant and critical). Running towards them, addressing them suddenly and personally, disrupt their personal being-there, their own way of part-taking. Disrupting their participation results in getting them and us participating together in the same situation: the disturbance (of what was going on) is the liminal situation where participation (in what will go on) arises. Disrupting participation in order to participate, is the ground for participation: outcome three. We the performers always have the possibility and duty, at any moment (except during the singing), to extract ourselves from the performers' group, walk up to a visitor and start talking to her, abruptly telling a personal story from our own life.

The result of this violent act of intrusion into a visitor's intimacy may be the reason why he becomes a participant (what many expressed like this: I feel participating with you, I feel co-author of the artwork with you). A deep participation feeling is involved here; the visitor becomes a participant not by contract or convention, but by flesh and bones, by blood and skin, a participant from the inside.[9]

Here the disturbances seem to play an ambiguous role. Under the apparent Brownian movement, and the apparent indistinctedness between visitors and performers, in a universe where borders seem to be deliberately blurred, there is a strict distribution of the sensible. Rancière (2000) calls "distribution of the sensible" a set of conventions that allows meaning to be shared, sense to be presented, but that at the same time distributes the shares, the rights, and legitimacy. Here there is a clear distinction between visitors and performers, each group being allowed to do certain things and forbidden to do others. A performer has the right to address directly, in a quasi-violent way, a visitor, but the contrary is impossible. Probably, for Tino Sehgal, we need such a distribution for the performance to "work."

What is at work here? In a way, it seems that performance has a general purpose of disturbance – it wants to disrupt our habits of seeing, behaving, and thinking. But for this to happen it would have to be immune to disruption; or rather, some uncertainties and disturbances are integrated into the general functioning, but it is necessary to be protected against external disturbances.

Rancière calls "police" everything that is done to preserve the distribution of the sensible in place and to prevent other speeches, other interventions than those planned. The distribution of the sensible is a form of organization that operates at the sensible/sensitive level. In the situation described, the police was very upfront and could have become as violent as the perturbation.

In the performer's notes the interpretation is more optimistic. The disturbances, caused by performers, would break the usual distribution of the sensible between visitors, who observe and evaluate, and performers, who play their role. This would allow real participation. Visitors would thus be part of the performance, part of the work of art. But disturbances from the outside are nuisances. They must be regulated, in order to be eliminated.

Another example given by the performer is the following: in what is performed, something happens that is not specified. Rules are not followed exactly; sequences of rules are modified by one person or the other. Who follows whom? This question is ongoing for the performer, who has to follow the group but can decide to create a diverging subgroup. No one among the performers or the visitors can have the real perception of the global event. This awareness is part of the individual local action in a way that is different from the distancing by reflection or reflexivity, critique or scepticism. It is a distancing-by-closeness, which the performers practice physically in every move they make. They come close to one another, very close, their bodies are never far from each other, but they distance themselves suddenly and keep their bodies apart, and at the same time keep the connection strongly. A game of closeness–distancing is played all along, which is fascinating in its strange pace and its metaphorical strength. Touching each other is not allowed. This strange rule given by Tino Sehgal makes full sense in relation to the necessity of distancing within the closeness, which appears as a practical manner of spacing. But once more, all such minor moves are included in the design of the performance and participate in its achievement.

Places to Dwell, Tarry, and Encounter

Getting closer and taking distance grounds all the moves in the performance. The group of performers move continuously, running, walking, speeding up and slowing down, standing still before they make the next move. And they also sing. Two songs, or perhaps better two psalms, rather like ritual melodies, rise from time to time from the group. The words are distorted, echoed, repeated, but two sentences emerge slowly if one listens carefully. One song tells:

> Today we have begun to create natural processes of our own, and instead of surrounding the world with defenses against nature's elementary forces, we have channeled these forces into the world itself.

The second song responds:

> Thus we ask now: if the old rootedness is lost in this age, may not a new ground be created, out of which humans' nature with all their work can flourish even in the technological age?

The first sentence is from Hannah Arendt (1958, pp. 148–149). The second was written by Heidegger (1955/1966, p. 55). Tino Sehgal claims his performance to be a reactivation of ancient forms of collective being, enabling (disturbing) new forms of encounters.[10]

Hannah Arendt, in *The Human Condition*, expresses her concerns about the technological age that arose more than sixty years ago. While tools until then helped the *homo faber* (the human maker) within the human world, machines now require man to be their servant. They even form a world in which human gestures and the human relation to the world are replaced by a mechanical world that becomes difficult to inhabit.

> For a society of laborers, the world of machines has become a substitute for the real world, even though this pseudo world cannot fulfil the most important task of the human artifice, which is to offer mortals a dwelling place more permanent and more stable than themselves.
>
> (Arendt, 1958, p. 152)

Heidegger redoubled this concern and saw the danger of a growing thoughtlessness, or rather that only calculative and optimizing thinking is possible: "the approaching tide of technological revolution in the atomic age could so captivate, bewitch, dazzle, and beguile man that calculative thinking may someday come to be accepted and practiced as the only way of thinking" (1955/1966, p. 56). For Heidegger, thought can only rise from a rootedness. And it is precisely the work of art that expresses the roots of a place, and it is likely that great works can only flourish if they are rooted. For him, therefore, it is not a question of rejecting any technique, but of adopting an attitude of equality of soul that leads to serenity: saying yes to the unavoidable use of technical devices, but strongly "deny them the right to dominate us, and so to warp, confuse, and lay waste our nature" (p. 54). Calculative thinking cannot grasp the meaning of technology, a meaning that at the same time shows itself and withdraws, that is, presents itself as a mystery. Release in relation to things and openness to the mystery might together be fit to recapture the old and now rapidly disappearing rootedness in a changed form.

If Tino Sehgal has chosen these two sentences and gives them to sing like a song from the depths, he certainly has something to tell us about technique, the world, and rootedness. Let's turn to another excerpt from the performer's diary:

> We meet in the dressing-room. Or in the lobby. Or at the bar. Or most often I meet the other performers by joining the running group – I was late and the group had already started. Catching the pace, I run besides Jacques, Emmanuelle or Anne, give them a little hello, a smile, a glance: no talk is allowed. And my running moves me close to other colleagues – are we workers, colleagues in the workplace? My place is moving, I move as the place moves and my moves carry me from place to place, looking for the right one. For example in the triangle exercise when I have to keep equidistant from two other runners, my moves result from trying (in vain) to keep in place, to stay still equidistant from both. An impossible task: they too try to achieve the same – with two other members. And it moves us continuously, catching up one with another and immediately separating. Is it exhausting? I think not. It's not funny either. The visitor curiously never laughs at us... It is work. Not a job (though I'm paid for it) but an activity, a vital activity although it is metaphorical. It's vital to stay tuned, stay in the group and keep my distance at the same time. Vital to play my part, in the spectacle but above all in my being here. A job consisting in working hard at making my presence valuable. A good metaphor of organizational contemporary life: where each employee has the freedom and pressure of continuously justifying her employment. My presence, like that of the others, creates a value because we create the group itself. The group to which I belong is created by my moves in the search for my place. Moving for searching where to belong creates my belonging to the move itself, that is to the life of our group. If we stopped moving, soon we would not be differentiated from the visitors, if we do not move in pace, idem. When I leave for encountering a visitor, I feel the elasticity of my connection with the group. While I talk,

> they move. In which place will I find them again? Where will my place be after the interruption? At the same time my place now is here, facing this visitor and chatting. Until it's time to run away, to a new place, from place to place.[11]

The performer expresses his attempts at place making, that is, at transforming the museum space into a place to dwell. His dwelling is not something he achieves alone; his place has to be in relation to the group – however each group member tries to make his place in relation to others. Place making appears as a task that is never achieved and at the same is already done. Very clearly, performing and attending are about creating the place where to be, where to ground our encountering. Encountering is the way by which the group's moves occur, always already missed encounters between the performers and between the performers and the visitors. They try to meet, to be together, but the run, walk, moves, and the distances keep them apart at the moment they gather. They have to "meet," to gather as a group; not a massive, unique, collective body, but a fluid shoal of moving bodies. The performers' bodies encounter each other in their distance and closeness, and above all, in their continuous attempt to get closer while escaping from the closeness.

For Casey (1996), place is an event, the coming together of people and things, and we experience the world always already from our emplacement. Place is thus an intrinsic part of our being-in-the-world. And as Ingold (2008, p. 1808) adds: "there would be no places were it not from the comings and goings of human beings and other organisms to and from them, from and to places elsewhere." Gatherings are making places occur, and "take place." Place happens by the coming together of people (and other beings) and will change or dissolve when they leave. As one moves, she goes from one place to another, and at the same time, finds her place in the new location: "To travel between places, is to move between a collection of trajectories and to reinsert yourself in the ones to which you relate" (Massey, 2005, p. 130; Pink, 2009, p. 31). Hence, we could have a joyful and exciting travel between places, leading to each time new encounters, discovering and making together places to share, which could well resemble our liquid modernity (Bauman, 2000).

However, this is not what Tino Sehgal wants us to feel, nor is it what the performer is experiencing. This jumping from place to place seems to prevent any lasting and satisfying encounter. And we might come back to Heidegger to get an insight. For Heidegger (1927), the "Dasein" space is not that of geometry or of science. It follows a personal geography of the places he has known or the elements useful to his activity. His space takes the shapes of his world making. When he later commented on sculpture, Heidegger (1969) related places to a clearing away that brings forth a locality preparing for dwelling. And sculpture can be seen as

> an embodying bringing-into-the-work of places, and with them a disclosing of regions of possible dwellings for man, regions of the possible tarrying of things surrounding and concerning man.
>
> (p. 8)

For Heidegger, even though places occur, they have to provide where to dwell and to tarry. And if in the sentence sung by the performers, Heidegger wonders about the possibility of new rootedness where human nature could flourish, the transient and never-lasting encounters performed there fail to provide a dwelling and tarrying place, for human nature to flourish – in the sense meant by Heidegger. We may have some suspicions when we refer to rootedness with Heidegger, as well as to the place of togetherness and the encounter in his thinking. But the sung phrase selected by Tino Sehgal as well as Hannah Arendt's both question the possibility of the flourishing of human nature in a new world of machines, calculative thinking, and technology – wondering if one can find a place one can live in, stay in, and create.

Both Hannah Arendt and Martin Heidegger's sentences were referring to the by then new stage of technology (the age of electricity and the atom). Tino Sehgal refers to our digital age, of ever more transience, liquidity, and jumping from place to place. One possibility is then to read the performance, as well as the performers' and visitors' experience, as a new way of dwelling, prophesied by Tino Sehgal, for our digital age; i.e. a dwelling less embedded in static places or cultures, a dwelling rather made of the search for dwelling; a dwelling made on moving ground, a kind of permanent "spacing" or place making that one must strive to rebuild every moment, but which allows communities and their work to flourish, as the performance manifests. Testimonies are that such a dwelling happened in Paris, but will it be felt as satisfactory? And can such a major event as the one in Paris, reproduced in other places, still keep something minor, or minoring? Can it lead to human dwelling and flourishing?

Conclusion

In Tino Sehgal's "situations," we are in a way witnessing the factory of organizing. Everyone acts and moves according to each other and according to a few simple rules. The empty space seems to take on different configurations from human movements. There are a few strong moments and intimate words. Our reading sees it as a metaphor for liquid modernity, new workspaces (flex-offices, open spaces, etc.), and generalized acceleration (Rosa). Then Tino Sehgal's work questions us about our organizations, about the place they can tolerate for the minor, the possibility of dwelling in them.

When we look at the academic literature linking space and organization, a huge proportion is about control or about making the organization more pleasant (or bearable). Spacing is above all a minor usage of the functional use of space, the insertion of a slowing down, of creating spaces where to live. It is about inventing some escape routes, some detour from and hijacking of control. But such steps aside are always threatened to be re-entered as functional and productive dynamics for the organization.

Are modern organizations places where human beings can dwell? Is there room for the minor? Toni Sehgal makes us see organizing as both a human-making and a quasi-inhuman place to be.

Spacing cannot be represented. It can happen (provided the police is not too powerful) as the search for place. There is always a minor usage of the major organization. While in many ways Tino Sehgal's performance was intended to make a minor usage of the space of the Palais de Tokyo, it did so by proposing an organization that in turn becomes major and tends to exclude other minor usages. But the same applies to academic research. Wanting to represent, program, or explain spacing, to explicitly want our research to produce spacing is probably immediately doomed to rendering it major. Wanting to explain everything, to know everything, to say everything does not leave room for spacing. Spacing sometimes occurs in some research texts. There is no recipe. One needs probably to connect to one's own pre-individual practices, one's flesh and imaginary to feel the political dimension inside, and then to try and express it. For Beyes and Steyaert, research has to be a performance. Research needs to experiment with the aesthetics and embodiment of research itself. There is no recipe. But it is in the possibility of spacing that there is still some space for freedom, breathing, and hope.

Notes

1 The authors would like to thank Eila Szendy-El-Khurdi for her inputs.
2 The title of one of his art pieces is "These Situations." Tino Sehgal likes to speak of creating situations, instead of performances or artworks.
3 Excerpts from field notes taken by the first author during his visit to Tino Sehgal's solo show, Palais de Tokyo, 18 October–10 December, 2016.
4 For this paragraph, we base ourselves on the interesting synthesis proposed by De Molli (2019).
5 Excerpts from the first author's field notes, November 2016. See note 2.
6 Excerpts from the second author's field notes, taken during his participation in Tino Sehgal's performance "These Associations," Palais de Tokyo, 18 October–10 December, 2016.
7 Ibid.
8 Second author's field notes, excerpts. See note 6.
9 Second author's field notes, excerpts. November 2016.

10 Excerpts from second author's field notes during rehearsal, October 2016.
11 Second author's field notes during his participation in the performance "These Associations," Tino Sehgal solo show, Palais de Tokyo, 18 October–10 December, 2016.

References

Arendt, H. (1958). *The human condition* (2nd ed.), Chicago, IL: The University of Chicago Press.

Bauman, Z. (2000). *Liquid modernity.* Cambridge, UK: Polity Press.

Beyes, T., & Steyaert, C. (2011). Spacing organization: Non-representational theory and performing organizational space. *Organization, 19*(1), 45–61.

Casey, E. (1996). How to get from space to place in a fairly short stretch of time. In S. Field & K. Basso (Eds.), *Senses of place* (pp. 13–52). Santa Fe, NM: School of American research Press.

De Molli, F. (2019). An aesthetic account of space: A report on recent developments in organizational research. *Studi Organizzativi, 1*, 36–63.

Fayard, A. L., & Weeks, J. (2011). Who moved my cube? Creating workspaces that actually foster collaboration. *Harvard Business Review, 89*(7–8), 102–110.

Gagliardi, P. (1990). *Symbols and artifacts: Views of the corporate landscape.* Berlin, Germany: De Gruyter.

Heidegger, M. (1969). "Art and space." In C. H. Seibert (trans.), *Man and world* (Vol. 6, pp. 3–8). Bloomington: Indiana University Press.

Heidegger, M. (1966). Memorial address. In M. Heidegger (Ed.), *Discourse on thinking* (pp. 43–57). New York, NY: Harper and Row.

Heidegger, M. (1927). *Sein und Zeit, Erste Halfte.* Tuebingen, Germany: Max Niemeyer.

Ingold, T. (2008). Binding against boundaries: Entanglements of life in an open world. *Environment and Planning* A, *40*, 1796–1810.

Lefebvre, H. (1991). *The production of space.* Trans. D. Nicholson-Smith. Oxford, UK: Blackwell.

Lefebvre, H. (2004). *Rhythmanalysis* Trans. S. Elden & G. Moore. London, UK: Continuum.

Letiche, H., & Lightfoot, G. (2014). *The relevant PhD.* Rotterdam, Netherlands: Sense Publisher.

Lorimer, H. (2008). Cultural geography: Non-representational conditions and concerns. *Progress in Human Geography, 32*(4), 551–559.

Massey, D. (2005). *For space.* London, UK: Sage.

Moriceau, J. L. (2016). Une approche affective de la communication organisationnelle. *Revue française des sciences de l'information et de la communication* [En ligne/online], n°9, accessed 07 juillet 2020. http://journals.openedition.org/rfsic/2478.

Paes, I. (2019). Le sens au carrefour des individuations : la construction du performer. In J. L. Moriceau, H. Letiche, & M. A. Le Theule (Eds.), *L'art du sens dans les organisations.* Laval: Presses de l'université Laval, pp. 217–235.

Pickering, A. (1994). After representation. Science studies in the performative idiom. *PSA: Proceedings of the Biennial Meeting of the Philosophy of Science Association, 2*, 413–419.

Pink, S. (2009). *Doing sensory ethnography*. London, UK: Sage Publications.
Rancière, J. (2000). *Le partage du sensible. Esthétique et politique*. Paris, France: La Fabrique Editions.
Schechner, R. (1988). *Performance theory*. New York, NY: Routledge.
Schechner, R. (2002). *Performance studies. An introduction*. London, UK: Routledge.
Sehgal, T. (2016a). Rencontre avec Tino Sehgal, l'artiste dont tout Paris va parler à la rentrée, *Numero*, June 01. Retrieved from https://www.numero.com/fr/art/tino-sehgal-place-jemaa-el-fna-marrakech-mouna-mekouar-bam-palais-de-tokyo#_
Sehgal, T. (2016b). « Le Gros Journal de Tino Sehgal : L'art comme vous ne l'avez jamais vu ». Interview with Mouloud Achour. *Le Gros Journal*, TV show, October 19, 2016. Retrieved from https://www.youtube.com/watch?v=mkFM-PkpmQc
Stengers, I. (2016). Another science is possible: A plea for slow science. In Letiche, Lightfoot, & Moriceau (Eds.), *Demo(s): Philosophy, pedagogy, politics* (pp. 53–70). Rotterdam, Netherlands: Sense Publishers.
Stewart, K. (1996). *A space on the side of the street*. Princeton, NJ: Princeton University Press.
Stewart, K. (2007). *Ordinary affects*. Durham, NC: Duke University Press.
Thrift, N. (2007). *Non-representational theory: Space, politics, affects*. London, UK: Routledge.
Turner, V. (1994). *Dramas, fields, and metaphors. Symbolic action in human society*. Ithaca, NY: Cornell University Press.
Ulmer, J. (2017). Writing slow ontology. *Qualitative Inquiry, 23*(3), 201–211.
van Marrewijk, A. (2009). Corporate headquarters as physical embodiments of organisational change. *Journal of Organizational Change Management, 22*(3), 290–306.
Vivant, E. (2009). *Qu'est-ce que la ville créative?*. Paris, France: Presses Universitaires de France.
Weick, K. E. (1979). *The social psychology of organizing* (2nd ed.). New York, NY: McGraw-Hill.
Yanow, D. (2006). How built spaces mean. In D. Yanow & P. Schwartz-Shea (Eds.), *Interpretation and method: Empirical research methods and the interpretive turn* (pp. 349–366). New York: M.E. Sharpe.

9 Aesthetic Learning in an Artistic Intervention Project for Organizational Creativity

Accepting Feelings of Uncertainty, Anxiety, and Fun

Marja Soila-Wadman

Introduction

The aim of this chapter is to increase the understanding of the aesthetic learning process during an artistic intervention project in an organization that does not belong to the art and cultural industries sphere. Artistic interventions have gained increased interest among several types of organizations in recent decades. The different mindsets that feature the organizational world and the art world can create a clash with the hope of promoting creativity in organizational action (Barry & Meisiek, 2010; Grzelec & Prata, 2013). In the management context, the goals often referred to are in co-operation with an artist and with the help of artistic methods to develop new management skills and to promote more creativity, play, and pleasure in everyday work (Berthoin Antal & Strauß, 2014; Taylor & Ladkin, 2009).

In this chapter, I refer to my case study on artistic interventions in a trade union organization (Soila-Wadman, 2017), here named the ARTin project. To increase creativity in the organization, the union engaged an artist who belongs to an artist organization that specializes in artistic interventions to lead creative workshops for a specially selected team of eight persons once a week for a year. I had an opportunity to follow the workshops. The organization sought to develop new recruitment and communication methods to guarantee membership numbers, which were not quite satisfactory. The team's learning would eventually be communicated throughout the main organization. Another aim of the intervention was to find more fun in everyday work practice and to reflect on how to achieve work–life balance, questions that aligned with the values that the union wanted to promote. These values are consistent with responsible management that pays attention to the aesthetic and ethical perspectives in organizational life (Strati, 2019b) and the humanistic management perspective, which advocates for the well-being and the development of human beings in organizational life (Höpfl, 1994).

However, encountering a work of art can touch one's feelings and involve the body, mind, heart, and spirit, and the experience is not necessarily a pleasant one (Beyes & Steyaert, 2013; Darsø, 2004; Köping, 2007). It can apply both to an artist's creation of artwork or to a recipient's experience of artwork. In an organization where everyday work has seemingly been characterized by clear routines and directives from higher hierarchical levels, confronting the varying experiences with artistic methods can be frustrating and induce anxiety. Moments when one does not know what it will be, if anything, can be an embarrassing and scary experience (Austin & Darsø, 2009; Darsø, 2004) that can create resistance in the participating group (Biehl-Missal, 2013; Styhre & Eriksson, 2008; Styhre & Fröberg, 2016). These types of reactions were observed in the case that I studied. I heard comments that questioned the meaning behind the "stupid games" that the artist introduced. These comments were not unlike the skeptical attitudes towards playfulness in serious organizational worlds (West 2015). The team had difficulties in adopting an open attitude to experiments with techniques without a direct connection to daily work tasks. Some months after the start, the process almost became locked.

However, when I interviewed the participants one year after the AR-Tin project had ended, they emphasized that they had learnt a lot about creativity. This concerned both the individual level and the collaborative work in the team. Learning with artistic methods had been an issue that throughout the project was often raised in my conversations with the participants. Following Gagliardi (1996) and Strati (1999, 2019a), who argue that the aesthetic dimension should be acknowledged in all types of organizations, not just in the art and cultural industries sphere, aesthetic learning and aesthetic sensitivity at work became some of the questions to focus on in the study. Accordingly, how can we understand the intervention process as aesthetic learning?

After this introduction, the theoretical frame concerning aesthetics in organizations and organizational learning with artistic interventions is presented. Then, the methodological notes are presented, followed by a description and analysis of some episodes to illustrate the learning process in practical situations, which are discussed further in the next section. The final section summarizes the chapter.

Aesthetics Is a Part of Our Everyday Life and Is Found in All Types of Organizations

Aesthetics has traditionally been related to theorizing about art, but aesthetics is a part of our everyday life and is found in all types of organizations (Gagliardi, 1996; Strati, 1999, 2019a). The aim of this chapter is not to review the history of aesthetic thinking, but a note can be made to Baumgarten, who in the eighteenth century spoke of philosophical aesthetics and sensual knowledge by emphasizing the mental ability to combine sensory impressions into a whole (Bale, 2010). Welsch (1997) writes about the double character of the concept that denotes both *sensation* and *perception*. How we get to know our world can be viewed as an aesthetic epistemological issue in the sense that our perceptions are based on the knowledge that we obtain through sensuous, bodily information, followed by the ability to make judgements (Gagliardi, 1996; Linstead & Höpfl, 2000; Strati, 1999, 2007, 2019a; Welsch, 1997). Welsch argues (1997) that there is no cognition without aesthetics. Currently, the concept of *extended aesthetics* is used, and it exceeds the connection solely to art and cultural questions (Wallenstein, 2001).

In organization studies, aesthetics has received increased interest in recent decades. Strati argues (1999) that, surely, organizations can be viewed as social and collective constructions, but they are not only cognitive constructions. Organizational life addresses emotions, imagination, improvisation, intuition, and so on, which are issues that are influenced through the aesthetic knowing of the world (Fineman, 2008; Hancock & Tyler, 2008; Linstead & Höpfl, 2000; Strati, 1999; Taylor & Hansen, 2005;). Accordingly, there are constant negotiations concerning the values, meanings, symbols, and organizational practices that refer to aesthetic aspects (Strati 1999, 2019a). This knowing has its origin in the knowledge-creating faculties of all the senses, which emphasizes the role of our bodies in these knowledge-creating processes (Burman, 2014; Gherardi, Meriläinen, Strati, & Valtonen, 2013; Ropo & Parviainen, 2001). Consequently, aesthetics can be used to discuss epistemological questions – how we link sensory impressions with bodily experience, affect, and knowledge (Danius, Sjöholm & Wallenstein, 2012).

Aesthetic Learning through Art – Finding One's Sensibility and Sensuality in Knowledge Creation

Aesthetic learning has become an academic discipline in recent decades, especially when the education for traditionally aesthetic disciplines such as visual and music studies has been developed (Lindstrand & Selander, 2010a,b,c). However, as aesthetics is a part of our world in general, it should be noticed in all types of education. Varying types of questions are raised in different disciplines, but one basis for aesthetic learning could be the idea that mankind is capable of creating forms and expressions from what is not there. Thus, a human being as a part of a social context not only has an ability to react and imitate but also an ability to create symbols, interpret them, and imagine the future, thereby being able to create and present something new (Lindstrand & Selander, 2010b,c).

Burman (2014) states that aesthetic learning can be understood as processual learning that focuses on the sensual part of a human being, as an experiencing and discerning human being with an ability in playful processes create something new. The fundamental aspect is *to find one's sensibility and sensuality*, but *reflexivity* is also necessary for deeper knowledge to come into being. According to Sutherland (2013), aesthetic reflexivity can be viewed as reflexive self-work, where the sensual and emotional characteristics of a (new or unknown) experience become cognitively objectified, which enables the development of self-knowledge. Rancière (2009) emphasizes the role of an active, already knowing student/spectator who is connected to one's surroundings and reflects on it by continuously searching, observing, and interpreting through bodily experiences. The role of the body in the aesthetic understanding of the world is also pointed out by Gherardi and Perrotta (2013). They write that when confronting our everyday practices for instance in work, our bodies are involved when interpreting sensory information when we think, discover, and learn. Aesthetic learning processes would then be described as an ongoing dialectical movement between the sensual, sensibility and reflexion (Burman, 2014).

The concept of aesthetic learning can obtain a wider understanding in connection with discussions on art. Either in the creation of a work of art or when encountering a piece of artwork as an audience, art can stimulate us to see, hear, and experience more of what is occurring within us and around us. Consequently, the discussion on how to understand art is relevant to note.

The history of theorizing on art, with a connection to a philosophical discussion on aesthetics, is long and has consisted of intensive debates. Similar to aesthetics, it is currently common to discuss an extended field in the arts without a final definition on what art is, as the phenomenon is multifaceted and changeable (Burman, 2014; Kalb, 2013). Art can be seen as human activity that combines creative ideas with technical know-how. The aim may be to influence our emotions by showing beauty, producing pleasure, or provoking our everyday understanding by asking unpleasant questions and offering sublime experiences (Stokstad & Cothren, 2014; Wallenstein, 2001; Wolff, 1993). Thereby questions can be raised about what we are able to think and imagine, pointing also to issues of disharmony, border states, and collapse (Wallenstein, 2001). In Bourriaud's opinion (2002), art should not just be viewed as something individual and private. He discusses relational art and argues that art is a phenomenon that has its origin in all human relations and their social context. Relational aesthetics would then take its departure "in judging art works on the basis of inter-human relations which they represent, produce and prompt" (Bourriaud, 2002, p. 112). In an artistic process, solutions are sought by the artist in an open, exploratory manner. Presumably, the final product is not defined in the beginning but is emerging in an iterative process during the making (Austin & Darsø, 2009; Austin & Devin, 2003). Artistic work processes can be frustrating and create anxiety (Austin & Darsø, 2009; Köping, 2007). An example is the rehearsal process of a symphony orchestra, where the fear of making mistakes and self-deprecation that faces depressives can be identified in the creative process (Köping, 2007). The artistic way of working would involve looking actively for these emotional tensions when seeking the moments when the artistic expressions are brought forth (Hjertström-Lappalainen, 2014). This process would mean being prepared to *stay in the experiences* of resistance and problems and to wait to hear what they say to one. The emotional tensions and uneasy experiences can give a hint of what is in becoming in the creative process. One way of accepting complex situations would be to cultivate playfulness (Guillet de Monthoux & Statler, 2008). Laughter and joking can help to achieve functioning group dynamics when the crew searches for creative expression, as reported in film production (Bechky, 2006; Soila-Wadman, 2007).

Organizational Learning by Artistic Interventions – To Use the Mindset and Methods from the Artistic World

One of the aims of artistic interventions is that the varying mindsets of the organizational world and the art world, when collaborating, can have a disruptive effect on everyday organizational performance with the hope of promoting creativity (Barry & Meisiek, 2010; Berthoin Antal, 2014; Grzelec & Prata, 2013). Artistic work processes are based on tacit knowledge where the sensual, intangible, and aesthetic values are at the core (Polanyi, 2009/1966). At the individual level of importance are soft skills such as self-knowledge and the ability to communicate and collaborate (Levasseur, 2013). These values can be difficult to appreciate in an organizational world dominated by quantitative, measurable results and where attention is not paid to emotions, imagination, and intuition (Darsø, 2004).

However, when more creativity is needed to meet the global economic, social, cultural, and environmental challenges in contemporary society, art can inspire people to learn to "see more and seeing differently" (Barry & Meisiek, 2010, p. 1505) by asking to see things deeply and widely and by changing the context. Art can have an organizing ability that can transcend everyday understanding in human life and thereby open up new opportunities (Guillet de Monthoux, 2004). What is understood with creativity is studied with different perspectives in several disciplines (Mumford, 2012), but in this chapter concerning organizational work, the focus is on creativity as a collective activity (Koivunen & Rehn, 2009).

An artistic intervention project emphasizes *working practically* with creative methods, not just thinking creatively (Taylor & Ladkin, 2009). The methods used may vary. Theatre methods can be used to develop leadership, while making sculptures can stimulate curiosity. Creating stories can promote communication, and film-making may support team building and the visualization of important questions. These activities can be performed as a short break in an everyday routine or over a long time, such as a month or a year (Berthoin Antal, 2013; Taylor & Ladkin, 2009).

Special workspaces can be designed where the familiar, both material and relational, interactional circumstances can be modified to enable employees to physically experiment with new methods. The changed circumstances can, in turn, facilitate in finding new working routines and training aesthetic reflexivity based on employees' aesthetic knowledge of the world (Friedman, 2011; Sutherland, 2013).

For an artistic intervention project to succeed, the people involved should open their mental spaces to exercise with different approaches, with the aim of finding interspaces between the artistic ways and the organization's routine activities (Berthoin Antal & Strauß, 2016). Styhre and Fröberg (2016) talk about liminal spaces, where the artist's professional expertise interacts with the participating organizational members' expertise. A high level of confidence in the artist helps to broaden a person's horizons on how to think, act, and approach challenges (Biehl-Missal & Berthoin Antal, 2011; Berthoin Antal & Strauß, 2016).

Taylor and Ladkin (2009, pp. 57–60) conceptualize the following four different processes that feature art-based methods in interventions and the manner in which they can contribute to organizational development: (1) *transfer of competence* – theatre techniques of listening and performing can develop greater empathy in a group; (2) *projective techniques* – participants' work with artistic methods can reveal inner thoughts and emotions, such as expressing strategic thoughts by building a model with LEGO bricks; (3) *illustration of essence* – methods that can enable meaning to be experienced and make tacit knowledge visible in a specific situation in a deeper way, such as reflecting on power relations in leadership as they are portrayed in a theatrical play; and (4) *making* – creating an art object, such as manufacturing an individual mask, can create a deep personal experience of belonging to a context.

Storytelling can be a way of making experiences visible and knowable, Gherardi and Perrotta (2013) write. These authors studied craftswomen's learning processes. When the women manufactured their artefacts, they simultaneously described their professional experiences. The knowledge between the craftswomen and the researchers emerged during the practical process.

Regarding the interaction between the individual and the environment in an artistic intervention project, Darsø (2004) proposes a processual approach for how art can teach the participants to reflect on their everyday view of the world and thereby develop a deeper understanding of oneself and one's context, hopefully leading to renewed actions.

However, art should not be reduced to only some instrumental tools, as Guillet de Monthoux (2004) emphasizes, which points out the danger of trivializing art, with a risk that it loses its attractive power of transcendence. Darsø (2004) believes that to create a change through an artistic process is about learning where emotions, visions, and passions should be involved when reflecting on different issues. This process can be described as aesthetic learning (Burman, 2014).

The artist's role as a supervisor then would be to convey his/her professional skills of continuously seeking, which would also mean to see the intervention participants as actively reflecting aesthetically to their world (Rancière, 2009). For these processes to occur, there should be space and time for reflexion, as well as support from the management of the organization so that the organizational participants can have the courage to go outside of their comfort zone; test new, unconventional methods; and have new, unexpected emotional experiences, with the aim of something new to materialize (Berthoin Antal & Strauß, 2014).

The Interactive Spaces between the Participants and the Researcher

I followed the workshops during the year they were conducted (Soila-Wadman, 2017). The study methodology was qualitative and was inspired by reflexive ethnography (Cunliffe, 2003; Soila-Wadman, 2019) and thoughts about organizational ethnography as a learning process in which imagination and new things coming into being are emphasized (Gaggiotti, Kostera, & Krzyworzeka, 2017). I wanted to be open to what was emerging during the research process.

The observation of the workshops can most often be described as shadowing (Czarniawska, 2007). That is, I was an outsider. I was not a part of the working team and did not participate in the creative and artistic exercises. However, I could follow the actions and movements quite freely, and my access eventually improved during the process. I was conscious of the role of sensitive, sensuous knowledge, and my purpose was to use all my senses, not just seeing and listening, thereby paying attention to tacit knowledge, intuition, feelings, and emotions as a basis for knowledge creation (Gherardi, Meriläinen, Strati, & Valtonen, 2013). When I first visited the team office, I reacted negatively to the cramped open office plan that had no privacy. However, I was told by the team members that it was not a problem, and the office also gave an impression of close and friendly relations; the team moved freely in the space.

With my basic assumptions in relational constructionism (Hosking, 2011; Stout & Staton, 2011), the relations between the researcher and the participants are fundamental to note. Both the material context and what emerges in the research process should be paid attention to

(Cunliffe & Karanayake, 2013). In knowledge creation, not only rational but also aesthetic understanding is fundamental (Burman, 2014; Strati, 1999, 2007, 2019a; Welsch, 1997). An aspect that became important in this study was to learn of the creative spaces in practical situations where the interpretative meanings emerged in negotiations and in interactions between the researcher and the participants. To acknowledge these situations was especially valuable when I conducted both semi-structured interviews with individuals and had somewhat structured conversations with them when I wanted to develop a deeper interpretation of something. Group interviews were also organized.

Some written documents were studied, and photos were taken. Sometimes, the method could be described as action research, when I actively participated with theoretical reflections in strategic meetings during discussions in conflict situations. Although the members did not consider it necessary, I chose to make the organization and the participants anonymous. My aim has been neither to point out especially this organization nor to focus on any individual participant. Instead, I want to give space for open discussions and reflexions on private, sometimes sensitive, experiences. The participants have also received opportunities to give feedback to the research report I have published (Soila-Wadman, 2017).

Episodes Illustrating Learning in Practice

In the beginning, the team members were enthusiastic about being selected to participate in the ARTin project. They met the exercises that the artist proposed with curiosity. At the start, the aim of the artist was to create trust in the group through playful exercises. An example was that the team would illustrate different mental themes, such as strength and togetherness, by building a tower with their bodies. These formations were then photographed. A lot of laughter from the group could be heard. The exercise can be analyzed by using the "illustration of essence" category (Taylor & Ladkin, 2009, p. 58), where the inner thoughts and feelings of the group concerning the theme were expressed.

However, after the initial phase of two months, the group became increasingly frustrated. There was a conflict between the artist and the team concerning the goals and methods of the project. Although I have experienced the turbulence that can emerge in an artistic process (Soila-Wadman, 2007), I was, nevertheless, astonished by the strength of the negative feelings and resistance among the group members. These emotions created inertia and, in one phase, almost a complete halting of the project. The team members talked of feeling useless if they used their time to play and could not show some measurable results in relation to their organizational task descriptions and to the goals of how many new members they had recruited into the union.

The manager of the participating team and the managers of the art organization arranged several meetings where the tense situations were discussed in quite excited, emotional language. According to Tsoukas (2009), dialogues are a way to create new knowledge in organizational action. Dialogues could indicate storytelling coming into being, according to an aesthetic method in practice where new knowledge can emerge (Gherardi & Perrotta, 2013). The discussions resulted in each workshop ending with a session where the participants together would try to find words for their experiences one at a time without being interrupted. Someone would write down the opinions in a logbook. In some of the meetings also the regional union manager participated, which gave the ARTin project legitimation from higher organizational level to continue, and the tense emotions and closed situations eventually were released.

During the autumn, the workshops focused on practical organizational topics conducted through playful and creative methods, which the co-workers said were satisfying. An event that exemplifies aesthetic learning, following Ranciére's (2009) thinking about participants' active, creative acts and where the ideas of individuals are externalized, was a graffiti painting workshop. A visual message for the union slogan would be created; no participant had done this before. The team went out of their office and out of their comfort zone to a place where both earlier graffiti and other artistic expressions could be seen. The atmosphere was exciting. The sky was bright blue and the sun was shining. The team wore black garbage bags over their clothes, conducted some brainstorming together, and then started to spray imaginative figures with strong colours on large walls. Much laughter and joking ensued. This activity could be an example of "making" (Taylor & Ladkin, 2009, p. 60). In the storytelling sessions afterwards, the participants indicated pleasure. The experience of personal presence was told to be deep. Belonging to the specific context different from the everyday office milieu was a meaningful experience. As Darsø (2004) notes, developing a deeper understanding of oneself and one's context can give a hint of transcendence to the participants' attitudes and make learning come into being.

Some of the workshops aimed at developing a new way to meet potential members and focused on the theme of manager. To work with an abstract concept of a manager and connect it to pictures to illustrate it was a new task for the team, and I heard comments that reminded me of the anxiety in the turbulent period during the spring of "Why should we do this job?" However, the team got along. In these workshops, it was easy to observe how the "transfer of artistic competence" worked (Taylor & Ladkin 2009, p. 57). The team members had become very skilful in using the visual and presentative methods, but they also actively searched for expressions for their thoughts (Ranciére, 2009). First, the participants in minor groups began by brainstorming and choosing images in journals and computer home pages that illustrated their ideas and imagination about the concept of a manager. Second, they tested poster collages concerning the theme. The third phase was to make an oral and visual presentation for some persons in manager position outside the union to test the ideas and get feedback from them before the team met potential new members.

Learning to Stay in the Experience of Uncertainty but Also Having Fun

It is difficult to know how an artistic intervention process develops. Consequences can be difficult to analyze on both the personal and organizational levels (Barry & Meisiek, 2010; Berthoin Antal & Strauss, 2014; Biehl-Missal & Berthoin Antal, 2011). It is understandable that an organization that invests in an artistic intervention project wants to evaluate whether the project has been successful. However, what effects there will evolve in an intervention project requires that the time issue should be considered. In an organizational development or change processes, as Langley, Smallman, Tsoukas, and Van de Ven (2013) argue, it takes differing time periods for changes to unfold. That an artistic intervention project focuses on learning and change processes which eventually will/can lead to materialized effects, like new organizational routines, was emphasized by the representatives of the artist organization when the contract was negotiated with the union. However, for the participants who were confronted by the new and sometimes scary situations in practice, it took time before they learnt the iterative, artistic way of work and had courage to test new issues.

Nevertheless, in interviews one year after the ARTin project had ended, the team members told me about their positive experiences concerning the project. They assured me that they had learnt a lot. To keep the creative mindset alive, they had incorporated creative meetings into their work schedules. They also continued to have some creative, playful tasks every week. For example, the team had a brainstorming session to find suggestions for weekly creative challenges, and the proposals were put on a slip of paper and placed in a creativity box, from which a task was drawn individually.

This learning became one of the themes to focus on that eventually emerged in the interactive conversations between the team members, the artist, and me. From the beginning of the project, the team talked about curiosity and a will to learn about creativity and new work methods, as guided by the artist. Surely, the meaning of the intervention was to get disrupted and in everyday understanding obtain new emotional experiences, which Ranciere (2009) points out to be fundamental in aesthetic learning. However, during the conflictual phase, when frustration ran high and insecurity concerning the meaning of the project was noticeable, the members hesitated about whether they were doing the right things according to the organizational norms and talked about ending the project. The artist discussed her frustration when the team did not trust her professional competence when describing the often indefinite, uncertain, artistic processes. The emotional engagement (Austin & Devin, 2003), however, increased in the project and, eventually, a change in attitudes could be observed. This indicates aesthetic learning at a deeper level (Austin & Darsø, 2009; Hjertström-Lappalainen, 2014; Ranciere, 2009).

Resistance to both artistic intervention projects and organizational development projects in general is observed by many (Bergström, Styhre, & Thilander, 2014; Biehl-Missal, 2013). In the organizational research on change, the situations where tension can be identified tell something important about the participating group (Thomas, Sargent, & Hardy, 2013). In the art world, frustrated feelings and conflict situations are considered to give emotional energy to further the artistic process (Austin & Darsø, 2009; Hjertström-Lappalainen, 2014). Furthermore, anxiety can be noted as a part of the creative process when something new is becoming (Köping, 2007).

A situation where the team showed that it had learnt about the artistic way of working iteratively (Austin & Darsø, 2009) is exemplified by the workshops with the manager theme. When the team members began the work, they once again experienced performance anxiety (Köping, 2007), and inertia was observed. However, I also observed that the participants quite soon actively started working, practically engaging in "cut and paste," according to the inspiring guidelines from the artist. In words, this exemplifies a transfer of competence (Taylor and Ladkin, 2009), and an exploring attitude was encouraged by the artist (Rancière, 2009). The artist did not know where the team's work would end up, but she could inspire the participants to continue to seek their understanding on ideas of what a manager could be by finding and interpreting visual images and testing different methods of collage making. A lot of joking and laughter could be heard. The team started to act with energy to find solutions, which in turn created even more action. I judged that some of the collages were very clever and visually pleasing. Thus, the participants had learnt to *stay in the experience* of resistance and problems to wait to hear what the situation said and what was in becoming (Austin & Darsø, 2009; Hjertström-Lappalainen, 2014). Regarding aesthetic learning, at the end of the workshops, the team discussed how the practical work had engaged their imagination, created new knowledge, and deepened their understanding, both emotionally and cognitively, of what it meant to be a manager.

The situations in which the team members sat together in the colourfully furnished meeting room can be described as aesthetic learning places and spaces (Friedman, 2011; Sutherland, 2013). The participants were emotionally affected by the new insights that they had garnered at the workshop and simultaneously searched for words to comprehend them, thereby participating in aesthetic knowledge creation. I could see and hear how the group had become more courageous when collaborating with one another. In dialogical roundtable meetings (Tsoukas, 2009) and through storytelling (Gherardi & Perrotta, 2013), the group eventually had become more open and learnt to put words both to their feelings and to reflections on what they had experienced during the workshops. Trust, which is considered to be important in interventions (Berthoin Antal & Strauß, 2016), had increased among the team members. Trust influenced the team members' courage to propose new ideas in the group and to test new methods and solutions in everyday work, which was described as rewarding in the team interviews one year after the project had ended.

Concerning playfulness in this ARTin project, it was slightly ironic to note that exercises to have fun, play games, and train humour were needed among the team. However, it is not uncommon to have a sceptical attitude towards playfulness in organizations used to conducting serious business (Darsø, 2004; West, 2015). Nevertheless, the artist continued to organize playful exercises such as Office Olympiads, where the team members competed to throw an eraser the farthest. The walls of the office even told of fun and play and increasingly got more creative visual contemplations both on work-related topics such as the statistics on new members and on funny illustrations on the team's work processes. The team said that during the project, the atmosphere eventually became more relaxed to play games and have fun. As noticed, laughter and playfulness can be a smoothing factor for group dynamics and an element for facilitating creativity (Bechky, 2006; Guillet de Monthoux & Statler, 2008).

Final Words

My aim has been to reflect on the artistic intervention project in an organization from an aesthetic learning perspective. If we agree that all knowledge creation in the world has an aesthetic dimension, then it is of value to increase aesthetic consciousness in society by facilitating aesthetic learning in variable contexts, that is, also outside the artistic and creative industries sector.

The fundamental aspect of aesthetic learning is to find one's sensibility and sensuality when reflecting on different issues concerning both oneself and the world. The lesson from this artistic intervention is that in addition to learning the artistic techniques in practice, the process enables unexpected experiences, including pleasure and the overwhelming anxiety and frustrations, when working with artistic methods in practice. At the individual level, art can help by opening one's mental space to see and experience more, which, in turn, can lead to a new way of creating one's world. In an organization, collaborative skills can be developed in creative, interactive work. This is facilitated by a trustful atmosphere that can increase the courage to express both positive and negative experiences and feelings when sharing ideas to create something new, such as new ideas, products, and work methods in an organizational context.

If more responsible management and a humanistic working life, as well as more creativity in organizational action is asked for, we should pay serious attention to both the sensual and sensible parts of human beings in organizational and in societal activities. That is, besides our rationality we should also be considered to be experiencing, improvising, discerning, and playful human beings with an ability to imagine the future.

References

Austin, R., & Darsø, L. (2009). Innovation processes and closure. In N. Koivunen & A. Rehn (Eds.), *Creativity and the contemporary economy* (pp. 55–81). Malmö, Sweden: Liber.

Austin, R., & Devin, L. (2003). *Artful making, what managers need to know about how artists work*. Upper Saddle River, NJ: FT Prentice Hall and Pearson Education.

Bale, K. (2010). *Estetik. En introduktion* (Aesthetics. An introduction). Göteborg, Sweden: Bokförlaget Daidalos.

Barry, D., & Meisiek, S. (2010). Seeing more and seeing differently. Sensemaking, mindfulness and the workarts. *Organization Studies, 31*(11), 1505–1530.

Bechky, B. (2006). "Gaffers, gofers, and grips: Role-based coordination in temporary organizations. *Organization Science, 17*(1), 3–21.

Bergström, O., Styhre, A., & Thilander, P. (2014). Paradoxifying organizational change: Cynicism and resistance in the Swedish armed forces. *Journal of Change Management, 14*(3), 384–404.

Berthoin Antal, A. (2013). Art-based research for engaging not-knowing in organizations. *Journal of Applied Arts and Health, 4*(1), 67–76.

Berthoin Antal, A. (2014). When arts enter organizational spaces: Implications for organizational learning. In A. Berthoin Antal, P. Meusburger, & L. Suarsana (Eds.), *Learning organizations: Extending the field* (pp. 177–201). Dordrecht, Netherlands: Springer.

Berthoin Antal, A., & Strauß, A. (2014). Not only art's task – Narrating bridges between unusual experiences with art and organizational identity. *Scandinavian Journal of Management, 30*(1), 114–123.

Berthoin Antal, A., & Strauß, A. (2016). Multi stakeholder perspectives on searching for evidence of values added in artistic interventions in organizations. In U. Johansson Sköldberg, J. Woodilla, & A. Berthoin Antal (Eds.), *Artistic interventions in organizations* (pp. 57–80). London, UK and New York, NY: Routledge.

Beyes, T., & Steyaert, C. (2013). "Strangely familiar: The uncanny and unsiting organizational analysis. *Organization Studies, 30*(10), 1445–1465.

Biehl-Missal, B. (2013). And if I don't want to work like an artist...?" How the study of artistic resistance enriches organizational studies. *Ephemera, Theory & Politics in Organization, 13*(1), 75–98.

Biehl-Missal, B., & Berthoin Antal, A. (2011). The impact of arts-based initiatives on people and organizations: Research findings, challenges for evaluation and research and caveats. *KEA-European Affairs*, Giełda Papierów Wartościowych (Eds.). Warsaw Stock Exchange.

Bourriaud, N. (2002). *Relational aesthetics.* Dijon, France: Les pressez du rèel.

Burman, A. (2014). Det estetiska, kunskapen och lärprocesserna" (The aesthetics, knowledge and learning processes). In A. Burman (Ed.), *Konst och lärande. Essäer om estetiska lärprocesser* (pp. 7–28). Södertörn Studies in Higher Education 3. Huddinge, Sweden: Södertörn University.

Cunliffe, A. L. (2003). Reflexive inquiry in organizational research: Questions and possibilities. *Human Relations, 56*, 983–1003.

Cunliffe, A. L., & Karunanayake, G. (2013). Working ithin hyphen-spaces in ethnographic research. *Organizational Research Methods, 16*(3), 364–392.

Czarniawska, B. (2007). *Shadowing and other techniques for doing fieldwork in modern societies.* Malmö, Sweden, Copenhagen, Denmark, and Oslo, Norway: Liber.

Danius, S., Sjöholm, C., & Wallenstein, S. O. (2012). Inledning. In *Aisthesis. Estetikens historia, del 1* (Introduction. Aesthesis. The history of aesthetics. Part 1) (pp. 9–15). Stockholm, Sweden: Thales bokförlag.

Darsø, L. (2004). *Artful creation: Learning-tales of art in business.* Fredriksberg, DK: Samfundslitteratur.

Fineman, S. (2008). *The emotional organization: Passions and power.* Oxford, UK and Malden, MA: Blackwell Publishing.

Friedman, V. J. (2011). Revisiting social space: Relational thinking about organizational change. *Research in organizational change and development, 19*(7), 233–257.

Gaggiotti, H., Kostera, M., & Krzyworzeka, P. (2017). More than a method? Organizational ethnography as a way of imagining the social. *Culture and Organization, 23*(5), 325–340.

Gagliardi, P. (1996). Exploring the aesthetic side of organizational life. In C. Clegg, C. Hardy, & W. Nord (Eds.), *Handbook of organization studies* (pp. 565–580). London, UK: Sage.

Gherardi, S., Meriläinen, S., Strati, A., & Valtonen, A. (2013). Editors introduction: A practice-based view on the body, senses and knowing in organization. *Scandinavian Journal of Management, 29*(4), 333–337.

Gherardi, S., & Perrotta, M. (2013). Between the hand and the head. How things get done, and how in doing the ways of doing are discovered. *Qualitative Research in Organizations and Management. An International Journal, 9*(2), 134–150.

Grzelec, A., & Prata, T. (2013). *Artists in organizations – Mapping of European producers of artistic interventions.* Göteborg, Sweden: TILLT, Creative Clash. (www.TILLT.se, 2014-05-16)

Guillet de Monthoux, P. (2004). *The art firm: Aesthetic management and metaphysical marketing.* Stanford, CA: Stanford University Press.

Guillet de Monthoux, P., & Statler, M. (2008). Aesthetic play as an organizing principle. In D. Barry & H. Hansen (Eds.), *The Sage handbook new approaches to management and organization* (pp. 423–435). London, UK and Los Angeles, CA: Sage.

Hancock, P., & Taylor, S. S. (2008). It's all too beautiful: Emotion and organization in the aesthetic economy. In S. Fineman (Ed.), *The emotional organization: Passions and power* (pp. 202–217). Oxford, UK and Malden, MA: Blackwell Publishing.

Hjertström-Lappalainen, J. (2014). Innan erfarenheten. Estetiska lärprocesser i ljuset av John Deweys estetik (Before the experience. Aesthetic learning processes in the light of Dewey's aesthetics). In A. Bjurman (Ed.), *Konst och lärande. Essäer om estetiska lärprocesser.* Södertörn studies in higher education 3 (pp. 29–46). Huddinge, Sweden: Södertörn University.

Höpfl, H. (1994). Learning by heart. *Management Learning, 25*(3), 463–474.

Hosking, D. M. (2011). Telling tales of relations: Appreciating relational constructionism. *Organization Studies, 32*(1), 47–65.

Kalb, P. R. (2013). *Art since 1980: Charting the contemporary.* London, UK: Laurence King Publishing.

Koivunen, N., & Rehn, A. (2009). *Creativity and the contemporary economy.* Malmö, Sweden: Liber.

Köping, A. S. (2007). The creative compost: Playing and conducting musical events In P. Guillet de Monthoux, C. Gustafsson, & S. E. Sjöstrand (Eds.), *Aesthetic leadership. Managing fields of flow in art and business* (pp. 15–32). London, UK and New York, NY: Palgrave Macmillan.

Langley, A., Smallman, C., Tsoukas, H., & Van de Ven, A. (2013). Process studies of change in organization and management. Unveiling temporality, activity and flow. *Academy of Management Journal, 56*(1), 1–13.

Levasseur, R. (2013). People skills: Developing soft skills: A change management perspective. *Interfaces, 43*(6), 566–571.

Linstead, S., & Höpfl, H. (2000). Introduction In S. Linstead & H. Höpfl (Eds.), *The aesthetics of organization* (pp. 1–11). London, UK and Thousand Oaks, CA: Sage.

Lindstrand, F., & Selander,S. (2010a). Förord. In F. Lindstrand & S. Selander (Eds.), *Estetiska lärprocesser – upplevelser, praktiker och kunskapsformer.* (Introduction, in aesthetic learning processes – Experiences, practices and forms of knowledge) (pp. 9–14). Lund, Sweden: Studentlitteratur.

Lindstrand, F., & Selander, S. (2010b). Estetiska upplevelser – estetiska praktiker. In F. Lindstrand & S. Selander (Eds.), *Estetiska lärprocesser – upplevelser, praktiker och kunskapsformer.* (Aesthetic experiences – aestethic practices) (pp. 16–18). Lund, Sweden: Studentlitteratur.

Lindstrand, F., & Selander, S. (2010c). *Estetiska lärprocesser – upplevelser, praktiker och kunskapsformer.* (Aestetic learning processes – Experiences, practices and forms of knowledge). Lund, Sweden: Studentlitteratur.

Mumford, M. D. (Ed.). (2012). *Handbook of organizational creativity.* London, UK: Elsevier.

Polanyi, M. (2009/1966). *The tacit dimension.* Chicago, IL: University of Chicago Press.

Rancière, J. (2009). *The emancipated spectator.* London, UK and New York, NY: Verso.
Ropo, A., & Parviainen, J. (2001). Leadership and bodily knowledge in expert organizations: Epistemological rethinking. *Scandinavian Journal of Management, 17*(1), 1–18.
Soila-Wadman, M. (2007). Can art be a Leader? Beyond heroic film directing. In P. Guillet de Monthoux, C. Gustafsson, & S. E. Sjöstrand (Eds.), *Aesthetic leadership. Managing fields of flow in art and business* (pp. 72–86). London, UK and New York, NY: Palgrave Macmillan.
Soila-Wadman, M. (2017). Konstnärliga interventioner för kreativitet och förändring i organisationer: lekfullt utforskande, motstånd och dialoger i läroprocessen. En fallstudie. (Artistic interventions for creativity and change in organizations: Playful exploration, resistance and dialogues in learning process. A case study). Gothenburg research institute report, 2017: 1. University of Gothenburg.
Soila-Wadman, M. (2019). Following artistic interventions for organizational creativity during a one-year-long case study. *Sage research methods cases.* London, UK: Sage.
Stokstad, M., & Cothren, M. W. (2014). *Art history.* Upper Saddle River, NJ: Pearson Education.
Stout, M., & Staton, C. M. (2011). The ontology of process philosophy in follet's administrative theory. *Administrative Theory & Praxis, 33*(2), 268–292.
Strati, A. (1999). *Organization and aesthetics.* London, UK and Thousand Oaks, CA: Sage.
Strati, A. (2007). Sensible knowledge and practice-based learning. *Management Learning, 38*(1), 61–77.
Strati, A. (2019a). *Organizational theory and aesthetic philosophies.* New York, NY and London, UK: Routledge.
Strati, A. (2019b). Beauty of responsible management: The lens and methodology of organizational aesthetics. In O. Laasch, D. Jamali, E. Freeman, & R. Suddaby (Eds.), *The research handbook of responsible management.* Cheltenham, UK: Edward Elgar. (2019 forthcoming)
Styhre, A., & Eriksson, M. (2008). Bring in the arts and get the creativity for free: A study of the artist in residence project. *Creativity and Innovation Management, 17*(1), 47–57.
Styhre, A., & Fröberg, J. (2016). Artistic interventions as détourment and constructed situations. In U. Johansson Sköldberg, J. Woodilla, & A. Berthoin Antal (Eds.), *Artistic interventions in organizations* (pp. 107–120). London, UK and New York, NY: Routledge.
Sutherland, I. (2013). Arts-based methods in leadership development: Affording aesthetic workspaces, reflexivity and memories with momentum. *Management Learning, 44*(1), 25–43.
Taylor, S. S., & Hansen, H. (2005). Finding form: Looking at the field of organizational aesthetics. *Journal of Management Studies, 42*(6), 1211–1232.
Taylor, S. S., & Ladkin, D. (2009). Understanding arts-based methods in managerial development. *Academy of Management Learning & Education, 8*(1), 55–69.

Thomas, R., Sargent, L., & Hardy, C. (2011). Managing organizational change: Negotiating meaning and power –Resistance relations. *Organization Science, 22*(1), 22–41.
Tsoukas, H. (2009). A dialogical approach to the creation of new knowledge in organizations. *Organization Science, 20*(6), 941–957.
Wallenstein, S. O. (2001). *Bildstrider: föreläsningar om estetisk teori*. Göteborg, Sweden: Alfabeta/Anamma.
Welsch, W. (1997). *Undoing aesthetics*. London, UK: Sage.
West, S. (2015). *Playing at work: Organizational play as a facilitator of creativity*. Lund, Sweden: Department of Psychology, Lund University.
Wolff, J. (1993). *The social production of art*. London, UK: The Macmillan Press.

10 The Art of Creating the Unthinkable

Connecting Processes of Engineering, Management, and Aesthetics

Alessandra Di Pisa and Robert Stasinski

Introduction

Since 2017, we – artist duo Di Pisa Stasinski – are leading the ongoing transdisciplinary art project *Being Unthinkable ... ...* (the last three words in the title are randomly artificial intelligence [AI] generated via a smartphone app) in close collaboration with IBM Sweden. *Being Unthinkable ... ...* is a permanent, interactive robotic sculpture, with an AI system core, based on philosophical data sets with the purpose of generating new and unique, synthetic questions. The aim of the robot sculpture is to interact with the audience via a smartphone app and using spatiotemporal choreographies in the form of colour and movement.

Although the main focus of this process has been constructing the artwork in close collaboration with coders, roboticists, and engineers, it has also spawned workshops, lectures, meetings, and many other experiences, both internally and externally to IBM, that by and large have been crucial for the development of the artwork itself. As suggested by some scholars, collaborations of this kind could sometimes lead to a separation of artistic work and broader "creative" contributions, making it harder for some artists to position themselves as autonomous artists in such a collaboration (Schnugg & Vesna, 2016). In our artistic practice, the separation of "artistic" and "creative" is not a very useful distinction, since our work emanates from the tradition of relational and dialogic art, where the creation of new relationships is not a side effect of the work, but rather the foundation of it. In other words, our practice shies away from the division between "artistic practice" and other "creative" work (Bourriaud, 2002; Kester, 2013).

The joint venture of developing and managing the various processes of training and building the entire artistic system has been documented through meeting notes, email conversations, PowerPoint presentations, interviews, conversations, and various creative processes, some of which will be described and reflected upon in this chapter.

Written by the artists of the project, this is a first person's account of the process from the start in 2017 to its near finish in 2019. The project can, on the one hand, be framed as part of a tradition of artistic organizational collaboration pioneered in the 1960s by the Artist Placement Group (APG) and E.A.T. (Experiments in Art and Technology), as well as in relation to the work by the Swedish artist Sture Johannesson together with engineer Sten Kallin at IBM during the 1970s. On the other hand, this project has presented many new and unique artistic challenges, such as the constant rebuilding of the project team's organizational structure, the close connections with the executive managers at IBM, and the nature of technical complexity of the work itself.

Historical precedents have both helped frame the initial artistic and organizational approach, and provided a backdrop of perspectives from which to analyze some of the key moments of the process.

Artistic Concept

The concept behind the artwork – to translate and augment the content of human–machine interaction through a physically interchangeable robotic form and a smartphone app – is both a continuation of current engineering practice and a major departure from it. It involves several software systems, some of which are based on machine learning, a subset of AI. Machine learning algorithms build mathematical models based on sample data, known as "training data," in order to make predictions without being explicitly programmed to perform the task. The data we have used in order to generate questions has consisted of digitized philosophy texts, going back 3,000 years, encompassing all continents and major traditions.

The data is not used as a base for a question answering system; rather, it aims to augment the curiosity and engagement of the audience. The reaction in the form of physical change in the robot sculpture comes about when a human engages with a synthetically generated philosophical question through a smartphone app. The change involves the dynamic movement of six robotic arms, as well as a shift in colour and light throughout the entire sculpture, including "the body." The movement is based on IBM Watson's ability to analyze written text emotionally and psychologically.

Much of the previous research on artists who collaborate or work within organizations has focused on what art can do for business, science, and organizations and seldom the other way around (Barry & Meisiek, 2010; Schnugg & Vesna, 2016). Whether it concerns art-based learning, creativity workshops, artistic interventions and commissions, or other kinds of collaborations, very few analyses give credible emphasis on what the artists stand to gain in a multidisciplinary collaboration, other than monetary remunerations. So much so, that we find it crucial to make explicit our artistic raison d'être for working with one of the biggest corporations in the world.

Context and Background

During 2016, one of us, Alessandra Di Pisa, was asked to perform an art historical tour of the IBM headquarters' art collection in Sweden, located at Kista, a suburb of Stockholm sometimes referred to as the "Silicon Valley of Europe." In connection with this, Anna-Lena Beckman, property manager at IBM, suggested that Di Pisa could curate a thematic new frame for the collection, in conjunction with moving to new facilities, closer to the centre of Kista. The commission included not only curating, researching, writing, and installing of artworks in the new seven-floor IBM headquarters, but also creating a complete inventory and eventually selling off remaining works.

The idea was suggested by Di Pisa to Beckman, that surplus from the artworks sold would be reinvested in a new art commission, which was met with great excitement, and Di Pisa initially researched a curatorially relevant artist. One of the most prominent figures in the IBM Collection is Sture Johannesson, a Swedish artist, who together with IBM employee Sten Kallin broke new ground with their early computer art experiments in the early 1970s. Connected to computers such as IBM 1130 and IBM 1620, they scripted lines of code, creating artistic digital images based on algorithms that were punched into a dot-matrix style printer and later screen printed. Their collaboration would last more than a decade, and the result was never-before-seen motifs based on Johannesson's vision of the digital media's relevance to art (Orrghen, 2015).

From this historical pairing of computers and art, a thought was born: would it be possible to reimagine the artistic collaboration between Johannesson and Sten Kallin? Would it makes sense artistically and for IBM? Although Johannesson today is regarded as a pioneer in Sweden for using computers in artistic creation, he was once shunned for collaborating with IBM and blending computers and art (Johannesson and Nacking, 2004). In dialogue with IBM, a proposal to utilize cutting-edge AI technology to create a new work of art came to light, and Watson, an overarching brand of several different software products utilizing AI, developed by IBM, was thought to fit well for this purpose. Watson's claim to fame was to masterfully beat the 74-time *Jeopardy!* champion Ken Jennings in several TV-broadcasted games in 2011; since then, it has been the rubric under which IBM's AI products have been marketed (Webb, 2019).

Following this, we started an artistic pilot study in order to find a conceptual angle from where to utilize the AI as a tool for producing art and to explore the potential aesthetic configurations that the technology could render possible.

Without any prior expertise in AI or more specifically IBM Watson, we initiated several parallel conversations with researchers and engineers in Sweden about the possibilities and limits of current technologies. What caught our attention was the theory and practice of *intelligence augmentation*, an often forgotten tradition of AI that regards technology not only as a servant of humans but as a means to enhance human attributes, skills, and curiosity, rather than replacing them (Roco & Montemagno, 2004). The artistic ground point became the reversal of the traditional function and understanding of AI, by not having the system providing answers, but instead training the Watson system with the aim to pose unsettling, but curious, questions to the audience.

Initial Project Development

The project, at the time of writing this chapter, is still a work in progress (we have effectively gotten rid of notions of specific deadlines, in favour of an open-ended timeline). Retrospectively, there have been several key moments that we wish to highlight.

In the initial phase of the project, the already established relationship between Di Pisa and Anna-Lena Beckman played a crucial role. Through the previous curatorial work with the IBM art collection, Di Pisa had already gained insight into the guidelines and values that the company praised and could effectively translate these into subject matter more ripe for artistic critique. Parallel to the initial role as curator, the trust earned by Di Pisa could successfully be transferred to a new, burgeoning project team.

As discussions about the new artistic commission took place, Di Pisa's approach was to listen to the intrinsic motivation expressed by IBM for supporting the project, knowing that if the organization's visions were not met, there would be slim chances of realizing the project. At the same time, the principle of providing quotas for IBM for specific assignments would no longer be valid if the new art project was to be created with any form of artistic autonomy. It would stifle the creative process and therefore we had find a more fluid workflow as well as a new remuneration structure. Still, the transition from working as a curator to working as an artist did not disrupt the management structure in the beginning, but would later turn out to be more problematic. It was at this stage (April 2017) that Robert Stasinski was introduced to IBM and joined the production team as a co-artist, as the two of us have collaborated as an artistic duo for more than a decade.

#ArtwithWatson and Value Framing

It was in the early spring of 2017 that Watson, IBM's AI platform, was offered to us as a possible tool for an artistic commission. We were subsequently introduced to an IBM Watson expert consultant, who played a crucial role in supporting the project from an early stage. It was through this dialogue that we developed the conceptual idea for the work, as far as coming to terms with what could be feasible when using AI and Watson as a tool for the production of the work.

Watson has, for several years, been branded through implementation in different domains, such as healthcare, finance, retail, and sports. IBM has also developed projects with musicians, designers, and architects as a way to market the breadth of the ecosystem. These projects were internationally branded under the name and hashtag *Art with Watson*, most of them realized in 2017. They included a "cognitive dress" by fashion label Marchesa; the exhibition *Art with Watson: Hidden Portraits,* sponsored by IBM at the Cadillac House gallery in New York; and a "cognitive sculpture" based on Antoni Gaudi by design studio SOFTlab, at the Mobile World Congress in Barcelona. The ad agency of IBM, Ogilvy & Mather, was involved in all of these projects, and thus puts the autonomous artistic merits into question, although the projects later on did receive limited coverage in news outlets such as *New York Magazine*, the Cut, and Engadget (*New York Magazine*, 2017).

We expressed the need to keep our project with IBM conceptually separate from the previous ones connecting art with Watson, for several reasons. First, due to the framing of our project as an autonomous proposal, presented to IBM as an art project, without an external mediator or stakeholder. Second, the aim of this project was and still is first and foremost cultural longevity and relevance, which the previous projects clearly lacked, in part because they were initialized by an external ad agency and partly due to the nature of the works as transient and event based. And third, this form of collaboration never intended to merely promote or experiment with a specific technology or product, but rather be an open conceptual approach to human–AI interaction, in which IBM Watson initially was an integral part, but would later on lose some of its significance.

As one of us (Stasinski) has the experience of working closely with the Stockholm School of Economics (SSE) Art Initiative – an organization initiated by the school's president, Lars Strannegård, to bridge the gap between arts and business by exposing students and faculty to new works, exhibitions, lectures, and seminars on art and culture as a complement to the primary curriculum – we invited IBM for a private view in order to facilitate a deeper understanding of how a business enterprise organization can work with art and artists without compromising the autonomy of the artwork (Stasinski & Guillet de Monthoux, 2017).

The enthusiasm and energy that the project team members at IBM expressed during the initial phase of the project was in many ways crucial for its development, but as the project grew, it needed further internal support. Beckman, therefore, introduced Kristina Ulander to the project who was working within the marketing department and proved to be important in communicating the idea of the project internally. Most important was the need to go beyond normative perspectives of business rationality and not to compromise the artistic autonomy of the project. We soon discovered that Ulander had a deeper knowledge and understanding of the artistic value system, being married to an artist whom she met while they both attended art school; hence, she had a great ability to bridge the gap between the two different cultural value systems, which proved to be fruitful. As soon as an agreement was drafted to execute the artistic idea, a set of baseline conditions were established for the implementation of the artistic vision, including, among many points, the following:

- For us as artists, it would be crucial to create a work that under no circumstances would compromise our artistic autonomy.
- IBM would be the owner of the work, providing its production costs including our artist fee, hardware and software, as well as developing and overseeing the production.
- IBM would offer all the technological resources needed to train and develop the software for the artwork, including training and coding of the artificial intelligence system.
- As we all could see the dangers of this project to develop indefinitely, we agreed to create a first possible result – a proposed version 1.0 – with the possibility to later on further develop the project generating subsequent versions of the artwork, 2.0, 3.0 and so on.
- Version 1.0 would not be considered ready for public unveiling without both parties giving their consent, both Di Pisa Stasinski and IBM.

RoboResearch

During the initial information research phase (April–December 2017), we gathered information about Watson and AI systems in general and through dialogue with IBM, and discussing the subject matter between ourselves, we ended up with the artistic concept to flip the normative question–answer structure around, through the idea of augmented curiosity. Based on the history of IBM Watson as a competitor in the television show *Jeopardy!*, this seemed from the outset to be an easy task. But we additionally also sought to create a dialogue between AI and humans that was not merely verbal in nature, but also visual, manifested into physical form – an interactive sculpture.

We met with several different parties – corporations and institutions – in search of a plausible way to develop and visualize our concept. We wanted to create a feedback loop based on language, movement, and aesthetic perception and suggested a three-dimensional sculpture hanging from the ceiling at the entrance of the IBM headquarters at Kista, based on a close dialogue with IBM. From here on, we envisioned using an application accessible on a smartphone device where a question could be posed by Watson to each member of the audience and in which an answer could be submitted to the system by a human. But instead of continuing the dialogue through verbal language, we wanted to continue the feedback by using an aesthetic response in the physical sculpture, so we looked into how Watson could interpret the answer given and react to it aesthetically. The hanging sculpture needed to be able to change in an almost infinite number of ways and interpret the signals of Watson in a precise manner. Eventually, we ended up with a sculptural form based on mechatronics and robotics, with very precise control and steering mechanisms.

Masters of Mechatronics

In order to build the robot sculpture, we needed to find a suitable third-party collaborator, since IBM has no robotics division. The company has a long history of engaging with research institutions and academia, and from the very beginning, expressed a wish for establishing collaboration of some kind with a university or a research institution. Soon we came in contact with two students from the master's level robotics programme at Mälardalen University, and a verbal agreement was made in which the students agreed to build the robot as part of their final examination course. Unfortunately, the students suddenly left the project right before the construction phase, putting the entire project at risk. From this we surmised that if we were to collaborate with academia, we could not rely on merely building relationships with the students, but also needed to approach the faculty.

But this was not the only problem we faced at this time (Dec 2017), since the projected costs of the robot had gradually grown past the initial budget ceiling. During the early stage of our collaboration, IBM referred to several projects under the *Art with Watson* rubric produced by IBM internationally. These works were, as discussed above, not in fact autonomous artworks, but more of marketing gimmicks. Nevertheless, these previous projects had raised the bar for our project, as far as the quality and impact of the envisioned physical structure was concerned. Therefore, nine months into the project and two days before New Year's Eve 2018, we had to seek out new solutions, both in order to secure a new financial plan and to establish new academic collaborators before the beginning of the spring semester, or else, the project would risk coming to an end.

One University's Loss Is Another's Gain

In the days to follow right after New Year's Eve, we held regular meetings with the project group at IBM, discussing preventative measures, making sure that if we were to enter new academic collaborations, we needed a different approach.

Fortunately, a few weeks into 2018, by chance we met with Björn Möller, researcher and director of the master's programme at the Mechatronics Department at KTH –Royal Institute of Technology in Stockholm. He showed immediate interest in the project and made room for it within the 2018 curriculum and secured nine students for the project, understanding its great complexity. Even though Möller was positive to the project he also expressed great concern as previous collaborations with corporations and artists had not always ended well, due to discrepancies between expectations and final outcomes. As one of us (Di Pisa) had ten years of experience teaching at KTH, we assured Möller that we were fully aware of what could be expected from the collaboration and our task was to make sure that IBM was in agreement on those conditions.

In order to get approval for a new financial plan in collaboration with KTH, a meeting was set up with the CFO and the global client executive at IBM Sweden. Briefing them on the project, we presented our ideas of realization of the project through the languages of different spheres of interest that we deemed relevant to IBM: culturally, we connected our project with the work of Johannesson and Kallin at IBM in the 1970s, as well as with art history at large. Architecturally, we argued for a powerful artistic element in the otherwise generic and empty entrance at IBM Kista. We furthermore argued for the opportunities of branding the Watson system as a creative tool for artists and engineers through this project, and finally we spoke about the possible new relationships that would be forged between institutions such as KTH and IBM, between various individuals and departments at IBM, as well as external organizations that could be connected to the project. We were then swiftly and without questions able to secure the financial means and other resources for the project, to everyone's surprise.

To further the connection of perspectives and translation of boundary objects we invited upper management as well as the project group at IBM, to Moderna Museet, introducing the work of Marcel Duchamp, Salvador Dalì, Niki de Saint Phalle, Hans Haacke, and Sture Johannesson, which was currently on display in the permanent collection. The aim was to educate and inspire, showing artworks that have emerged from the conjunction between art and technology. This is when we first met the country technical leader at IBM Sweden, who eventually would come to play an important part within the project.

A similar approach was taken with the master's level engineering students from KTH, with a tour given both at Moderna Museet and at the collections of the SSE Art Initiative, to communicate the knowledge base of our artistic practice.

Inversion of Artificial Intelligence

A full year into the project (April 2018), we finally met the team at KTH, starting the construction of the robot sculpture, but we were also keen on initiating the actual training of the software system at IBM, which was a separate process altogether. The project team was at this time expanded with a technical sales specialist at IBM. This is the first time the concept of training the AI system in order to flip the question–answer system architecture was met with doubts about its feasibility. Up until this point the project was still built around the idea of Watson's capacity to deliver questions analogous to the *Jeopardy!* exposition in 2011, but the first time we met an actual IBM engineer working with the Watson ecosystem, the project turned out to be far more complicated than previously anticipated by anyone within the project group.

During summer, we started the first AI training process, meaning we started uploading data, in this case philosophical articles and books in PDF format, in order to train the algorithm, following the guidelines of IBM. We were also in contact with international IBM support teams, who turned out to be very confused about the way we intended to use Watson for our artwork.

In late September 2018, the newly appointed country technical leader for IBM Sweden, Anders Westberg, became a core member of our project group, bringing with him the necessary resources to proceed with the project. As a result, the engineer connected to the project at IBM was given the task to continue training Watson together with a team of four IBM student employees ("Blue smarties") working part time during their studies.

Regular meetings were held, sometimes on a weekly basis. We relied heavily on the skills of our technical team, and as a result, our artistic role during this period was mainly reduced to that of observers of engineering processes driven by ideals of linear management (IBM) and rational engineering (KTH), but still overseeing the implementation of the artistic vision.

With no clear technical plan for getting Watson to pose the desirable AI-generated questions, the training proceeded according to a traditional view of systems architecture, based on the pre-packaged products in the Watson ecosystem. The aim at this point was to get as close as possible to a result that would be acceptable within the artistic vision. Obstacles were dealt with based on existing models for solutions, even though our problem was unique in kind.

Meanwhile, the robot sculpture came into being in its first iteration through regular meetings at KTH. In dialogue with the students, we made sure that the sculpture was constructed in line with the artistic vision. By mid-December 2018, the robot sculpture was ready for trial runs based on the time frame given by KTH. It was finally tested and except for what was then thought to be minor errors, it was working fine; the audience who happened to be in the lab during the first test found it remarkable. The six-armed robot with a diameter of three metres performed a complex choreography set in motion via the Watson algorithm. The movement could only be triggered manually at the time, as the AI system was still not connected to the sculpture.

Prototype Almost Gets Launched

As the work picked up after the Christmas holidays (Jan 2019), we led a workshop at IBM with some fifty participants, including Johan Rittner, general manager at IBM Sweden, who all along had expressed his support for the project.

But as time passed, the internal project group at IBM was under immense pressure to showcase the result, which eventually led to a conflict in the project team. While we as artists considered the training of the AI to still be in prototype or sketch phase in relation to our artistic concept, IBM was quite content with the achieved result, given the limits of the existing Watson ecosystem, and was keen to declare that version 1.0 had been reached.

The situation soon became even more tense, and from our artistic standpoint, we were by no means close to the underlying vision of the project; therefore, we could not agree to release the current version of the work as version 1.0, especially as there were no guarantees for securing further resources to be able to continue the development of the work.

This was the first time in the project that the generic relationship between client and consultant was not applicable. Even though as artists we had agreed to produce a work of art for IBM, which would eventually be the owner of the artwork, we made it clear to IBM that we would not give our artistic blessing if the quality of the entire system, software and hardware, was not guaranteed. The differences in epistemic outlooks were brought forth and intensely discussed, as the underlying core values of the project surfaced in meetings and discussions.

Somehow, we needed to switch the underlying managerial approach, where systems architects at IBM delineated the process, and instead strengthen our position as artistic leaders of the project. We felt the need to set the project on track with the artistic vision, but to do so, we needed the internal support of IBM. A meeting was set to discuss how to further continue with the work, and for this meeting, we asked the country technical leader and the AI and business development expert to join, with the hope of creating a situation where they, as insiders at IBM but outsiders to the project, could bring some valuable input.

The meeting pitted different ideas and perspectives forth and several misunderstandings or concepts "lost in translation" between management, engineering, and art were debated and discussed. The meeting concluded with an agreement to postpone the release date indefinitely and to take new action and freely explore new possible alternative ways for moving the project forward.

Killed Our Darling

As the Watson system had shown to have limitations with regard to our vision of generating unique questions, the next step was to "kill our darling," that is, think beyond the utilization of the Watson ecosystem in search of a technical solution. By doing so we could at this point engage in more open-ended and creative meetings with the team members, leading to several different possible solutions to generate questions based on the existing philosophical texts. The reason why this had not happened earlier was due to the fact that focus had been put on including Watson as the core technology of the project instead of viewing it as one of many possible tools.

Once we looked beyond using one specific technical tool as the questions generator, the team quickly found effective solutions to the problem that we had tried to resolve for almost six months with no success. Watson would still play a crucial part in the work by intermediating the interaction between people and the robot sculpture, by translating the response given in verbal form into an aesthetic expression – colour, form, and movement. But IBM's artificial intelligence system would not be utilized in the creation of the synthetic queries.

As the robotic sculpture was installed at the IBM headquarters at Kista (June 2019) and tested for a longer period of time, it turned out that what were previously seen as minor glitches in the construction were in fact major problems that needed a complete overhaul, which started a new process of making the robot sculpture more durable and safe.

When Artists Collaborate with Organizations

Our challenge as artists in this project has mainly been to balance a leadership role with a creative artistic role, from which we can pursue our conceptual vision despite inherent cultural differences. Of grave significance for anchoring the project at IBM early on was the historical collaboration at the company between Sture Johannesson and Sten Kallin almost fifty years earlier, serving as a narrative backdrop from which our project could grow (Bang Larsen & Johannesson, 2002). Barry and Meisiek (2010) and many others have studied artistic contributions to development in organizations during the last half century and found that the aesthetic skills of artists can, among many things, help to bridge some of the gaps in conversations through artistic media, discover blind spots and present new perspectives, help to create new hybrid fields or push the boundaries of existing ones, as well as bring in new conceptual and practical knowledge (Taylor, 2014). In short, a plethora of research exists suggesting the benefits for an organization in collaborating with an artist.

Although previous research on this topic finds positive effects of artists' collaborations, it is glaringly obvious that it seldom focuses on what is gained artistically, especially in regard to immaterial exchange. Our initial idea was focused on the material and technological advantages of a collaboration with IBM, but soon focus shifted towards the more conceptual and artistic aspects of the collaboration, more specifically the dialogic approach to artistic technological development.

Several issues arise in multidisciplinary partnerships. One of the most obvious is translation. The various backgrounds, perspectives, and points of departure of the different actors in a team are challenging to converge into a common language or nomenclature, shared by all. Instead, these perspectives tend to congregate around new and constantly emerging modus operandi, organic development of issues and problems (Strauss, 1978). Occupying liminal spaces in between well-established concepts and practices, as artists we realized that these constructed objects and processes meant different things for different actors in the project, and in order to reconcile the various meanings, we set out to build a common but simple, flexible language of references and ideas (Callon, 1985).

One example regarding the issue of translation of commonly shared concepts, centered around the phrase "sufficiently meaningful interaction between art and audience," as one of the stated criteria for the public launch of the project. It was first introduced in our initial draft of agreement with IBM in 2018, where we needed to establish a legally clear definition for when to launch the project publically. Initially, this was solved by contractually referring to the artists' denomination of "meaningful interaction," that is, the artwork would reach a sufficient degree of meaningfulness when the artists deemed it so. But as the project developed, we looked for more objectively communicable criteria. Since the artwork itself will occupy a liminal space both physically and mentally, we proposed the concept of "meaningful interaction" as a starting point of development of the system. The working definition was based around the idea of "returning interaction," meaning we envisioned a sufficiently large percentage of the audience to come back to the artwork or the app after their initial interaction. To put differently, we created a concept with a measurable component – percentage of viewers who return to work – as well as an immeasurable and unknowable part – what part of the system the viewers would find meaningful or engaging. Both parties would agree to this definition.

Here, Susan Leigh Star's and James R. Griesemer's notion of the boundary object seems to us useful in describing our process. Boundary objects are a sort of arrangement that allows different groups to work together without consensus, in a liminal, constructed sphere of references and meaning. These are not only physical objects but could be conceptual as well. Conceptually plastic and always adapting to local needs and with dynamic interpretations across fields of thought, they are also robust enough to carry and maintain conceptual integrity. Leigh Star and Griesemer (1989) regard the creation and management of these boundary objects as key in developing and maintaining coherence across intersecting social worlds, describing them as the "stuff of action."

Historical Precedents

Many collaborations have been documented between artists, businesses, and scientists. One of the most significant and systematic approaches was made under the umbrella of E.A.T – a non-profit organization founded in 1966 by the Swedish engineer Billy Klüver and American Fred Waldhauer, both working at Bell Telephone Laboratories at that time. The aim of E.A.T. was to forge connections between the arts and the technology industry by matching artists with engineers in order to stimulate a creative exchange between the fields equally beneficial for both parties. E.A.T. soon grew into a worldwide network of more than 4,000 members by 1969 (Hatch & Schultz, 2004)

Among many works that came from these collaborations were *Silver Clouds* (1966) by Andy Warhol and *Mud Muse* (1968–1971) by Robert Rauschenberg, works that arguably would not otherwise exist, and in return, the engineers would learn how to utilize the existing technologies in new ways, sometimes developing new products and services (Schnugg, 2019). In our interview with Sten Kallin in 2019, he testified to the importance of his experience working with art, when later in his career, expertise was needed to handle challenging engineering tasks at IBM. Kallin describes a commission for Kockums AB where he was tasked to convert the Steer Bear System to another programming language, a mission that was only rendered possible, according to Kallin, thanks to the knowledge he had acquired making computer-generated art, giving him the intellectual flexibility required for the task (Kallin, 2019).

The other significant precedent of collaboration emanated from the 1960s in Great Britain by artists Barbara Steveni and John Latham. The APG, founded in 1966, sought to establish artists within governmental, commercial, and industrial organizations for a limited period of time, hoping for new kinds of art to emerge that could be of interest both from an artistic perspective and for the institutions hosting the artist. For example, artist Ian Breakwell produced the film *The Journey* in 1970 as a result of his placement with the British Rail, and George Levantis travelled with the shipping company Ocean Fleets, ending up making a poetic book as well as an art installation that was thrown overboard (Breakwell & Midland Group Nottingham, 1977). In 2004, the APG records were purchased by Tate Archive, further emphasizing its art historical significance.

In Sweden, non-profit organization TILLT has been commissioning artists to cooperate with organizations, producing projects focused "on social issues where artists are a creative engine" (TILLT webpage 2019), but with little or no focus on the non-monetary gains of the participating artists. Apart from TILLT, there have mainly been two initiatives offering placements for artists: Skiss (Contemporary Artist in the Contemporary Society) and Airis (Artist in Residence). These temporary initiatives facilitated contact with organizations of various kinds, such as schools, hospitals, elderly care, business, and councils. The participant artists operated at their designated workplaces for eight to ten months, part time, usually in a team with other artists (Eriksson, 2009; Widoff & Lobell, 2011).

In the Swedish government-issued report *Artist – Regardless of Conditions?* 2018, one of the propositions made was to develop several new artist placements in state organizations, with TILLT as intermediary. The stated goal in the report was that, by 2020, 10% of state authorities should have employed an artist, although up to the point of writing this chapter, no policy bills have been introduced to make it a reality.

Initiatives such as Skiss and Airis have shown some positive effects on the organization, but have been suggested to affect the artists' creative processes (Stenberg, 2016). Their main goal seems to have been as an employment measure, funded by the state and local governments to get more artists integrated into the labour market, and not as initiatives based on artists' preferences, needs, or desires.

Translating Epistemologies

Epistemology is about *how we know*, and differing epistemologies can be associated with statements about the knowledge of concepts, acts (such as representation), entities, and systems. In this context, we wish to apply it onto practical production as it pertains to the project *Being Unthinkable* … … …. We posit that knowledge in a temporary project is both part of the organizational structure and dispersed among the individuals and their respective networks, both implicitly and explicitly as-it-happens (Tsoukas, 2004). We also assert that knowledge in an organization (both a long-term and a short-term project team) is an emergent phenomenon, meaning knowledge reveals itself through practical tasks, meetings, and discussions (Kijne & Spender, 1996). Although the artistic project management, in this case, to a certain extent demanded a balkanization of knowledge and skills, early on it became clear that learning, thinking, and acting meshed together as a sort of situated practice, through boundary objects rather than as the acquisition of propositional knowledge (Lave & Wenger 1991).

Matteo Valleriani uses the term "practical knowledge," referring to the knowledge that follows a defined workflow needed to obtain an outcome, such as the making of an artefact or a theoretical calculation (Valleriani, 2017). At the same time, he stresses the continuum and fluidity between practical and theoretical knowledge in organizations. In our project, we have seen many instances where this notion is useful since we constantly have tried to push the technology and the means of production to their artistic and/or conceptual limits, rather than their organizational or economic limits. Knowledge was in large part acquired through workshops and trails runs of the software and other parts of the artwork. In the project team this was usually met with great interest and psychological safety, since we mostly could challenge the technical solutions of a specific engineer, pushing the envelope of IBM technology in general, rather than the limits of specific knowledge in individual team members.

Furthermore, viewing organizations as systems of knowledge highlights the role of interpretation and communication and also points to the skills required for generating effective action (Tsoukas, 2004). Here we are describing knowledge within both an existing organizational structure at IBM and a newly formed organizational structure, namely, the organically evolving art project team, constantly changing with regard to its individual members based on the requested knowledge and skills. At times, these two types of organizations have worked in tandem; at other times, they have presented conflicting values, time frames, and systems of knowledge production, directly referencing the notion of the boundary object by Leigh Star and Griesemer (1989) and Leigh Star (2010). When those fault lines have surfaced, we usually have had to pause the process in order to find common ground within the project team, basically realigning the core values at play. The method we as artists have used in order to do this is through a steady flow of communication of the premises of the project, which has always been the artistic vision.

Thus, the creation and management of the project's boundary objects have been the starting point in developing and maintaining coherence across intersecting value systems and worlds. In the case of the relationship between us and IBM, it has been fortified through discussions, museum visits, presentations, texts, and workshops. These "acts of translation" have been initiated by us, the artists, and could be argued to have qualities of what Ariane Berthoin Antal (Johansson, Woodilla, & Antal, 2004) calls "intellectual entrepreneurship." She purports that organizations and individuals bridge this translational gap by the new ideas and the energy born when people from different organizations come together. In our case, this has been expressed most clearly in the establishing of a safe space for dialogue, characterized by a nonhierarchical relationship with participants. The team members often possessed a high level of independence when discussing various ideas and issues, regardless of whether members of the executive team and/or junior coders and employees were present or not.

Tsoukas's idea of the organization as a system of knowledge directly comes back to Billy Klüver, founder of E.A.T., who argued that organizational development is never predetermined or completely rational in nature, but rather organic through the change in knowledge of individuals in the organization:

> A general system can never control or steer the growth or change of individual reality according to a predetermined schedule. In order to

> do so, the general system must have the capacity to anticipate and shape any change in the individual realities that support it. Such control is impossible because every person's perception of reality will evolve faster than the common reality of a general system.
>
> (Hatch & Schultz, 2004)

Concluding Discussion

It is tempting to retrospectively view mistakes made in this project as glitches or fault lines that could have been eliminated, but as we have oscillated between physical, psychosocial, and epistemological spaces, the mistakes, detours and conflicts look more as a necessary part of a holistic system. As artists, we have spent much time on this project thoroughly analyzing meetings, emails, terms and concepts, agreements, and other information always thinking about how to approach the next ones. Because, although we could not eliminate the circulation of boundary objects, we could at least make sure that we updated our point of departure in between meetings and discussions with the other team members. We found the concept of Leigh Star and Griesemer (1989) useful in this analysis since it moves away from the idea of consensus as a prerequisite for cooperation. We have always found that working in transdisciplinary projects starts with dissensus between heterogeneous groups or individuals, but cooperation can still work if the means of communication are developed early on. If mistakes and conflicts are considered to be negative obstacles by the project team, which they often have been in larger structures and organizations, the entire endeavour risks being driven by negation (fear of making mistakes) rather than affirmation (the satisfaction of finding new solutions), which will stifle creative and artistic growth.

Being Unthinkable ... ... has grown and developed for almost three years and has all in all involved several dozen people, brought together to ponder problems in art and technology. The process has engendered new knowledge, organizational constellations, individual relationships and ideas, even before the artwork is finalized. It has forced us and the other team members to solve hitherto unknown problems.

When we asked the team members to reflect upon the process of our artistic collaboration with IBM, Anna-Lena Beckman wrote: "We have had to think very much outside everyone's comfort zones and challenge structures to find ways that no one else has used through our process flows. This is a very useful experience for everyone involved" (Interview Anna-Lena Beckman, 2019).

During the scope of this artistic process so far we have had to balance the artists' role with the role of project manager and systems architect, as well as the roles of pedagogues, communicators, and coordinators, among many others. For us as artists, this is not a negative outcome since we ground our work in historical research, new relationships, and contextual knowledge. This project has tested our ability to manage teams of coders, managers, and engineers through complex processes without having expert knowledge in any of those fields.

The project has moved forward, due to three specific points that we have discerned: first, we have moved forward through and because of dissenting discussions and heterogeneous perspectives rather than consensus and homogeneity. Second, as artistic leaders our focus has been durational, meaning we have sometimes shied away from or postponed engaging in smaller conflicts or disagreements for the sake of the bigger artistic vision and social safety. Third, we have throughout the project focused on how it will benefit us artistically, rather than financially or otherwise. This last point has been crucial to keep us on track when conflicts have arisen or technical problems have surfaced.

Lennart Malm, PR and external relations lead for IBM Sweden, who has been part of the team for most of the project, described the experience like this: "I really like how the project has challenged everyone involved to see things from other perspectives than from what one might normally be accustomed to – and comfortable with" (Interview Lennart Malm, 2019).

The organic network of team members at IBM has been of crucial importance to find support during different stages of the process, where various people in different roles have been asked to step forward. Reversely, a lot of the team members have come and gone through different stages of the process, in effect being part of a passive advisory team around the active core team at IBM.

As artists, we usually work outside the scope of hierarchical ideation and creation processes, and here, we injected ourselves among employees, students, and researchers to build new and holarchical teams and structures, in contrast to hierarchical ones. Holarchies, or collections of simultaneously integrated and autonomous individuals working together, sometimes seem hard to manage or control, but our version of holarchy entails less of managing people and less local control, but rather constantly rebuilding the larger process and vision, in which people can take on interchangeable or multiple roles.

When asked to reflect upon the differences of this project with more custom workflows, processes, and project structures at IBM, Country Technical Leader Anders Westberg concluded:

> The big differences I see are that most projects IBM is involved in have both a clear end goal, based on a number of well-defined functional and non-functional requirements, and have a defined end time. This open-ended process where the goal both in function and time are more open is very different from what IBM traditionally does.

Westberg continuous: "It would be very interesting to see if we can encourage clients to enter projects together with IBM where the goal is more of an exploratory journey rather than a well-defined 'end product'" (Interview Anders Westberg, 2019).

Susanna Salwen, corporate citizenship and corporate affairs manager as well as university relations manager at IBM Sweden reflected on the process as follows: "Well, we know this project has had some challenges. One lesson from this engagement is to embrace those; you learn and grow through overcoming challenges, and often end up in solutions that were better than your original design or idea" (Salwen, 2019) (Figures 10.1–10.3).

Figure 10.1 Robotic sketch workshop at KTH Royal Institute of Technology, 2018. Photo Credit: Di Pisa Stasinski.

Figure 10.2 Artistic process meeting at IBM Headquarters in Sweden, 2019. Photo Credit: Di Pisa Stasinski.

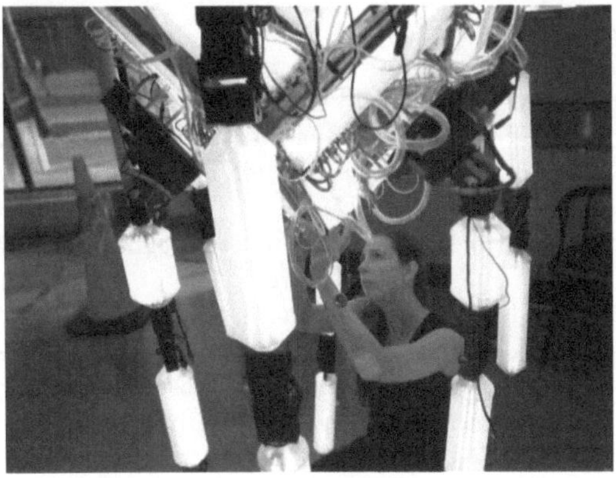

Figure 10.3 Installation work, IBM Headquarters in Sweden, 2019. Photo Credit: Di Pisa Stasinski.

References

Bang Larsen, L., & Johannesson, S. (2002). *Sture Johannesson*. New York, NY: Lukas & Sternberg.

Barry, D., & Meisiek, S. (2010). Seeing more and seeing differently: Sensemaking, mindfulness and the workarts. *Organization Studies, 31*(11), 1505–1530.

Beckman, A. (2019, August 20). Email interview.

Bourriaud, N. (2002). *Relational aesthetics*. Dijon, France: Presses du Réel.

Breakwell, I., & Midland Group Nottingham. (1977). *Diary extracts, 1968–1976 / Ian Breakwell*. Nottingham] ([11 East Circus St., Nottingham NG1 5AF]) Nottingham, England: Midland Group.

Callon, M. (1985). Some elements of a sociology of translation: Domestication of the scallops and the fishermen of St. Brieuc Bay. In J. Law (Ed.), *Power, Action and Belief, Sociological Review Monograph, 32*(1), 196–233.

Eriksson, M. (2009). *Expanding your confort zone – The effects of artistic cultural intervention on the workplace. A study of AIRIS 2005–2008 (Including Genklang Vara 2006–2008)*. Göteborg: Institute for Management of Innovation and Technology.

Great Britain, Department of the Environment, PUP. (1977). *You and me here we are: Artist placement group project*. Dept. Env. Inner Area Study, Birmingham; IAS/B/14. S.l.]

Goldman, A. I. (1986). *Epistemology and cognition*. Cambridge, MA: Harvard University Press.

Hatch, M. J., & Schultz, M. (red.) (2004). *Organizational identity: A reader*. Oxford: Oxford University Press.

Johannesson, S., & Nacking, Å. (2004). *Sture Johannesson: Lund konsthall*. Lund: Lunds konsthall.

Johansson, U., Woodilla, J., & Antal, A. B. (red.) (2016). *Artistic interventions in organizations: Research, theory and practice*. Abingdon: Routledge.

Johnson, P., & Duberley, J. (2000). *Understanding management research: An introduction to epistemology*. London, UK: SAGE.

Kallin, S. (2019, January 15). Personal interview.

Kester, G. H. (2013). Conversation pieces: Community and communication in modern art. Berkeley: University of California Press.

Konstnär – oavsett villkor?, Statens offentliga utredningar 2018, 23.

Krogh, G., & Roos, J. (1995). *Organizational epistemology*. Basingstoke, UK: Macmillan.

Lave, J., & Wenger, E. (1991). *Situated learning: Legitimate peripheral participation*. Cambridge: Cambridge Univ. Press.

Leigh Star, S. (2010). This is not a boundary object: Reflections on the origin of a concept. *Science, Technology, & Human Values, 35*(5), 601–617.

Leigh Star, S., & Griesemer, J. R. (1989). Institutional ecology, `translations' and boundary objects: Amateurs and professionals in Berkeley's museum of vertebrate zoology 1907–1939. *Social Studies of Science, 19*(3), 387–420.

Lindqvist, K. (2004). *Att göra det främmande till sitt. Konstnärer och arbetsplatser i samarbetsprojekt. Erfarenheter från projektet Airis, fas I och II*, 2002–2004.

Malm, L. (2019, August 20). Email interview.

Meyer, J. W., & Rowan, B. (1977). "Institutionalized organizations: Formal structure as myth and ceremony." *American Journal of Sociology, 83*(2), 340–363.

New York Magazine (2017). Art of data – How artists with IBM Watson turned data into unusually insightful portraits.

Nonaka, I. (1991). The knowledge creating company. *Harvard Business Review, 69*, 96–104.

Orrghen, A. (2015). Driven by visualization: Sten Kallin's collaborations with Astrid Sampe, Sture Johannesson and Mats Amundin as explorations of computer technology. *Konsthistorisk Tidskrift, 84*(2), 93–107.

Polanyi, M. (1967). *The tacit dimension*. London, UK: Routledge.

Pollan, M. (2018). *How to change your mind: What the new science of psychedelics teaches us about consciousness, dying, addiction, depression, and transcendence*. New York, NY: Penguin Press.

Roco, M. C., & Montemagno, C. D. (red.) (2004). *The coevolution of human potential and converging technologies*. New York, N.Y.: The New York Academy of Sciences.

Salwen, S. (2019, August 20). Email interview.

Schnugg, C., & Vesna, V. (2017). Media art in the context of art, science and the market. In E. Raviola & P. Zackariasson (Ed.), *Arts and business: Building a common ground for understanding society* (pp. 28–38). New York, NY: Routledge.

Schnugg, C. (2019). *Creating ArtScience collaboration: Bringing value to organizations*. Cham, Switzerland: Palgrave Macmillan.

SOU (2018). Konstnär – oavsett villkor?. *Statens offentliga utredningar*, 23, retrieved on 11-08-2019 from https://www.regeringen.se/rattsliga-dokument/statens-offentliga-utredningar/2018/03/sou-201823/

Spender, J., & Kijne, H. J. (1996). Villain, Victim or Visionary?: The Insights and Flaws in F. W. Taylor's Ideas. In J.-C. Spender & H. J. Kijne (Eds.), *Scientific management: Frederick Winslow Taylor's gift to the world*? Boston; London: Kluwer Academic.

Stasinski, R., & Guillet de Monthoux, P. (Eds.). (2017). *SSE Art Initiative*, SSE Art Initiative, Stockholm.

Stenberg, H. (2016). How is the artist role affected when artists are participating in projects in work life?. *International Journal of Qualitative Studies on Health and Well-being, 11*(1), 30549.

Strauss, A. (1978). A social world perspective. *Studies in Symbolic Interaction, 1*, 119–128.

Sułkowski, Ł. (2010). Two paradigms in management epistemology. *Journal of Intercultural Management, 2*(1), 109–119.

Tate (1977). *Artist placement group: You and me here we are: Artist placement group project*. London, UK: Tate Archives, Department of the Environment.

Tate (2005). Artist placement group chronology. retrieved on 11-08-2019 from http://www2.tate.org.uk/artistplacementgroup/chronology.htm

Taylor, G. D. (2014). *When the machine made art. The troubled history of computer art*. New York, NY: Bloomsbury.

Tillt (2019). About us. retrieved on 11-08-2019 from https://www.tillt.se/sv-SE/om-oss/vad-%C3%A4r-tillt--40709284

Tsoukas, H. (2004). *Complex knowledge: Studies in organizational epistemology*. Oxford, UK: Oxford University Press.

Valleriani, M. (Ed.). (2017). *The structures of practical knowledge*. New York, NY: Springer Berlin Heidelberg.

Webb, A. (2019). *The Big Nine: How the tech titans and their thinking machines could warp humanity*. (First edition). New York: PublicAffairs.

Westberg, A. (2019, August 20). Email interview.

Widoff, A., & Lobell, M. (Eds.). (2011). *Skiss: konst, arbetsliv, forskning: nio rapporter*. Konstfrämjandet.

11 Monuments to Enterprises in Communist-era Poland

The Creation and Consolidation of an Organizational Identity through Art

Marcin Laberschek

A Social Identity

Each society has a particular "something" thanks to which it can be distinguished from other societies, "something" that makes it stand out. That "something" makes it a separate and internally cohesive entity and hence endows it with its own identity. This "something" cannot then be accidental. It should be considered significant from the point of view of all its members. It should also have a certain inherent, intrinsic value and be protected as a unique, one-of-a-kind cultural "artefact." As a result, there are a wide range of elements to choose from that may constitute a society's identity. The elements might include a separate language, social practices and customs, a place – or places – and monuments of natural and/or historical significance, with which a given society is inherently connected. These elements also might include people of a particular cultural lineage, symbols, purpose-built structures, and a host of other elements of significant importance to the members of the society. On the whole, one might claim that natural and cultural heritage (both material and immaterial) in a wide sense constitute a social identity, by which a given society may identify itself and be identified.

An identity is constructed of elements that are significant for a given group within society. The aforementioned elements create a so-called image of an identity. Different social groups (and this applies equally to social groups on the scale of a nation, as well as to groups on the level of a cultural movement or a club membership) have separate, distinct images of their identity, because they emphasize different elements. That is because people representing those social groups are different. For example, Joanna d'Arc is a hugely significant person for France, Abraham Lincoln for the United States, and King Jan III Sobieski for Poland. Historical events also have different levels of significance for each society (the French Revolution, the American Civil War, the Warsaw Uprising), as well as places (Versailles, the White House, and Wawel

Castle, respectively for each society) and many others. These elements are of such importance that cultural representatives and authorities are engaged in a never-ending task of consolidating their position in social/cultural memory. This can be done both through the teaching of history and by having symbolic messages deliberately created, involving the sphere of art and culture practitioners, who usually are native to the culture in question. A significant body of work in this field already exists, including movies, music, paintings, and sculptures. These works are of particular significance to the identity and self-worth of a nation. Monuments created by renowned artists to honour figures of national significance and importance are an example of this. By way of illustration, there is a statue of Joanna d'Arc in Place des Pyramides in Paris, created by the French sculptor Emmanuel Frémiet. In Lincoln's Mausoleum in Washington, there stands a statue of the president made by Daniel Chester French, one of the most renowned American sculptors at the turn of the nineteenth to the twentieth century. Franciszek Pinck, King Stanisław August Poniatowski's sculptor, created a statue of King Jan III Sobieski, located in Warsaw. It needs to be emphasized that artists are not "accidentally" engaged in the creation of an image/sculpture/musical score (a medium for the transmission/creation of a national ideal). A work of art, a work of high aesthetic value is – in effect – a distillation of a symbolic message that is to be conveyed. It is brought together in such a way as to be accessible to the greatest number of people within a given nation or who have membership to a particular cultural group within a nation. It is also clear – yet often forgotten – that particular artists are chosen to produce such a work. High-profile artists have a reputation that will intrinsically empower a given work in the eyes of the social group in question.

The purpose of these activities, then, is to consolidate an identity and strengthen a feeling of social distinction. Consolidation is cultivating – or even cementing – what values a given society recognizes as significant. However, an identity can also be created, namely, its future shape might be defined. It can be done by pointing out to a society what is significant for it, and by doing so, creating a new cultural destination. This is a powerful moment, because it presents all others who are engaged in the same cultural journey towards the defined destination, as friends, compatriots, and allies, irrespective of where they may have originated. Such activities may also happen in a symbolic form and emerge in two situations. These situations are (A) a declaration, in which a community recognizes itself and concludes that this recognition is important enough to create its own identity and (B) a concrete and definite need to change the group's identity.

Macedonia, which gained its independence in 1991, illustrates the first case. A new and independent country needed to create a new and coherent cultural foundation. Consequently, clean-cut symbolic references were made to ancient (distinct) cultural heritage and to territory. In Macedonia's capital, about 130 "neo-baroque" purpose-built structures, designed to make reference to ancient Rome and Greece, were erected as part of the Skopje 2014 project, at a cost of 700 million euros. A meaningful example of such an "ancient-making" process (Matyjanka, 2019) is a 25 metre-high statue-fountain of a Warrior on a Horse, inspired by Alexander the Great, set at the centre of Skopje (ibid.).

An example of the second case can be seen among the countries that would constitute "the Eastern European bloc" after World War II. After the war, these nations were deep within the Soviet Union's "sphere of influence." Through symbolic activities, including – but not limited to – erecting statues to icons of the communist system (e.g. Stalin or Lenin), the previous "native" identity of these nations was remoulded and made to fit an ideologically appropriate form and posture.

The Relation between Organizational Identity and Monuments of an Organization

A reference to examples of monuments and their significance in the creation and consolidation of a social identity is not accidental – it is of fundamental significance from the point of view of the topic of this chapter, since the topic in question is of organizational identity and the roles of monuments in its creation and maintenance. An organizational identity is an identity of a particular social group – members of the organization (including enterprise). In the same way that a cultural community (e.g. a nation) creates and establishes an identity, so do various organizations, by using a broad scope of activities to shape their image, including symbolic ones.

It is worth mentioning that pondering on the topic of identity and also on the symbolic activities an organization engages in, its values, history, cultural heritage, the ideology it pursues, as well as works of art (e.g. monuments) or artists connected with it, constitutes an area of non-economic – and so humanistic and aesthetic – perspective (Strati, 1999). It is the humanistic approach, especially in the context of organizational identity, and organizational symbolism (Kostera, 1996; Turner, 1986) and the cultural heritage of the organization (Carnegie & Kociatkiewicz, 2019; Gaweł, 2009), that constitute the theoretical framework of this chapter.

Organizational identity can be seen as a response by the members of an organization to the following question: "Who are we as an organisation?" (Cornelissen, 2002; Cornelissen, Haslam, & Balmer, 2007; Gioia, 1998; Hatch & Schultz, 2002). An organizational identity, as highlighted by Krzysztof Konecki (2002), is about the "perception of the main, and distinct features of an organisation, encompassing also its status in comparison with other organisations" (p. 82). Distinct features of an organization might refer to elements such as its name, activity, the place where its activity is based, or the place where the organization was founded. Particular elements carry a greater amount of significance, such as the history of its establishment, special individuals connected with it, breakthrough moments, and many more aspects of symbolic meaning for an organization.

It has been pointed out that monuments refer to the features and attributes that are significant from the point of view of a community (Gurler & Ozer, 2013; Praczyk, 2015). As a result, one might conclude that monuments "focus" or "unify" organizational identity, because they support and promote the fundamental values of the organization. As well as in the case of other communities (e.g. nations (Osborne, 2001)), there are monuments of different groups of organizations: state (military memorials are an example of this), non-governmental sectors (e.g. the monument of Wikipedia in Słubice, Poland), as well as enterprises.

This chapter is dedicated to the monuments erected by organizations, and more specifically, to the monuments of enterprises. Particularly, this work addresses the following important question: which monuments were created by artists in cooperation with Polish enterprises during the communist era, and how did they contribute to the creation and consolidation of the identity of these enterprises?

There are monuments of various types of enterprises: classic enterprises (mines, steel mills, factories, banks) and contemporary ones (new technologies or start-ups); all these monuments may be of interest to management sciences researchers. Enterprises' monuments do not really stand out from other monuments. They too can present prominent figures, symbolize events, refer to historical places, and present objects and artefacts significant to a particular community. Monuments of enterprises can aspire to be works of art, as in many cases renowned artists create them. As with the others, they also can be divided among the three categories that Kowalewski presented: (A) the "monument-icon," which "does not cause any doubt at the level of perception, as to the purpose of a built structure" (Kowalewski, 2007, p. 4); (B) the "monument-symbol," which "is considered on many more levels than realistic paintings"; (ibid., p. 5) and (C) the "monumental work of art," namely, an abstract object, where meanings are ambiguous and "'difficult for a viewer to recognize" (ibid., p. 6).

An Outline of the Research

There is not much research focusing on organizational monuments currently, and yet, this is a fascinating topic that is worthy of attention, investigation, and reflection. As there is no catalogue of monuments for enterprises, I have undertaken (and I'm still carrying it out) a query of such purpose-built structures, guided by a definition of them that I formulated by myself, where a monument of/to an organization (in this case, an enterprise) is an exposed and a one-of-a-kind spatial purpose-built structure with a symbolic meaning, connected with "a life" of an organization. In the period from March 2018 to June 2019, I collected data on over 160 monuments from all over Poland. I was interested in all enterprises' monuments, both made on their own initiative (such as by the management or the workers) and by people in their environment (such as local authorities or inhabitants). I searched for this data online, initially using the Google search engine. I began by typing certain terms (e.g. monument of an enterprise, a monument of a factory). In this way I identified specific monuments, and then I continued my search on the internet, but only for each individual purpose-built structure. I looked for all kinds of source materials (articles, documents, reports) that referred to a relationship between a monument and an enterprise, its creation, creators, the materials used for its creation, as well as various events connected with it. I also collected entries on internet forums made under articles about purpose-built structures. In these entries, I found lots of meaningful stories regarding particular purpose-built structures related to enterprises. They were often made by people connected with the enterprise or the town in which it was based. Some structures, especially those that no longer exist, I researched by reading publications dedicated to the monuments of specific towns, for instance, *Pomniki Warszawy* (Monuments of Warsaw) (Sobieraj, 1985), *Warszawskie pomniki* (Warsaw Monuments) (Głębocki, 1990), and *Pomniki Wrocławia* (Monuments of Wroclaw) (Antkowiak, 1985).

This database of over 160 structures can be complemented by information about several dozen other monuments (due to the fact that some of these monuments no longer exist, a precise number cannot be offered), which were not made as a single project (as an individual monument) but in a group, during artistic biennales in Poland. Information about these monument-sculptures was obtained from scientific and specialist publications, for example, *Spatial Forms as the Centre of Everything*, edited by Karolina Breguła (2013a), *Artysta w fabryce. Dwa oblicza mecenatu przemysłowego w PRL* (The Artist in a Factory. Two Faces of Industrial Patronage) (Stano, 2019) and *Puławy 66* (Leśniewska, 2006).

I assigned eight categories to each monument in the database. These categories are (1) the name of the enterprise with which the monument is associated; (2) activity profile of the enterprise; (3) name of the region where the monument is located; (4) name of the place; (5) address; (6) date of erection of the monument; (7) name of the sculptor/designer; (8) information about what the monument represents (e.g. machines and their components, products, people – owners, managers, employees, and patrons – company logos and symbols, abstract monuments). A database prepared in such a way can be used in many different respects;

everything depends on how a research query is formulated. My question dealing with monuments erected during the communist era, specifically those created by artists in cooperation with Polish enterprises, and aiming to understand if and how these monuments contributed to the creation and consolidation of those organizations' identities required me to carry out an appropriate reorganization of my database of monuments. First, Communist-era monuments made in Poland needed to be separated from the ones made before and after that period of time. The time frame considered was between 8 May 1945 (the date of the end of the Second World War, specifically, the date of the signing of the capitulation treaty by the Germans) and 4 June 1989 (when the first partially democratic parliamentary elections took place in Poland). Second, it was necessary to remove monuments that were not created by artists (it was sometimes the case that they were made by the workers) or consisted of structure-souvenirs, vehicles, machines, or other elements of technical infrastructure that had lost their initial function but somehow gained a sentimental or symbolic value and were left in situ as monuments-by-default on the premises or in the surrounding area. Finally, those monuments whose construction required/received no participation from the enterprise, or which were erected without the enterprise knowing (yet still made reference to their activity), were removed from consideration as well. In this way, a shortlist of forty-five purpose-built structures was drawn up (and to which the aforementioned group of purpose-built structures made within the bounds of an artistic biennale was added), which was then subjected to an analysis looking for deeper meanings in the context of communist identities of business entities, according to the presumption of the interpretative paradigm. What the monuments represent was identified by me, the author; next, a connection between what was depicted in the monument and the business activity was sought out, and a decision was made whether a given purpose-built structure should be viewed in the context of consolidation of an organizational identity or maybe with reference to its creation. In the area of identity consolidation – nurturing what is significant and valuable for communities contributing to enterprises – the following structures were found: statues of people connected with the enterprise, – purpose-built structures making reference to important events or to the activity profile of the enterprise or its products, as well as to signs, trademarks, and symbols that identified it. In contrast, abstract structures and statues of patrons who at the same time were icons of communist ideology can be included among structures creating an identity.

The role of the researcher is vast and requires personal commitment. First, before beginning to analyze the data for the purpose of this research, a carefully prepared database of all monuments needed to be created. Then editing the list according to the needs of this research, and finally, interpreting what the monument represents in the context of the enterprise. At this last stage, the researcher interprets the collected material. As this research takes an interpretative perspective, the researcher understands that subjective factors affect the explanation and interpretation of the monuments' symbolism and significance.

Consolidation of the Identity of Communist-Era Enterprises through Monuments

Heroes of an organization are people who left an indelible mark on the history of these communities (Sułkowski, 2012). Of course, this is not about people who are heroic, but about those people who can be called "personalities of organization" (ibid., p. 74). Making use of cooperation with artists, communist-era enterprises erected monuments of people who were of importance for various reasons. It could have been distinguished workers or individuals in charge of people. In case of the latter, it was not a common practice, since "common" workers were given greater recognition, since they carried out ideologically valuable "work at the grassroots level" or "the nitty-gritty." By contrast, the position of a person in charge was more of a functional character, and a person holding it did not become somebody special for that reason. Only one monument of such a person was identified. It is a bust of Ignacy Łukasiewicz – a co-owner of a partnership established in 1862 and a director of the first mineral oil mine in the world – at Bóbrka. close to Gorlice, made by the sculptor Stanisław Kandefer in 1982. As a shareholder, Łukasiewicz could have been perceived by communist authorities as a capitalist, and it is worth mentioning that after World War II, the memory of such individuals was censured, and the companies they had established were nationalized, cutting the company away from its "un-praiseworthy" past. Łukasiewicz was however a world-famous engineer; he was the one to build the first kerosene lamp (Mierzecki, 1999). Such a potent figure could not be easily disregarded and could be made use of in a pragmatic way. Łukasiewicz's figure was therefore "rehabilitated," and it became one of the icons of the Polish mineral oil industry of communist-era Poland. Supposedly for this reason, the erection of a statue of the engineer on the premises of the mine, operating also in the times of People's Poland, did not rise any objections; on the contrary, it was in line with the communist narrative. Simultaneously, it consolidated an enterprise's identity, since it made reference to a particular figure in the organization's history, specifically, to its founding father and also to its founding myth – the story of its establishment. Organizations have inherent "stories," "legends" even, that carry enormous significance and meaning for the organization and directly shape its self-identity (Laberschek & Popiołek, 2019,

p. 202) – the way in which it sees itself and where it is going, or at least its aims and ambitions.

From the cooperation between the community of an enterprise and an artist, monuments to other significant individuals were also made, namely, workers. Two such monuments were identified. One is located near the "Wieczorek" anthracite coal mine in Katowice and was made by Stanisław Marcinów, who specialized in socialist realism sculpture. The second monument was in Warsaw, and it stood in front of the Precision Products Factory. It was made by Gustaw Zemła, one of the most recognizable Polish sculptors. The Katowice monument is dedicated to Józef Wieczorek, a miner who worked in that coal mine. The second one was dedicated to Karol Świerczewski, who used to be an apprentice at the factory between 1912 and 1915. It should be mentioned here that those monuments contributed to the consolidation of organizational identity, since they referred to the memory of workers and thus to the history of the company. Every monument that refers to the past of a particular social group strengthen the identity of this group. This is, after all, an important goal of erecting monuments. On the other hand, both Józef Wieczorek and Karol Świerczewski were individuals – icons of the ideology of those times. The first was involved in creating the structures of communist organizations; the second was a general of the Red Army. Those particular achievements, more than their performance at work, were decisive in terms of monument erection. From that standpoint, one can claim that the identity of the organization was not only reinforced, but also created, since the monument, in a certain symbolic sense, imposed a communist ideology on the whole community of the organization.

Monuments to individuals connected with enterprises indirectly made reference to various kinds of stories, tales, and memories. But there have also been cases of monuments that directly referred to significant moments for an enterprise, or were erected to commemorate significant events, which would serve as a reminder of important memories of the past. Purpose-built structures of this type were of considerable significance to the consolidation of organizational identity. A particular example of this kind of work was an enormous "Monument to the Fallen Shipyard Workers of 1970" in Gdansk. It was erected in 1980 to commemorate striking shipyard workers who were killed in clashes with the security forces. A special team of artists was commissioned to work on the concept. The dimensions of the monument are impressive. The monument is forty-two metres high and weighs thirty-six tons; it consists of three crosses, three anchors, and bas-reliefs. It is surely a monument that reinforces the identity of an organization, an identity based on a traumatic experience of the shipyard community. It is worth mentioning that the erection of such a monument in the communist era was practically impossible. This monument can be also viewed as a symbol of workers' resistance against communist violence.

Other monuments that have referred to significant events in a given enterprise's history might not have stood out with such expressive symbolism. However, they would still be meaningful from the point of view of cementing the internal integrity of an enterprise's community. This applies especially to monuments that were erected on the occasion of important anniversaries, where a monument's unveiling could have been an important element of bigger celebrations. An abstract monument erected in 1988 close to a foundry in Śrem, on the Day of a Foundry Worker, can be a good example of this, or the previously mentioned statue of Karol Świerczewski, which was unveiled on the seventieth anniversary of the Precision Products Factory.

In the communist era, there have also been monuments that referred to an enterprise's profile or activity. A purpose-built structure in the shape of the chemical symbol for copper (as it appears in the Periodic Table – a large rendering of the letters "'Cu") was created in Lubin, in front of the headquarters of an organization whose business was copper extraction. There was a similar purpose-built structure (Figure 11.1) at the premises of the "Machów" Mines and Sulphur Processing Plant in Tarnobrzeg, which was erected in 1962 by Magdalena Więcek (Leśniewska, 2013). It can be claimed that this kind of monument – even though a sculptor's aesthetic can be seen within the work – can be (and is) identified as a visual motif that encompasses "the complete symbolism the colour scheme, the logo, the logotypes used by the company in order to be properly recognized" (Szulc & Bunk, 2009, p. 279). This "recognition" is of special importance, since – as has been previously stated – everything

Figure 11.1 A monument of the sign "S" – sulphur, made by Magdalena Więcek in 1962 for Mines and Sulfur Processing Plant Enterprise in Machów, Tarnobrzeg.

Source: from the archives of Magdalena Więcek.

that allows an organization to be identified and distinguished from others (enterprises with a similar activity profile) strengthens its unique identity. Such is also the case with these deliberately erected structures and monuments.

In the group of visual elements that distinguish an organization from other organizations (e.g. headquarters' architecture, employee dress code), one of the simplest but most effective visual identifiers is the logo. In the communist era, some enterprises erected monuments that presented their logo. This was the case for "Igloopol" Agro-Industrial Combine in Dębica, "Stargard" Rolling Stock Repair Plant, and "Łucznik" (Archer) Metal Plants, in front of whose headquarters a figure of an archer was unveiled in the 1970s. This image was displayed on all the products manufactured by the enterprise (e. g. sewing machines). This monument was made by a sculptor duo, Aleksander Śliwa and Wiesław Jelonek, who were connected with the Academy of Fine Arts in Kraków. Even though monuments that referred to the symbolism of a given enterprise were created, there was a strong emphasis on the improvisation element in the artists' creative output. A figure of a "reindeer" is such an example, making a reference to the now vanished Lower Silesian "Renifer" (Reindeer) White-Leather Gloves Plant in Świdnica. This was designed and erected by Maria Bor, who revealed that

> ...the sculpture obviously was inspired by the name of the plant. However, it would never occur to me to make it in the literal form, so having four legs and two antlers. It mattered to me to make it in a spacious, symbolic form, and a bit humorous.
>
> (Swidnica24, 2005)

A similar story is connected with a statue that was installed in 1989 by the sculptor Ryszard Chachulski at the "Światowit" Enamelware Factory in Myszków (Figure 11.2). The statue of "Światowit" is on the one hand a clear reference to the trademark of the enterprise, and on the other, the four human faces that look out into the four cardinal directions are probably (there is no certainty here) the faces of the workers at the enterprise (Bączyński, 2013). This kind of preservation of employees' images at the monument of the Myszków factory consolidates its organizational identity. However, the monument also presents the figure and character of Światowit. This character makes a direct reference to another – earlier – community, the Slavs, to whom Światowit (in truth, Świętowit) was the highest and most potent deity.

As noted, monuments that referred to enterprises' activity profile contributed to the consolidation of their identity in communist Poland. Examples of purpose-built structures have been given, and it has been shown that the form of these structures sometimes made reference to the names of chemical elements associated with the industry the enterprise

Figure 11.2 A statue of Światowit made by Ryszard Chachulski in 1989 for enamelware factory "Światowit" in Myszków.

was engaged in (e.g. copper and sulphur). There were, however, other kinds of monuments that did not always make a direct reference to enterprises' activity. In the first half of the 1960s, a sculpture titled "Flight" was made by Henryk Burzec. It depicted a man with wings, the figure being a reference to a neighbouring enterprise, the Polskie Zakłady Lotnicze, where planes were manufactured. Meanwhile, the meaning of a dinosaur erected in the 1970s on the premises of the Polish Oil and Gas Company (now "Orlen") is far more complicated. The explanation of its connection with the activity profile of the enterprise can however be found in the words of Jacek Borkowski, a member of the research and development group at the Department of Refinery Technology within "Orlen" (Stachurska, 2019):

> A dinosaur was a reptile which – as we all know – lived in prehistoric times and died out. In PKN ORLEN we process crude oil, which comes from (among others) these reptiles. As a result of processes such as kerogen, diagenesis, or a metamorphism which takes place in the earth's crust, the organic matter of such creatures – over many thousands of years – broke down and slowly recombined, resulting in the crude oil, which we today extract and process.

It is also worth paying attention to statues of real people who were not themselves in any way directly connected with any particular enterprise, and yet because of what they themselves were engaged in, their figure/persona is being referred to and promoted, as it corresponded to the enterprise's activity profile, industry, and ethics. In a neighbourhood that is close to the aforementioned "Orlen" site stands another monument.

This one is for Wiktor Zglenicki, who was not connected with any enterprise, but as a geologist and the engineer who created and pioneered oil rig technology, his "figure" was utilized. He ideally matched the values of the enterprise, which were focused on crude oil extraction and processing, and it certainly was a decisive reason when erecting the monument. A similar but different example comes from Olsztyn. In the second half of the 1960s, a bust of Seweryn Pieniężny was unveiled close to the Olsztyn Graphic Plant. Pieniężny was the manager of the editing pool at the *Gazeta Olsztynska* from 1918 through to 1939. In 1939, he was arrested by the Gestapo, then murdered in the Hohenbruch concentration camp. He was not in any way connected with the Olsztyn Graphic Plant (which was established sometime after his death); however, his activities as a journalist and publisher – together with local socio-patriotic activity – were in line with the enterprise's activity of printing. It cannot be doubted that this kind of monument also strengthens and consolidates organizational identity.

Other purpose-built structures have also made references to enterprises' activity profile, referring to the products and/or services provided. Three interesting examples of this are to be found in Osowa Sień, Biesiekierz, and Łódź.

Osowa Sien is a village; near the Animal Husbandry for Breeding complex stands a monument to a bull called Ilon. It was erected in 1982 (Machnik & Kurczewski, 2014). This animal was a one-of-a-kind in a way, becoming a symbol of the enterprise. The bull had a remarkable – unusual even – reproductive prowess, illustrated in a 97% success rate (Polskie Radio, 1999).

In front of the Plant Cultivation Station in Biesiekierz, a nine-metre-high sculpture of a potato was unveiled, created by the sculptor Wiesław Adamski. The structure commemorated the fact that nine previously unknown varieties of potatoes had been cultivated at the plant.

In Łódź, meanwhile, a monument in the form of stacked bobbins used to coil threads and yarn was erected in front of the Cetech plant, these bobbins being their primary product. Each of the monuments listed clearly shows that enterprises strove to consolidate what was special and valuable for them and set about this by strengthening their identity in creative, monumental ways.

A final group of monuments needs to be mentioned, which also served as a focus and consolidated enterprises' identity, but with a single significant difference: the structures were intended to present a modified (if not brand new) version of their identity by focusing on the labourers, especially in those occupations that were surrounded by some kind of a "cult of work," for instance, miners, steelmakers, and foundry men. "Images" of this variety can be viewed from the context of archetype, which – from the point of view of this chapter – is of significant importance. In Figure 11.3, a figure of a miner can be seen. This sculpture was

Figure 11.3 A statue: an archetypical presentation of a miner, located in front of Daniłowicz Mineshaft at the Wieliczka Salt Mine; installed in 1958 and removed in 2016.

most probably made by Jan Siek while under the supervision of his master, Jacek Puget. The sculpture was erected in front of the Daniłowicz Mineshaft, part of the Wieliczka Salt Mine (Duda, 2016), in which two archetypal perspectives can be found.

In the first archetypal perspective, the figure is presented in such a way as to identify as a man-titan: it has a lean, well-built body, and clearly visible musculature. This archetype presents a labourer, a "Worker." The nature of the work is a secondary concern. The primary concern is to present the labourer as someone who is working to some great purpose, a cause, a calling that they are persevering with, and are sacrificing themselves to complete.

In the second archetypal perspective, the figure does not portray a particular person. The figure is an "Everyman"; yet, it is clear that this "Everyman" is a miner because they have the equipment and attributes of a miner – the helmet, the pickaxe, and the mining lamp. Where the first archetype presented a "Worker," this archetype presents a "Miner." In this second archetype, we are presented with a completely basic and universal image of a miner.

Both of these archetypes corresponded with the mine's identity, and the monument was installed in 1958. It should be noted that although both archetypes are present in this work, one might well have the impression that the archetype of the "Miner" is stronger and contributes more to it than the "personality" archetype of the "Worker."

A job as a miner constituted – and continues to constitute – the very foundation of a mine's identity. A second image of a "Worker" was promoted across all the communist countries – including Poland – and this was the image of an employee as some sort of a demon for work.

This second image is not in line with the mine's image because it stems from central communist ideologies, based on the ethos of the labouring man. A monument for Wieliczka constructed from this secondary image would severely distort the mine's identity from a place of work and into a place for really unusual people; a kind of colony for people who deserved recognition for who/what they are and not for anything that they may have done/will do.

Many such monuments depicting archetypal images of miners were erected in Poland. Representatives of the world of art were often commissioned to create them, just as in case of the Wieliczka statue. However, sometimes monuments were not created by artists, but by talented and educated workers. An example of this would be Antoni Wyrodek from the Wieliczka Salt Mine (Wolańska, 2018), who made the statue of a miner, that was unveiled in front of Anthracite-Coal Mine in Nowa Ruda in 1960.

In the meantime, in the 1970s, another archetypical monument was unveiled in Plock, on Orlen's premises. It was a statue of a peasant, which was a symbolic thank you gesture to farmers, on whose land the enterprise was established (Stachurska, 2019). It is a special case of an organization modulating its identity by connecting with the identity of another social group.

Creating an Identity of Enterprises in the Communist Era through Monuments

The modulation that Orlen engaged in is actually creating a new identity. Thanks to new monuments, a "shape" can be achieved that did not exist before. In Poland, between 1945 and 1989 lots of purpose-built structures were erected, thanks to which a new image of enterprises' identity was created.

The structures discussed consolidated organizational identity. These include monuments of the activity profile of enterprises or their products. There are also purpose-built structures of signs, trademarks, and symbols that identified them, as well as statues of people connected with the enterprise and monuments making reference to important events. Some of them, as was highlighted, both consolidated previous identity and created its new image. Monuments consolidating and creating include both figures of labourers and specific workers within an enterprise also being officially involved in communist activity.

However, some of the structures of communist-era Poland should only be perceived from the perspective of creating an identity. Two groups of monuments can be distinguished here: (A) structures directly in line with communist ideology and (B) structures that are entirely different, because they are monuments – works of art, abstract, spatial forms. Each of those two groups created a different kind of identity. The first one created an identity based on communist ideology, while the second one sprang from values such as social engagement and creative activity. I looked for stories about social engagement and creative activity in existing sources regarding enterprises that in the communist era collaborated with the artistic community.

Much of it boils down to the benefactors of a given enterprise's monument. Clearly, patrons were not randomly chosen people, but individuals whose activity was not only ideally in line with communist ideology, but also consolidated it. Apart from two instances mentioned of people who had been workers before becoming sponsors of the enterprises' monument, this was not the norm. One other case like this is the statue of Władysław Gomułka (who was also a member of the enterprise's communist body), which was erected in 1986 in front of FSO (Factory of Personal Cars) in Warsaw. However, the majority of individuals were not connected with the history of the organization of which they were patrons. In one case, however, there was an interesting relationship between a patron and a place.

Marcin Kasprzak – whose bust was unveiled in 1975 in front of Radio Works in Warsaw – used to run a printing house in which illegal proletarian activities were carried out. What is most interesting is that the printing house used to operate in the same place on which (half a century later) the "Radio Works under the Patronage of Marcin Kasprzak" were established. This seemingly insignificant relationship had a great symbolic meaning, as it was another element for creating a communist identity for the enterprise.

Statues of various representatives of the Eastern European communist bloc, nominated to be patrons for various enterprises, were erected. These were Soviet heroes, both ideological champions, like Wlodzimierz Ilicz Lenin (his bust stands in front of the Skawina Metallurgical Works), and representatives of the Soviet Union's security apparatus, such as Feliks Dzierżyński (his bust stands in front of the Moscice Nitrogen Works). There were also monuments of icons of Polish communism (except for the above): a statue of Bolesław Bierut, which was unveiled close to Częstochowa Ironworks; a statue of Marceli Nowotko, which stands in front of Warsaw Mechanical Works (Figure 11.4); a statue of Ludwik Waryński, which stands in front of the ZMB Works in Warsaw (Construction Machinery Enterprise); and the statue of Julian Marchlewski, beside the Pulp and Paper Plant in Włocławek. Meanwhile, in front of the High Voltage Apparatus Plant ZWAR in Warsaw, a monument to Georgi Dymitrov, a Bulgarian communist activist, was erected.

While the patrons, for the most part, were not connected with the enterprise itself, the erection of their figures outside organizations was a telltale symbol for the desire to connect the enterprise to the strong political ideology of that particular patron. Selecting them as patrons and erecting monuments for them in front of the headquarters of various

Figure 11.4 A statue of Marceli Nowotko, a patron of Warsaw Mechanical Works.

Source: digital archive of Narodowe Archiwum Cyfrowe. Photographer: Grażyna Rutkowska.

trade organizations was a symbolic tool to impose a concrete ideology. These kinds of monuments can therefore be perceived as tools for ideological labelling, stigmatizing particular communities, or as Florian Zieliński (2005) would put it, "stamping." Of course, this phenomenon had a broader dimension, as it applied not only to enterprise communities but also to larger social groups.

Creating a new identity is obviously a certain process. It was not about erecting a purpose-built structure itself, but what happened afterwards. It needs to be impressed upon the reader that the statues of patrons were often placed in front of the main gate of an enterprise, which was the place where workers gathered every day before and after their shifts. It was here that the symbolic interaction between a worker and a monument took place. The interaction was in the form of an everyday ritual, a ritual of workers being greeted by their "patron." In this way the worker was subjected to a sort of perpetual, long-lasting symbolic indoctrination, designed to impose a proper image of the place and work in a communist climate. Beside the monuments, various kinds of enterprise–party celebrations took place, and these were of a cyclical nature, such as 1 May parades, celebrations on 22 July (a communist festival), or the patron's birthday anniversaries.

It also needs to be underlined that the force of the symbolic effect of a monument was boosted by commissioning distinguished artists to create them (e.g. the sculptor Gabriel Hajdas made a monument to Bierut in Częstochowa, and Edmund Matuszek created a statue of Marcin Kasprzak in Warsaw). The work of one such artist, Gustaw Zemła, needs to be emphasized. As the sculptor who worked on statues of patrons (Świerczewski, Nowotko, Waryński), his sculptures have been ascribed to a pantheon of the most important and are the most recognizable ones in Poland.

Abstract, purpose-built structures of plants constituted a totally different group of monuments for communist enterprises, but, like the communist patrons monuments, they also created a new organizational identity of enterprises.

Some of them were erected on special occasions, and they were commissioned by a board. A monument created by an artist named Stanisław Słodowy for the Moszczenica Anthracite-Coal Mine in Jastrzębie-Zdrój is an interesting example. It had been planned to inaugurate a new coal mine in December 1965, and representatives of the highest state authorities had been invited (e. g. the first secretary of KC PZPR, Władysław Gomułka). The monument had been created for this occasion.

> However, it turned out that the final effect shocked the personnel of the mine as well as the board. The sculpture was considered too bold and not compatible with such a serious institution. The first instinct was to destroy the work of art. The director, Chlebik, was strongly opposed to that, claiming that one cannot demolish something that cost such a big amount of money. Brainstorming started what to do instead. And a solution was found! Chlebik contacted the board of the health resort and suggested making a "duo" sculpture (a "Duo" became the name of the structure) in the Park Zdrojowy (Health Resort Park) as a gift from workers of the new coal mine.
>
> (Boratyn, 2015)

Abstract monuments could therefore be commissioned by an enterprise, but they were supposed to serve a particular function. On the one hand, as in the case of sponsorship (Colbert, d'Astous, & Parmentier, 2005; Swanson & Davis, 2006) or patronage (O'Hagan & Harvey, 2000) of various arts projects, they raised the prestige of the event organized by a plant (e. g. plant inauguration), and on the other, they also raised the prestige of the plant itself and gave it a unique character. Such monuments served to create the plant's identity, especially where a certain element of spirituality or artistic sublimeness became significant. In the case of the Jastrzębie-Zdrój coal mine, that attempt turned out to be unsuccessful though.

Unknown to general opinion, enterprises in the communist era – though focused on the realization of their basic production and service targets – also engaged in community-centric operations, including helping and cooperating with artists. Such an approach is called "corporate philanthropy," which with time became planned and organized and a form of "corporate community involvement" (Hess, Rogovsky, & Dunfee, 2002, p. 111). It is claimed that practical corporate philanthropy originated in the 1980s. Earlier, help was mostly financial in character (ibid.). In contrast, in the communist reality (which for unknown reasons is not taken into consideration by Western researchers on the topic of an organization), a direct form of support existed much earlier. Since 1965, Biennales of Spatial Forms were taking place in Elblag, within which monumental structures were erected across the whole town. Up to this day, there are still a few dozen of such purpose-built abstract structures. A founding father and a person who implemented this idea was Gerard Kwiatkowski, an artist employed in Zamech plant in Elbląg. He invited well-known – and also less widely recognized – artists to each biennale; Zamech in turn provided everything that was necessary to create a work of art: a place, machines, tools, raw materials, and people above all, namely, its employees. Participation of the last group was of particular significance (Breguła, 2013, p. 6):

> The worker-artist integration made the Biennale a hugely popular event. The Zamech specialists involved in the project quickly pass on word about the strange sculptures to their families and friends, causing the – non-utilitarian and seemingly incomprehensible – purpose-built structures to become their next location and openings attracted large crowds.

Zamech's involvement in artistic activity, as well as the participation of its employees in the event – and indirectly of their families, friends, and inhabitants – surely contributed to creating a new identity for the enterprise, not only of a manufacturing plant, but a place (or maybe even a creative centre), a unit contributing to the development of avant-garde art and triggering aesthetic needs in the social environment. It needs to be highlighted that, as a result of the success of the biennale in Elblag, similar initiatives were set up – in 1966 at Puławy Nitrogen Plants (Leśniewska, 2006) and in 1968 in Warsaw, organized under the auspices of Marcin Kasprzak Radio Works. The fact that enterprises were entering the world of art and contacting artists could then change an organizational identity because artistic projects realized on their premises became a part of the history of the community contributing to the project (especially if it involved workers).

It might be obvious to claim that all enterprises in the communist era were encumbered with a mission of spreading and modernizing culture, a culture imposed upon them by the state and proclaimed in 1947 by its then president Bolesław Bierut (Stano, 2019). If, however, some of the monuments (even if only of the workers) actually had been realized according to the requirements of a modernization process (the process of adapting creative artistic output to the needs of a working-class recipient), then we can assume with a degree of certainty that this did not apply to non-single-meaning abstract monuments. Thanks to them, enterprises could self-determine their own independent identity and prevent it being imposed upon them by an outside influence.

Conclusions

Those artistic purpose-built structures on the one hand might have helped in preserving what was important for an enterprise (identity consolidation); yet, on the other hand, they might have pointed out or even imposed what should be important, especially in a situation where workers and artists participated in creating monuments. They themselves could have become an important part of the enterprise's identity (creating an identity). In the first case, it was about statues of founding fathers (to be precise, there was only one such case) or an element of the history of an enterprise, as well as monuments referring to their activity profile (such as monuments of logos or products). As far as monuments creating an identity are concerned, there have been statues of communist patrons for organizations (an identity created by external forces) and abstract purpose-built structures (an identity created by the organization itself). It needs to be highlighted that there have been monuments that have had both an identity consolidating and creating potential; these were the statues of enterprise workers who were connected with the communist apparatus, as well as to the archetypal figures of working men.

Monuments are an element of the cultural heritage of an organization; they are an example of artistic heritage (works of art) as well as historical pedigree (pictures of the past), but also symbols of a material and immaterial heritage. In this sense, monuments can be treated, as Pierre Nora would say, as "sites of memory" (*les lieux de mémoire*) (Nora, 1989) – important events for the organization (company rituals, employee meetings) take place here. The heroes and patrons of the organization were also mentioned. It is possible to expand this topic and ask why – in the context of the organization's identity – just these and not other people "deserved" to erect monuments. Similar questions can be asked in relation to archetypes of professions (miner, steelworker, railwayman) that are "hidden" in monuments, as well as within another topic discussed: the stories and myths of the organization. As indicated, monuments are also a special kind of organizational symbol; importantly, the symbols help to understand what norms and values are fundamental to the organization and why. An important issue raised in the chapter is also ideology; as noted, monuments contain an ideological message. This chapter mentioned a communist ideology, but in today's monuments of enterprises, one can look out for the threads of neoliberal, post-colonial, or consumerist ideology. Comparative studies on the involvement of communist and capitalist enterprises in artistic projects (not only monuments) would also be interesting. The more so because the slowly discovered subject of Europe's communist art and enterprises is absent in Western scientific debates.

It would be also interesting to see what role organizational monuments play in the process of sense making in organizations (Weick, 1995). Do they engage with organizational spirituality (Bell & Taylor, 2003)? Are they a way of reflecting the feelings of employees, or perhaps are they an expression of the management of meaning (Morgan, 1986)? These questions all remain to be asked and explored, but one thing is certain, I believe: such monuments are an important artistic feature of organizational space, an expression of its symbolic dimension (Yanov, 1995). As such, they invite a large number of possible understandings and uses; however, it should be emphasized that each research process and each question asked must be associated with the proper reorganization of the database of monuments.

References

Antkowiak, Z. (1985). *Pomniki Wrocławia*. Wrocław, Poland: Ossolineum.

Bączyński, R. (2013). *Światowita wyrzeźbił artysta z Myszkowa*. Retrieved on 11-07-2019 from http://gazetamyszkowska.pl/artykul/swiatowita-wyrzezbil-artysta-z-myszkowa

Bell, E., & Taylor, S. (2003). The elevation of work: Pastoral power and the new age work ethic. *Organization, 10*(2), 39–349.

Boratyn, M. (2015). *Tańcząca para*. Retrieved on 11-07-2019 from http://jasnet.pl/?m=publicystyka&id=2943

Breguła, K. (Ed.). (2013a). *Spatial forms as the centre of everything*. Warszawa, Poland: Fundacja Bęc Zmiana.

Breguła, K. (2013b). Introduction. In K. Breguła (Ed.), *Spatial forms as the centre of everything* (pp. 5–8). Warszawa, Poland: Fundacja Bęc Zmiana.

Carnegie, E., & Kociatkiewicz, J. (2019). Occupying whateverland: Journeys to museums in the Baltic. *Annals of Tourism Research, 75*(2019), 238–247.

Colbert, F., d'Astous, A., & Parmentier, M. A. (2005). Consumer perceptions of sponsorship in the art. *International Journal of Cultural Policy, 11*(2), 215–228.

Cornelissen, J. P. (2002). On the "organisational identity" metaphor. *British Journal of Management, 13*(3), 259–268.

Cornelissen, J. P., Haslam, A., & Balmer, J. M. T. (2007). Social identity, organizational identity and corporate identity: Towards an integrated understanding of processes, patternings and products. *British Journal of Management, 18*(s1), S1–S16.

Duda, J. (2016). 218 spotkanie z cyklu "Wieliczka-Wieliczanie" pt. "Górnicy rzeźbiarze Kopalni Soli Wieliczka". Wieliczka, Poland: Wydawnictwo Powiatowej i Miejskiej Biblioteki Publicznej.

Gaweł, Ł. (2009). Czy zapałki są dziedzictwem kulturowym?. *Zarządzanie w Kulturze, Tom 10*, 2009, 13–18.

Gioia, D. A. (1998). From individual to organisational identity. In D. Whetten & P. Godfrey (Eds.), *Identity in organizations: Building theory through conversations* (pp. 17–31). Thousand Oaks, CA: Sage.

Głębock,i W. (1990). *Warszawskie pomniki.* Warszawa, Poland: Wydawnictwo PTTK „Kraj".

Gurler, E. E., & Ozer, B. (2013). The effects of public memorials on social memory and urban identity. *Procedia – Social and Behavioral Sciences, 82*(2013), 858–863.

Hatch, M. J., & Schultz, M. (2002). The dynamics of organisational identity. *Human Relations, 55*(8), 989–1018.

Hess, D., Rogovsky, N., & Dunfee, T. W. (2002). The next wave of corporate community involvement: Corporate social initiatives. *California Management Review, 44*(2), 110–125.

Konecki, K. (2002). Tożsamość organizacyjna. In K. Konecki & P. Tobera (Eds.), *Szkice z socjologii zarządzania* (pp. 82–102). Łódź, Poland: Wydawnictwo Uniwersytetu Łódzkiego.

Kostera, M. (1996). *Postmodernizm w zarządzaniu.* Warszawa, Poland: Polskie Wydawnictwo Ekonomiczne.

Kowalewski, M. (2007). Zmiany na cokołach. Uwagi o funkcjach pomników w przestrzeni miasta. *Obóz. Problemy narodów byłego obozu komunistycznego, 49*, 125–137.

Laberschek, M., & Popiołek, M. (2019). Three dimensions of myth in post advertising: A case of an advertising spot of the reserved brand. In J. Kreft, S. Kuczamer-Kłopotowska, & A. Kalinowska-Żeleźnik (Eds.), *Myth in modern media management and marketing* (pp. 195–222). Hershy, PA: IGI Global.

Leśniewska, A. M. (2006). *Puławy 66.* Puławy, Poland: Towarzystwo Przyjaciół Puław.

Leśniewska, A. M. (2013). *Magdalena Więcek. Przestrzeń jako narzędzie poznania.* Orońsko, Poland: Wydawnictwo Centrum Rzeźby Polskiej.

Machnik, A., & Kurczewski, R. (2014). Dziedzictwo przyrodnicze w rozwoju turystyki kulturowej na terenach wiejskich. *Turystyka kulturowa,* 7(2014), 35–48.

Matyjanka, M. (2019). Projekt Skopje 2014. In A. Tarasiuk & A. Miczko (Eds.), *Pomnik. Europa Środkowo-Wschodnia 1918–2018* (pp. 58–61). Warszawa, Poland: Muzeum Rzeźby im. Xawerego Dunikowskiego w Królikarni.

Mierzecki, R. (1999). Przemysł naftowy w Polsce w XIX i XX wieku. *Analecta, 8*/2(16), 55–71.

Morgan, G. (1986). *Images of organisation.* Newbury Park, CA, London, UK, and New Delhi, India: Sage.

Nora, P. (1989). Between memory and history: Les Lieux de Mémoire. *Representations*, No. 26, Special Issue: Memory and Counter-Memory (Spring, 1989), 7–24.

O'Hagan J., & Harvey, D. (2000). Why do companies sponsor arts events? Some evidence and a proposed classification. *Journal of Cultural Economics, 24*(3), 205–224.

Osborne, B. S. (2001). Landscapes, memory, monuments, and commemoration: Putting identity in its place. *Canadian Ethnic Studies, 33*(3), 39–77.

Polskie Radio (1999). *Byki i pomniki* (broadcast: Polskie Radio). Retrieved on 11-07-2019 from https://www.polskieradio.pl/80/4198/Artykul/1321563,Byki-i-pomniki

Praczyk, M. (2015). Materia pomnika. Studium porównawcze na przykładzie monumentów w Poznaniu i Strasburgu w XIX i XX wieku. Poznań, Poland: Instytut Historii UAM.

Sobieraj, T. (1985). *Pomniki Warszawy*. Warszawa, Poland: Wydawnictwo Sport i Turystyka.

Stachurska, A. (2019). *ORLEN bez tajemnic: Co robi dinozaur na terenie zakładu produkcyjnego?* Retrieved on 11-07-2019 from http://petronews.pl/orlen-bez-tajemnic-co-robi-dinozaur-na-terenie-zakladu-produkcyjnego

Stano, B. (2019). *Artysta w fabryce. Dwa oblicza mecenatu przemysłowego*. Kraków, Poland: Wydawnictwo Naukowe Uniwersytetu Pedagogicznego.

Strati, A. (1999). *Organization and aesthetics*. London, UK, Thousand Oaks, CA, and New Delhi, India: Sage.

Sułkowski, Ł. (2012). *Kulturowe procesy zarządzania*. Warszawa, Poland: Difin.

Swanson S. R., & Davis, C. (2006). Arts patronage: A social identity perspective. *Journal of Marketing Theory and Practice, 14*(2), 125–138.

Swidnica24 (2005). *Autorka rzeźby renifera w Świdnicy*. Retrieved on 11-07-2019 from https://swidnica24.pl/2015/02/autorka-rzezby-renifera-w-swidnicy/

Szulc, R., & Bunk, K. (2009). Realizacja strategii kształtowania relacji z otoczeniem z wykorzystaniem księgi identyfikacji wizualnej przedsiębiorstwa. *Zeszyty Naukowe Uniwersytetu Szczecińskiego. Ekonomiczne Problemy Usług, 42*(2009), 279–286.

Turner, B. A. (1986). Sociological aspects of organizational symbolism. *Organization Studies, 7*(2), 101–115.

Weick, K. (1995). *Sensemaking in organisation*. Thousand Oaks, CA: Sage.

Wolańska, A. (2018). *Wiara i patriotyzm w rzeźbach wielickich górników*. Kraków, Poland: Kopalnia Soli „Wieliczka" Trasa Turystyczna Sp. z o. o.

Yanov, D. (1995). Built space as story: The policy stories that buildings tell. *Policy Studies Journal, 23*(3), 407–422.

Zieliński, F. (2005). Szata ideologiczna miasta–pomniki. In B. Jałowiecki, A. Majer, & M. S. Szczepański (Eds.), *Przemiany miasta. Wokół socjologii A. Wallisa* (pp. 219–234). Warszawa, Poland: Scholar.

12 The Lure of the East in the Empires of Sight

Does Changing Ownership of Colonial Art Challenge the Notion of Being "Colonized by the Gaze"?

Elizabeth Carnegie

Introduction

Many decade ago, Edward Said observed:

> One ought never to assume that that the structure of orientalism is nothing more than a structure of lies or of myths, which if the truth about them were to be told, would simply blow away...Orientalism is more particularly valuable as a sign of European-Atlantic power over the orient than it is a veridic discourse about the Orient.
>
> (Said, 1979, p. 6)

Art may function as a commodity that is impacted by fashion, the political present, and contemporary ideologies and reflects the movements of peoples, shown as both subject and object; its market is influenced by the "rules" of cultural diplomacy as well as value. This chapter is concerned with the narrative shift and ways of seeing and understanding nineteenth-century Orientalist art and looks at the factors that influence and impact on current interpretations.

A key question to be debated is whether Orientalist art is always colonial art and indeed is colonial art always Orientalist art and what impact this labelling has on the way such art is viewed, interpreted, and displayed by the work's current owners in a contemporary context. In other words, if we take Said's Orientalist reading (1979) as Western-generated colonial art where the East is muse, then this forces a particular reading from a Western perspective. One of the purposes of this chapter is to see whether the shift of ownership from West to East can also change the meaning and cultural value of the images. Colonial art so defined by Said (1979) as Orientalist art predates the nineteenth century and the international market for such works within a long and complex history and a wide geographical spread. Colonial art has its roots in the Napoleonic Wars (1803–1815), where art directly commissioned for or purchased by the state served the aims of Empire (Porterfield, 1998, pp. 132–133). During the nineteenth century what we now term Orientalist art was being bought by private collectors in the Middle East and North Africa as contemporary art (Volait, 2014, p. 254). The impact of decolonization from the 1950s changed the market with a resurgence of interest in the nineteenth-century works, and a growing overseas market from the 1970s Oil Crisis onwards led to the location of major auctions within the eastern Mediterranean and the Arabian Peninsula. Volait notes that:

> In 2009 Sotheby's opened a branch in Istanbul, and that same year (March 18–19, 2009) held its first auction of Islamic, contemporary and Orientalist art in Qatar. Other major houses have developed similar strategies: Christie's has been operating in Dubai since 2006; Bonhams since 2007. And there is the more recent invention of the acronym MENASA (Middle East, North Africa, South Asia), used now by gallery owners to promote their quest for emerging markets.
> (Volait, 2014, p. 257)

At the same time, over the last 10–15 years, major exhibitions of Orientalist art have been held in the United Kingdom, the United States, France, and Germany, seeking to reappraise and reposition such art for present-day Western audiences. Such reappraisals of "basement dwelling" collections may well constitute a shift in "ways of seeing" and organizations' willingness to enter into debates about Orientalism, but such high-profile exhibitions also serve the growing art market in the Middle East and North Africa, pushing up prices for known artists amidst the resurgence of interest in reassessing Western-generated images of the East within the West. These two approaches to Orientalist art while seeming polar opposites in terms of geography and audiences impacts on how such works are viewed. However, a third path is clearly evidenced in the rise of the "international" museum developed through intergovernmental agreements (Louvre Abu Dhabi) or developed by nations keen to embrace the notion of national museums intended to have an international reach. These museums are a triumph of cultural diplomacy and national expression of soft power through flagship cultural organizations. These serve the wider purpose of allowing narratives of space and place to become internationalized and therefore seeming to herald a new openness in confronting the past and thus reinterpreting it. Does this allow for an organizational reappraisal of Orientalist art removed from the need to also define it as colonal art? Is it indeed possible to separate the two?

Volait (2014) makes the wider point:

> there can be no doubt that Orientalist painting's return to fashion owes much to the Middle East. This is of course not the only facet

> of the phenomenon: pictorial Orientalism came to be reassessed in the larger framework of a rehabilitation of the nineteenth century as a whole.
>
> (p. 252)

Although record prices have been paid within these emerging markets in recent years (Ma, 2011), I am less interested in the notion of "value" of nineteenth-century Orientalist art in the present day, as "value" is constructed by markets as a reflection of quality. Rather, in this chapter, I focus on the general culture of aesthetics under which such art was created and how government-funded or -endorsed museums in Europe, the United States, the Middle East, and North Africa purchase, present, represent, hid, or hide these works from public view as they fit their current strategic aims or otherwise. Curators remain "inspectors of quality" (Phillips, 1997, p. 7) in that they hold or are assumed to hold the knowledge about the works, the period and context of their creation. Curators determine the narratives and grouping of works within exhibition spaces, although they are also limited by the institutional values and associated donors and funders (Carnegie, 2006). Yes, curatorial authority is subject to peer review, and influential curators at highly regarded institutions can and do shape value. Their reach therefore extends beyond the organization they represent and indeed many are freelance or guest curators.

The way in which cultural diplomacy is exercised at the institutional level has shifted to reflect both organizational values and narratives of time and place. That is to say, Western critiques of such art within Western museums serve to align the museum with decolonization agendas. This can happen in several ways: the most obvious of these is to interpret Colonial art in an open way that serves the needs of the political present. Part of the act of cultural diplomacy is to admit to a problematic past in order to move forward, building new relationships. Art serves as a conduit for ideas they contain. As noted above, reappriasals can change and challenge those original ideas about place and peoples who have been an assumed part of the work's creation. Representations of Orientalist art within the emerging global museum complexes are here discussed as a meeting point of cultures, allowing a joint reframing of the past based on notions of humanity. The (re)framing of such works when the ownership of ideas and images constructed in the West becomes owned by galleries in the countries they represent offers a third way in which potentially the artist is owned and thus the work changes the relationship of time to space and place.

I will first consider the culture of aesthetics within the Western context under which Orientalist art was created, before going on to determine how intergovernmental museums frame such art within international diplomacy agendas. I also debate current approaches to decolonization and the notions of cultural theft, before focusing on the key questions raised by this reappraisal of Orientalist art. Does the change of ownership of Orientalist art change or neutralize the power structures of the context of its creation? Do such works lose their original and essential "aura" as works of art (Benjamin in Arendt, 1968) once the context of their creation has been changed by time, political and cultural change? If so, are such works being reappraised to offer what MacCannell (1999) terms "reconstructed ethnicity"? As will be determined later, the answer to these questions may differ according to context.

As I write this, the British Museum, the flagship of the United Kingdom's soft power, opened their 2019 autumn special exhibition curated in partnership with Islamic Arts Museum, Malaysia, with a focus on Orientalism from the point of view of shared influence. The exhibition is entitled *Inspired by the East: How the Islamic World Influenced Western Art*, their website argues that

> Artistic exchange between East and West has a long and intertwined history, and the exhibition picks these stories up from the 15th century, following cultural interactions that can still be felt today (2019). Extending the frame to before the 19th century and including crafts within the distinction, of Orientalist art and emphasizing a mutual influence between the two world, is a change of tone from the tenets of post Saidain discourse which is referred to in passing as a complex form of criticism beyond the scope of the exhibition.
>
> (British Museum, 2019)

Instead, we are told, the British Museum exhibition

> takes a deeper look at the art movement of "Orientalism" – specifically the way in which North Africa and the Middle East were represented as lands of beauty and intrigue, especially in European and North American art. Often blurring the lines between fantasy and reality.
>
> (British Museum, 2019)

This is a reminder that language creates the culture of display. For example, in an online blog about the exhibition, the curators determined that "from around 1500, as Europeans became both increasingly curious and aggressive in their dealings with those outside their borders, there was a sustained awareness of the empires of the Middle East" (British Museum, 2019).

The loaded words "curious" and "aggressive" serve to set the stage for an artistic response to the world. In this they are not alone in seeing "travel" for reasons of curiosity mixed with fantasy as the key reason behind such art. The Orientalist Museum, Qatar, which is still at the planning stage, encouraged the public to consider

> How travel can further understanding between religions, nations, cultures and traditions. It illustrated the importance of European and Ottoman relations in the 16th century, focusing on one adventurer's travel album.
>
> (Orientalist Museum, Qatar, 2019)

People were invited to contribute personal photos from their own travels onto the museum's social media channels, with the most "liked" images winning international flights (Orientalism Museum, Qatar, 2019). Travel is here framed as a way to understand other cultures and herald a willingness to open up to other cultures.

The inclusion in the British Museum exhibition of works from the fifteenth century onwards, and their curatorial argument that Orientalism – or rather the influence of the Middle East on arts and crafts in Europe – predates the nineteenth-century that became the focus of Orientalist debates in Said's 1979 study. I will discuss the impacts of language as a tool of cultural diplomacy at a later stage in this chapter, but now seek to frame the study in the nineteenth-century growth of aestheticism, born of industrialization that led to the desire for and need to travel.

Art Museums and the Culture of Aesthetics

Fraser notes how art from the nineteenth century onwards became dominated by aesthetics. She determines that "the aesthetic discipline institutionalised in the museum has been exemplified by the aestheticism, silence and stillness associated with art museums until very recently" (Fraser, 2006, p. 142). In this way, art was different from the objects of everyday life and indeed the role of art museums was to create spaces where such objects could be safe from the noise of everyday life in an increasingly industrialized society (Fraser, 2006). Art museums and the art they contained were initially intended to be understood on aesthetic terms by those visitors able to access their meanings (Bourdieu, 1984). Bennett (2006) argues that the "exhibition practices of Western Art museums have functioned as mechanisms of social triage – that is sorting people into different groups and arranging them hierarchically – they have also operated along racial lines as well as class lines." At the same time, he notes that "in other kinds of museums" "the Western or white self" is not concerned with class distinction but is defined against the other cultures being represented (p. 55). He argues that art museums were founded with different intentions and for different audiences than "historymaking" or other kinds of artefact-led museums (p. 56). Art was organized aesthetically within these calm spaces as an end in itself. Artists sought ways in which to rise above the everyday life of an increasingly mechanized society, and travel was as much a way of getting away from an increasingly industrialized society as it was about going to visit other cultures.

Much of Orientalist art under consideration in this chapter can be viewed as a product of such thinking, although it can reflect Western artists' journeys of selfhood explored through the frame of other cultures. King (2002, p. 13) highlights the Eurocentric bias of much Orientalist historiography, which makes interpretation of work such artists produced problematic in the present, although he later argues that

> expunging or exorcizing the mystical aspects of Western culture post-Enlightenment thought has also tended to project these same characteristics onto "the Mystic East."
>
> (p. 33)

And it can be argued that this manipulation of the East as muse offered artists a way to rise above the "boundedness" and constraints of rational Western culture as well as simply place. There are clear differences between individual artists being inspired by the "East," which they might imagine as a more authentic and natural space in which to situate themselves, and the conscious construction of place by commissioned artists, which serves political ambitions of the time. The latter offering the political value of "othering" nations that they were in the act of colonizing. Ma (2011) determines that "Orientalist art, as an important component of French empire-building demonstrates that the West's invention of the East is inseparable from the creation of its own identity" (p. 22). Space does not allow for a discussion of artists but it is important to note key tropes associated with Orientalist art. These are landscapes (with real or imagined use of bright colours that denote exotism and climate difference), female nudes, bathers and the harem (more usually within French colonialist works and rarely if ever in situ because of taboos), and locals painted to imply an unsophisticated, even backward, people. The framing of the East as the (never wholly) penetrable female muse to the West is to Volait (2014) evidence of complexity of both a desire for what cannot be known (behind the veil) and a desire to ensure that the West is framed as rational and superior, a necessary condition of colonialization. Such art, "colonised by the gaze" (Claessen & Howes, 2006, p. 200), remains shaped by a complex set of circumstances – from individual agency and national empire building at the point of its creation to the possibilities for reframing such art on the international stage.

"International" Art Spaces and the Meeting Point of Cultures

In the previous section, I discussed the ways in which Western-generated visions and versions of the real or imagined "East" supported Western identity shaping by defining the East as the "other." This raises two questions: whether art remains influential in identity and indeed nation shaping in contemporary society and whether the change of ownership or reappraisal of nineteenth-century colonial art reverses this notion of "who is the 'other'" when such art is owned and displayed within the Middle East and North Africa. Chaplin (2004) argues that in contemporary Western society, visual representation is "increasingly influential in shaping our views of the world" (p. 1) and Hackforth-Jones and Roberts (2005) determine that "changing definitions of the self [of both the individual and the state]...find expression in visual culture" (p. 4).

The predominance of visual forms, and clearly their impact, is not confined to those areas previously deemed "high culture" but is evident within popular culture and its expressive forms of film and television, media, and increasingly the internet. Indeed, the blurring of media and art is arguably creating new art forms, with a potentially global reach. Within this fast-changing society, Hanquinet and Savage (2012) note that "art museums have shifted from being central bastions of 'high culture' to become part of a post-modern commercial complex offering an 'experience'" (p. 42).

Such art experiences are now commonplace in major cities as governments invest in gallery spaces and are increasingly seeking to focus on global markets and indeed transnational agreements. Kirschenblatt-Gimblett (2006) determines that the Guggenheim Bilbao signalled a sea change in intergovernmental global art relationships when

> instead of recycling a dead industrial economy as heritage by making it into an exhibition of itself, the city purchased a Guggenheim franchise and became a Guggenheim outpost along with Venice, Berlin, and Las Vegas...Now on the map of World Cities and part of the grand tour of our time. Guggenheim Bilbao remaps not only the museum but its political economy.
>
> (p. 37)

While the "Guggenheim effect" remains subject to debate, the development of major new art gallery and museum complexes worldwide continues unabated with major developments in the Middle East and North Africa. The Louvre Abu Dhabi, the result of an intergovernmental relationship with France in 2007, frames itself as an international space, a "new cultural beacon bringing different cultures together to shine fresh light on the shared stories of humanity" (Louvre Abu Dhabi, 2019).

The conscious framing of the Louvre Abu Dhabi aiming to be a cultural beacon shedding "fresh light on the shared stories of humanity" is at once a statement of intent in the present but also forms the basis under which Orientalist art can be freed from the mantle of being colonial art. "Shared stories of humanity" implies equality and indeed rises above the limitations of nationhood, just as World Heritage Sites attempt to do in their claim towards universality (Tucker and Carnegie, 2013).

Despite the tendency for spaces such as the Louvre Abu Dhabi and other developments to be initially termed as Western "outposts," these modern museum complexes, while a testament to cultural diplomacy, with their aims to be "universal" in scope and vision, are forcing reappraisals of "domestic" art in the modern world and indeed shaping the potential for "global" art. This constitutes a power shift evidenced from the outset by the Arab world funding these ventures on their terms. It is in the context of these costly and showcasing developments that I consider how this shift affects Orientalist art both within the nations that the artists under scrutiny here represent and also within these emerging complexes.

Contemporary Debates in Object Ownership and Access

As museums and galleries increasingly focus on facilitating "cross-cultural exchange ...according respect and recognition to previously marginalised or repressed histories and cultures" (Bennett, 2006, p. 59), this has inevitably led to discussions about ownership of objects and repatriation of objects rather than the conditions under which such works were created (p. 59). This is evident in "Museums Serve Every Nation" debates, a combined response from national museum directors to the vexed question of ownership of contested cultural property that forms a part of, or is even the basis of, all significant museum collections. They determined that while "objects and monumental works were installed decades and even centuries ago in museums through Europe and America they were acquired under conditions that are not comparable with current ones" (pp. 247–248); their continued existence within the cultural institutions that housed them over this time means they have strong associations with the heritage of those nations. The above words drawn from the Declaration of European and American Museums directors and printed in full in *Museum Frictions* (2002, pp. 247–248) go on to argue that "their" museums offer a valuable context for displaced objects.

Despite increasing international external and indeed sectorial pressure and spoliation claims, the concept that holding of objects in collections equates to institutional claims of ownership of them remains deeply entrenched, albeit determined as a supportive way to ensure knowledge is shared. The length of time that objects have been in a collection is additionally used as an argument to "keep" such objects on the basis that the objects have an often long history as a museum object in the collection – potentially a longer time as a museum object that in the country of place of their origin.

Little has changed in the intervening years. Former politician Tristram Hunt, now director of the Victoria and Albert Museum, London, still argues that

> There remains something essentially valuable about the ability of museums to position objects beyond particular cultural or ethnic identities, curate them within a broader intellectual or aesthetic lineage, and situate them within a wider, richer framework of relationships while allowing free and open access, physically and digitally.
>
> (Hunt, 2019)

Of course, these debates are not confined to art museums, and in 2019, a number of international natural history museums were fielding repatriation requests for human remains and fossils, which Vogel (2019) argues challenges the notion of "discovery" – one of the key narratives deployed in colonization and cultural property debates. Indeed, it is the extent to which such narratives of "discovery" become accepted or acceptable Western forms of object collecting that enables organizations to avoid a closer examination of cultural theft.

What all of the aforementioned debates about cultural ownership have in common is that the movement of culturally and often spiritually significant objects is interpreted within the context of their containment. If possession changes meaning, can this reasoning be applied to understanding how objects created by, in this case, Western artists can then become understood and reinterpreted by the very culture that unwittingly played muse to a particular view of their people and place?

This is an important point in the context of this chapter for a number of reasons. Drawing on the "tactical museology" (Kratz & Karp, 2006, p. 25) of the Declaration of European and American Museums' statement above, objects are defined, interpreted, and understood within the context of the museums and galleries, and by extension, cultures that "own" them. This suggests that Orientalist art, as Western-generated images of the East, can be interpreted within the European context in situ and can be "owed" and reappraised and re-envisioned within the emerging "Orientalist" museums in the Middle East and North Africa.

I will now go on to consider whether these arguments about ownership can equally be applied to "the East." Does the possession of these works within the context of, for example, the Orientalist Art Museum, Qatar, over time allow for their meaning to be changed? Can their context be understood not as trophies of the East that fulfilled a colonial artistic imaginary where the East was muse to the masculine gaze, but as interesting reflections on place created not of the "other" but by the "other," where artist becomes object? If so, this shift in both ownership and interpretation can create "new" dominant narratives (Bennett, 1995). In this way can "visual repatriation" (MacDonald, 2005, p. 173) be achieved? This reappraisal of works previously understood within a particular context as essentially British works of art can be reassessed based on new knowledge that arises from the changing context. Moreover, this development of having cultural diplomacy at the "core" of the organization allows for reinterpretations such as that deployed by the British Museum in their 2019 exhibition and by the new flagship and emerging museums in the Middle East as discussed.

Grincheva (2013, p. 40), drawing on Bennett (1995), argues that museums have always had, and indeed "exercised," the power to interpret and create meanings for the objects in their care. In the case of nationally funded or endorsed museums, fear that misrepresentations of other cultures "can distort meanings and alter facts, encouraging dangerous and destructive attitudes in the national community towards the other cultures" can make staff wary. For this reason, Crang and Tolia-Kelly argue that the nationally funded and internationally significant British Museum "appeals to a putatively de-ethnicised sense of identity" (2010, p. 2316) which can function as a meeting point of institutional and community values, merged with those of curatorial staff (Bryce & Carnegie, 2013).

Reappraising Orientalist Art – Case of the United Kingdom

Despite this apparent willingness for museums and galleries to address contemporary issues and debates within society, see, for example, exhibitions devoted to the holocaust, or more recently, the reframing of slavery, Edwards and Mead (2013) note that colonialism remains more problematic simply because of the extent to which the colonial past has shaped contemporary Britain and France in particular. They argue that "the narrative of the colonial past lacks discursive unity, apparent closure and moral certainty" (p. 19) and that the "colonial" cannot be safely contained in the past (p. 20). Therefore, it is interesting to observe that prior to the British Museum's forthcoming exhibition (2019), in recent years, attempts to reclaim Orientalist art from the stores is happening seemingly in tandem with such developments overseas. Such is the challenge to create self-conscious exhibitions acceptable to gallery, curatorial, and art critics' sensitivities around artistic quality and amidst embarrassment of what such works might stand for within colonial history.

It is almost a cliché that Orientalist art has been viewed as "bad art," which in part serves to explain the banishment to the basement of collections. As is evident in reviews of the exhibition "The Lure of the East"

(2008), being able to label it as such makes it easier to deal with the problematics of subject matter and the colonial gaze. Thus, it is twice damned but reviewers while paying lip service to these tropes, thereafter, feel free to contradict them as they appraise the art afresh. Colin Wilson in the *Socialist Review*, for example, draws on the context and content to see them as flawed historic documents: "The Lure of the East includes dozens of paintings from this period, none of them great works of art, but fascinating none the less as a document of British attitudes to 'the Orient'" (Wilson, 2008).

Similarly, Johnathon Jones, in a rare five-star review in the *Guardian*, determines that

> None of these painters is a great artist, and yet the exhibition is full of great art. In Holman Hunt's view of the Sphinx at Giza, he shows us the famous ancient Egyptian sculpture from behind. We do not recognise it; we are just looking at a strange geological formation, sculpted perhaps by windblown sand. A familiar view of power relationships in art – the idea that representing the "other" is necessarily oppressive – becomes unrecognisable here.
>
> (Jones, 2008)

And,

> At first glance, you might conclude that when a Victorian artist like William Holman Hunt visited the Middle East, what he saw was indeed predetermined by imperial fantasy. In his painting of a Cairo street scene, a young man playfully tries to pull away a young woman's veil – it is a somewhat shallow view of Islam. And yet spend a little time in this show, and you will find these Victorians surprisingly sensitive traveling companions.
>
> (Jones, 2008)

What is clear is the degree of uncertainty felt by contemporary critics, and indeed academics, and curators about how they should feel when reappraising works that so fully reflect a period in history that Edwards and Mead (2013) agree remains problematic in the colonial present. Interestingly, Jones (2008) praises this exhibition because "Of all the attempts by Britain's museums to take on the divisive issues of world culture, this is the best, because it is the least platitudinous. It provokes a complex response to a complex history." This complexity, easily reduced to cultural stereotyping, is challenged by Hackforth-Jones and Roberts (2005) in the *New Interventions in Art History* as they argue against "the stasis and fixidity of the colonial stereotype to examine the processes of translation that occur as artists, artworks, and iconic conventions shift across the boundaries between East and West" (2005, p. 1). They argue that

> in recent years there has been a major shift, as Western Orientalist visual culture is resituated within an expanded field that encompasses non-Western artists and patrons. A reassessment of the central terms in the Orientalist debate has gone hand in hand with this crucial project of historical recovery.
>
> (Hackforth & Jones, 2005, p. 2)

They go on to note that these reassessments encompass not just art but are evidenced across visual cultures – including photography, architecture, urban geography, and museology – mapping aspects of the colonial encounter and resulting in an emerging body of work that creates new dialogues between "colonial" institutions in contemporary society and local responses to works. This reappraisal of art created by Western artists suggests that it can be viewed not just as an expression of European colonial authority but as a "vehicle for indigenous self-expression" (p. 2). Volait (2014) equates this to colonial nostalgia. "We find it compelling because it goes against our received ideas, however politically correct – and profitable on the academic market – they may be. Received ideas and distastes are both worthy of investigation" (p. 271). Therefore, exhibitions located within Western galleries were perhaps not mounted to be, or expected to be, unproblematically received public "successes" (Bryce & Carnegie, 2013).

In the contemporary context of international museums, understanding the past through visual representations of the West and the "other" allows on the one hand for interplay between the Orientalist art and exhibitions and institutional authority held in Western museums and galleries and on the other hand works being bought and interpreted from within the contemporary and emerging galleries in the Near East. What is perhaps interesting about the 2019 British Museum exhibition is the way the organization has chosen to address problematic tropes such as the representation of women in nineteenth-century colonial art. They intend that the exhibition will conclude with four contemporary reactions to the imagery of Orientalism by Middle Eastern and North African female artists. One of these artists (Essayadi) we are told "replaces the bright colours, nudity and luxury of Orientalist paintings with monochrome settings, fully clothed women and strings of Arabic letters, taking back ownership of their representation." In this, the museum exhibition comes up to date challenging also the criticisms of women in Islam, where the artist shows women as having agency, active subjects rather than the objects of the nineteenth-century male gaze and the gendered imaginary of the "other" (British Museum, 2019).

Malik (2019) in an early review of the exhibition determines that

> this is an attempt to reclaim orientalist art from its sinister connotations and strip it back to what the exhibition nudges you towards thinking it was: curiosity and interest in a different culture when the west was beginning to pass from one era to the next.

What the exhibition succeeds in doing is to evidence a successful inter-governmental relationship between two nations via the exhibition partner, the Islamic Arts Museum, Malaysia. This 2019 exhibition takes what was problematic subject matter in the political present within the Western context, and it then becomes an exercise in cultural diplomacy highlighting inter-governmental loans and relationships.

The Lure of the East in the East

As has been noted above, the biggest market for Orientalist art in the present day comes from the Middle East and North Africa. Volait (2014, p. 271) makes an interesting point when she determines that such debates about content and historic context might well be more important to academics than to private collectors or indeed modern museum complexes.

As such, criticisms of the reception of such art within museums in the Far East and Africa seem out of place – rather like Western academics are now saying – but you realize these works are inauthentic and need to be interpreted as such. That implies that the context under which the works were originally curated forces an overlay of complexity, embarrassment, and even shame onto the works, which owners, collectors, and curators in other contexts may well not feel necessary. Indeed, that range of emotions linked to the specifics of Empires debates about the colonial past and the ideas they contain about people and place that are reflected in Orientalist art need to be part of Western reflection if they are to be able to reposition the art as simply art. According to Volait (2014),

> the way Orientalist painting is currently received in the Middle East may be perceived as a kind of well-deserved return to the lands that inspired it – a civilized version of the restoration of antiques clamorously demanded by the political authorities.
>
> (p. 270)

Theorists such as Ma (2011) emphasize the ways in which Orientalist art consciously represents subjects taboo in the Arab World. She notes that

> officials at the Louvre Abu Dhabi are ritually questioned on the supposed impossibility of such acquisitions for the future collection, and on the importance of keeping Christian iconography to a

> minimum – two received ideas that simply are not borne out by the purchases made.
>
> (p. 55)

These debates, largely overlaid onto the people and subjects of the contemporary Middle East, miss the essential point. Namely, the right to interpret, to view these works as authentic or inauthentic, as valorized art or as social documents, to collect taboos subject such as depictions of the harem and yet have them remain taboos in the wider society, lies with the organizations, collectors, and curators, who *now* determine their role and value.

Conclusion

In this chapter, I have considered how ideas about place and people, and the construction of such representations in colonialist art, have framed enduring images of the East as a reflection of the Western gaze. I have argued how political and cultural changes allow for – or even force – a reappraisal of the context under which such art was created. I have determined that Western-generated images of the East from the nineteenth century onwards sit within the wider culture of aesthetics that influenced art during this time of rapid change in the industrialized West. I acknowledge the many complex influences from individual journeys of selfhood and fantasies of a real or imagined East, and the machinery of colonialism and the demands of Empire across Europe make the range of works highly problematic to easily define.

I then considered how nationally funded or endorsed museums in both the West and in the developing complexes in the Middle East use interpretation or the lack of it, performing cultural diplomacy at intergovernmental level in praise of the notion of a wider humanity. Lastly, I considered how museums in the Middle East and North Africa have bought and are continuing to buy colonialist art even when it covers taboo subjects within the culture being represented. I conclude that owning such works may close the circle and that there is a power shift in the act of owning, which in turn allows the artist and the art to become the property of the culture depicted. Though the works are themselves mobile just as the artists that painted them were (or sought to be), these visions and versions of the real and imagined East were created to represent the East within the West. Yet, museums are themselves static spaces, where objects once owned can only then be mobile through reinterpretation. That many of these works have now gone into collections in the Middle East and East Africa, where there is little or no interpretation for the context of the art in terms of its creation, this feels like the ultimate way to both silence and immobilize them.

However, this is not borne out by Curator Zakryat Matouk of the Qatar Museum about the 2009 Exhibition "The Lure of the East." She determines that colonialist art need not be framed in the light of contemporary thinking in the West and does not impact the way that the museum can organize or enjoy such works in the present. She argues, "They have not dented our self-esteem." Matouk says:

> We feel flattered that people came all this way to paint us. They say, "Look, isn't this place wonderful? So different from home." They certainly don't put us down in our own eyes.
>
> (Smith, 2009)

Ultimately, it seems that the debates about appropriateness and the wider political and philosophical issues that are constructed in Said's (1979) text exist in "the Western mind." Thus, the British Museum, for example, needs to create new ways of representing and organizing arts and crafts that can be deemed Orientalist, making them acceptable to modern audiences within the United Kingdom. In so doing they are required to reflect self, organizational, and cultural awareness, based on an understanding of Saidian discourses if not directly addressing them in their displays as such. Within the new and emerging context of Middle Eastern museums, such works are enjoyed on both aesthetic grounds and because they offer insights into place and peoples and not the artists as such. (Although, of course, ownership of works that demand high prizes from French Orientalists such as Gericault also reflects the power of individual and national wealth.) This approach, evidenced in website information and blogs that are currently heralding the opening of the Qatar Museum of Orientalism, does not read as "othering" the Western artists. Rather, it reads like an inclusivist response to both owning the works and being willing to share them on an international stage.

All of which suggests that the aura of the art remains (Benjamin in Arendt, 1968) and ownership of such works allows for a reinterpretation that does neutralize, even trivialize them into harmless travelogues rather than representations that served political ideologies of a colonializing nation. Removed from that political context of their creation, and mindful of the values of diplomacy and global reach of nations, there is no need for their current owners to interpret them in the way Western culture must continue to do so.

References

Arendt, H. (Ed.). (1968) *The work of art in the age of mechanical reproduction, illuminations*. London, UK: Fontana.

Bennett, T. (1995). *The birth of the museum: History, theory, politics*. London, UK: Routledge.

Bennett, T. (2006). Exhibition, difference and the logic of culture. In I. Karp, C. Kratz, A. L. Szwaja, & T. Ybarra-Frausto (Eds.), *Museum frictions: Public culture/global transformations* (pp. 46–69). Durham, NC: Duke University Press.

Bourdieu, P. (1984). *La distinction*. Paris, France: Minuit.

Bryce, D., & Carnegie, E. (2013). Exhibiting the 'orient': Historicising theory and curatorial practice in UK museums and galleries. *Environment and Planning A, 45*(7), 1734–1752.

Carnegie, E. (2006). 'It wasn't all bad': Representations of working class cultures within social history museums and their impacts on audiences. *Museum and Society, 4*(2), 69–83.

Chaplin, E. (2004). *Sociology and visual representation*. New York, NY: Routledge.

Classen, C., & Howes, D. (2006). The museum as sensescape: Western sensibilities and indigenous artefacts. In: E. Edwards, C. Gosden, & R.B. Philips (Eds.), *Sensible objects: Colonialism, museums and material culture* (pp. 199–222.) Oxford: Bloomsbury Academic.

Crang, M., & Tolia-Kelly, D. P. (2010). Nation, race, and affect: Senses and sensibilities at national heritage sites. *Environment and Planning A, 42*(10), 2315–2331.

"Declaration on the importance and value of universal museums: Museums serve every nation". (2002). In I. Karp, C. Kratz, A. L. Szwaja, & T. Ybarra-Frausto (Eds.), *Museum frictions: Public culture/global transformations* (pp. 247–249). Durham, NC: Duke University Press.

Edwards, E., & Mead, M. (2013). Absent histories and absent images: Photographs, museums and the colonial past. *Museum and Society, 11*(1), 19–38.

Fraser, A. (2006). Isn't this a wonderful place? (A tour of a tour of the Guggenheim Bilbao). In I. Karp, C. Kratz, A. L. Szwaja, & T. Ybarra-Frausto (Eds.), *Museum frictions: Public culture/global transformations* (pp. 135–160). Durham, NC: Duke University Press.

Grincheva, N. (2013). Cultural diplomacy 2.0: Challenges and opportunities in museum international practices. *Museum and Society, 11*(1), 39–49.

Hackforth-Jones, J., & Roberts, M. (2005). Introduction: Visualising cultures across the edges of empire. In J. Hackforth-Jones & M. Roberts (Eds.), *Edges of empire: Orientalism and visual culture. (New interventions in art history)* (pp. 1–19). Malden, MA: Blackwell.

Hanquinet, L., & Savage, M. (2012). "'Educative leisure' and the art museum. *Museum and Society, 10*(1), 42–59.

Hunt, T. (2019). Should museums return their colonial artefacts?. *The Guardian*, accessed 5/7/2019 at: https://www.theguardian.com/culture/2019/jun/29/should-museums-return-their-colonial-artefacts

Jones, J. (2008). The lure of the east: British orientalist painting. *The Guardian*, accessed 17/1/2014 at: http://www.theguardian.com/artanddesign/2008/jun/04/art.tatebritain

King, R., (2002). *Orientalism and religion: Postcolonial theory, India and the 'Mystic East'*. New York, NY: Routledge.

Kirschenblatt-Gimblett, B. (2006). "Exhibitionary complexes. In I. Karp, C. Kratz, A. L. Szwaja, & T. Ybarra-Frausto (Eds.), *Museum frictions: Public culture/global transformations* (pp. 35–45). Durham, NC: Duke University Press.

Kratz, C. A., & Karp, I. (2006). Museum frictions: Public cultures/global transformations I. In I. Karp, C. Kratz, A. L. Szwaja, & T. Ybarra-Frausto (Eds.), *Museum frictions: Public culture/global transformations* (pp. 1–31). Durham, NC: Duke University Press.

Ma, L. (2011). The real and imaginary harem: Assessing delacroix's women of algiers as an imperialist apparatus. *Penn History Review, 19*(1), 9–26.

MacCannell, D. (1999). *The tourist.* New York, NY: Schocken.

MacDonald, S. (2005). Stolen or shared: Ancient Egypt at the petrie museum. In J. Hackforth-Jones & M. Roberts (Eds.), *Edges of empire: Orientalism and visual culture. (New interventions in art history)* (pp. 162–180). Malden, MA: Blackwell.

Malik, N. (2019). Inspired by the East: Fertile fascination or racist Pastiche? https://www.theguardian.com/artanddesign/2019/oct/11/inspired-by-the-east-british-museum-exhibition

Orientalist Museum (2019). Accessed 1/9/2019 at: https://www.qm.org.qa/en/project/orientalist-museum

Phillips, D. (1997). *Exhibiting authenticity.* Manchester: Manchester University Press.

Porterfield, T. (1998). *The allure of empire: Art in the service of French imperialism 1798–1836.* Princeton, NJ: Princeton University Press.

Said, E.W. (1979). *Orientalism.* New York: Vintage Books.

The British Museum (2019). *Inspired by the east, how the Islamic world influenced western art*, accessed 1/9/2019 at: https://www.britishmuseum.org/whats_on/exhibitions/east.aspx

The Louvre Abu Dhabi (2019). Accessed 8/7/2019 at: https://www.louvreabudhabi.ae/en/about-us/our-story

Tucker, H., & Carnegie, E. (2014). World heritage and the contradictions of 'universal value'. *Annals of Tourism Research, 47*, 63–76.

Vogel, G. (2019). Countries demand their fossils back, forcing natural history museums to confront their past. *Science Magazine*, accessed 6/9/2019 at: https://www.sciencemag.org/news/2019/03/countries-demand-their-fossils-back-forcing-natural-history-museums-confront-their-past

Volait, M. (2014). Middle Eastern collections of Orientalist painting at the turn of the 21st century: Paradoxical reversal or persistent misunderstanding?. In F Pouillon & J. C. Vatin (Eds.), *After orientalism: Critical perspectives on western agency and eastern re-appropriations. (Leiden studies in Islam and society)* (pp. 251–271). 2. Leiden, Netherlands: Brill.

Wilson, C. (2008). The lure of the east. *Socialist Review*, July/August, 327.

13 Exercises in Sensemaking

3,628,800 Ways of Writing Organization and Management

Daniel Ericsson

Organization and management studies have in many ways been influenced by the past decades' many post-positivist turns, making ideas on objectivity, deduction, linearity, reliability, validity, and generalized truth claims somewhat outdated. On the one hand, the postmodernist notion of fragmented knowledge has gained a strong foothold, and on the other hand, the constructionist idea that reality is constituted by language, and as such is a matter of intersubjective meaning-making processes, has for many organization and management scholars almost become a truism.

Despite the impact of the post-positivist turns, however, writing (about) management and organization is largely still a positivist activity. Out in the empirical fields, researchers on management and organization seem to have no trouble in acting as full-fledged hermeneuticians, paying close attention to their pre-understandings, reflecting upon the abductive unfolding of their subjective experiences in relation to the people they interact with, or engaging in the co-creation of knowledge together with their informants. But back at their offices, in front of their computers, they tend to "write up the results" as if the post-positivist turns never occurred, creating "out-there-ness" (Potter, 1996) and telling "realist tales" (Van Maanen, 1988). The reader is simply left out of the epistemological picture.

In this chapter, I would like to remedy this situation by engaging in an impressionist writing (Van Maanen, 1988) that not only acknowledges the arbitrary character of knowledge representations, but also draws upon Karl Weick's (1979, 1995) ideas on enactment and sensemaking. These ideas suggest that every act of interpretation is a product of past experiences and that knowledge is immanently subjective and processual in character. This in turn draws attention to the importance of narrative knowing, that is, the "organizing (of) one's experience around the intentionality of human action" (Czarniawska, 1999, p. 14) and to the difference between story and plot. In contrast to story, which is the chronological order of things that have happened, plot represents the author's sequencing of things that have happened; it is the basic means by which authors try to create a meaningful whole for the reader (p. 14). This means that different plots trigger different enactments and sensemaking processes (p. 14) – and different types of narrative knowledge.

But what if the reader had the opportunity to write the plot? And what if there were not one story to tell, but multiple versions of it? What becomes then of the reader's sensemaking?

To elaborate upon such questions I turn for inspiration to Raymond Queneau and two of his most famous works: *Exercises in Style* (1947/1981) and *One Hundred Thousand Billion Poems* (1961/1983). In the former, Queneau retells "the same story" in ninety-nine different styles; in the latter, Queneau arranges ten 10-line sonnets so that each line in each sonnet could be replaced by nine other lines, summing up to a total of 10^{14} combinations. With these two books as sources of inspiration, it is my intent to invite the reader to the reading of ten different versions of "the same event," retold from different angles and perspectives, presented in a non-linear manner without a ready-made plot. It is simply up to the reader to create the plot by deciding the reading order of the ten different versions, thus engaging in one specific sensemaking process out of 3,628,800 possible ones.

In the next section, *Exercises in Style* and *One Hundred Thousand Billion Poems* are introduced more thoroughly, and contextualized in relation to Queneau's overall writing projects and ambitions. In the following section, Queneau's works are read from an epistemological angle in order to chisel out the basic hermeneutic principles on interpretation and sensemaking that will guide my endeavour. This in turn is followed by my attempt to write in Queneauan style, inviting the reader to make sense of "a case" in a subjectivist manner. In the concluding section, I elaborate upon Queneauan writing in relation to impressionist writing (Van Maanen, 1988) and storytelling in organizations (Boje, 1995).

The Potentiality of Writing

Throughout his career, French novelist and poet Raymond Queneau (1903–1976) was fascinated by the potentialities of literature. He, therefore, one the one hand, turned to mathematics to explore the calculative aspects of writing, from the numbering of chapters and paragraphs to syntax and morphology (Shorley, 1985); on the other hand, he turned to *pataphysics* (the science of exceptions), experimenting with imagination and creativity to transform the French language in a speculative manner. Not for nothing, he was one of the founding forces of the artistic collective Oulipo (Ouvroir de litérature potentielle), Workshop for Potential Literature, including notable members such as Italo Calvino, Georges Perec, and Marcel Duchamp (cf. Motte, 1986), who all took an interest in being as creative as possible under given constraints.

The mathematical aspects of writing, or rather the stochastic aspects of poetry, lie at the heart of Queneau's (1961/1983) *One Hundred Thousand Billion Poems*. The book begins with a quote attributed to Alan Turing, "Only a machine can appreciate a sonnet written by another machine," and it highlights Queneau's intention to invent a machine designed to produce poetry. The quote, however, is also a riposte to one of Queneau's colleagues, who had "dismissed the creative potential of artificial intelligence" (Duncan, 2019, p. 27). As such it stands not only in sharp contradiction to Queneau's pataphysic position, but also to his seemingly democratic and emancipatory ambitions, that poetry – in the words of Lautréamont referred to in the book's introduction –"should be made by all and not by one." By (re)combining the book's shredded ten-by-ten sonnet lines, the reader simply becomes her own author – and she becomes so eternally. If it takes forty-five seconds to read a specific combination of the lines, and fifteen seconds to recombine them, then – Queneau calculates – the reader will be occupied for 190,258,751 years, all day and all night (Queneau, 1961/1983).

One way of conceptualizing *One Hundred Thousand Billion Poems* is to say that it is a project intended to blur the boundaries between man and machine, as well as between reader and writer. In one way or the other, Queneau seems to propose, we are all one, construed and connected through language, and constrained by its arbitrary syntactic and grammatical conventions. The arbitrariness of language, and specifically the arbitrariness between signifier and signified, is also the topic of *Exercises in Style* (1947/1981), in which Queneau describes a situation (the signified) in ninety-nine different ways (the signifiers).

Queneau illustrates these exercises with a seemingly realistic account under the heading of "Notation":

> In the S bus, in the rush hour. A chap of about 26, felt hat with a cord instead of a ribbon, neck too long, as if someone's been having a tug-of-war with it. People getting off. The chap in question gets annoyed with one of the men standing next to him. He accuses him of jostling him every time anyone goes past. A snivelling tone which is meant to be aggressive. When he sees a vacant seat he throws himself on to it. Two hours later, I meet him in the Cour de Rome, in front of the gare Saint-Lazare. He's with a friend who's saying: "You ought to get an extra button put on your overcoat." He shows him where (at the lapels) and why.

The realism of the situation is, however, questioned, as the "subjective side" is accounted for not only from the chap's perspective but also from a bystander's perspective – and as Queneau continues to play around with different genres and styles. The very "same" story is, for instance, accounted for "philosophically"...

> Great cities alone can provide phenomenological spirituality with the essentialities of temporal and improbabilistic coincidences. The philosopher who occasionally ascends into the futile and utilitarian inexistentiality of an S bus can perceive therein with the lucidity of his pineal eye the transitory and faded appearance of a profane consciousness afflicted by the long neck of vanity and the hatly plait of ignorance. This matter, void of true entelechy, occasionally plunges into the categorical imperative of its recriminatory life force against the neo-Berkeleyan unreality of a corporeal mechanism unburdened by conscience. This moral attitude then carries the more unconscious of the two towards a void spatiality where it disintegrates into its primary and crooked elements. Philosophical research is then pursued normally by the fortuitous but anagogic encounter of the same being accompanied by its inessential and sartorial replica, which is noumenally advising it to transpose on the level of the understanding the concept of overcoat button situated sociologically too low.

...in haiku...

> Summer S long neck
> plait hat toes abuse retreat
> station button friend

...and in mathematical terms...

> In a rectangular parallelepiped moving along a line representing an integral solution of the second-order differential equation:
>
> $$y + PPTB(x)y + S = 84$$
>
> two homeoids (of which only one, the homeoid A, manifests a cylindrical element of length $L > N$ encircled by two sine waves of period immediately below its crowning hemisphere) cannot suffer point contact at their lower extremities without proceeding upon divergent courses. The oscillation of two homeoids tangentially to the above trajectory has as a consequence the small but significant displacement of all significantly small spheres tangential to a perpendicular of length $I < L$ described on the supra-median line of the homeoid A's shirtfront.

The inspiration for these playful accounts Queneau seems to have got from hearing Johann Sebastian Bach's *The Art of Fugue* (Hagström, 1990). In this piece, the musical theme is repeated over and over again, although each time in an altered form. Bach's piece thus lacks an original theme; all there is are variations – or exercises, to use Queneau's choice of words.

Epistemological Considerations

In *Exercises in Style*, Queneau inculcates the precariousness of describing the world, but also the precariousness of knowledge and what is often referred to as "truth." According to Kenneth Gergen (1999, p. 24 ff), who uses *Exercises in Style* to make his point, "truth" is nothing but "being in style." It is not a matter of representing the outside world in an unequivocal manner, but instead a matter of making sense in relation to a linguistic domain – be it a discourse, a genre, a convention, or a conversation – in which descriptive accounts, words, and phrases gain their meaning in relation to other accounts, words, and phrases. Truth is thus ultimately a matter of a language-mediated intersubjectivity and legitimacy – with accompanying privileged rights of interpretation and attributed powers to speak or to be silent.

From an epistemological angle, Queneau could in this sense be said to pinpoint some basic fundamental hermeneutic principles with his writings. On the one hand, he stresses the relational aspects between the interpreter and the interpreted, and on the other hand, he accentuates the importance of language as the constraining medium through which interpretation thrives. One could also argue that he illustrates in his writing the power of the hermeneutic circle in the sense that his two works, as parts, in a dialectic manner together constitute a meaningful whole. Read separately, his pataphysic writing project would simply not stand out the way it does: *One Hundred Thousand Billion Poems* and *Exercises in Style* are woven together intertextually, and acquire their meaning in tandem.

Processual aspects of interpretation are, however, not problematized in Queneau's two *magna opera*. There are seemingly no intended dynamics to be traced either within the works themselves or between them: interpretation and understanding is not something that is intended to unfold over time, altering the reader's interpretations and understandings of the texts and contexts little by little, from one page to the other. The ninety-nine exercises are no more, no less stand-alone pieces, just as the innumerable poems are discrete in character. They are, in other words, texts without plots and narratives.

Another way of conceptualizing this lack of processual aspects is to say that Queneau refrains from envisioning the reading experience as a case of abduction, that is, the pragmatist idea that every act of interpretation is mediated by the interpreter's evolving experience, and that every act of interpretation changes the interpreter's experience as it evolves into the future (cf. Alvesson & Sköldberg, 2000). A reader, according to this abductive idea, does not interpret a text "as it is"; rather, the text materializes in and through the reader's past experiences as "something" and is in relation to those past experiences attributed meaning. In this regard, it makes sense to talk about interpretation not only in terms of pre-interpretation or pre-understanding (Alvesson & Sköldberg, 2000) but also in terms of pro-interpretation and pro-understanding. Past experiences direct our experiences, interpretations, and understandings of the present, which in turn form our expectations of what to encounter in the future.

Within organization and management studies this abductive idea has most meritoriously been capitalized upon by Karl E. Weick. It is, for instance, built into his organizing model "enactment–selection–retention" (Weick, 1979), which conveys the idea that reality is enacted in and through the active selection and retention of prior experiences – or, put slightly differently, that every (inter)subjective interpretation of reality is biased and based on previous (inter)subjective experiences and interpretations. And, it forms the backbone of his ideas on sensemaking as a relational activity betwixt cues and frames:

> Frames tend to be past moments of socialization and cues tend to be present moments of experience. If a person can construct a relation between these two moments, meaning is created. This means that the content of sensemaking is to be found in the frames and categories that summarise past experience, in the cues and labels that snare specifics of present experience, and the ways these two settings of experience are connected.
>
> (Weick, 1995, p. 111)

The overall abductive message sent from Weick is thus that we tend to see only those things that we have seen before. When confronted with something unexpected, shocking, or ambiguous, however, Weick argues that a process of sensemaking is triggered, inducing us to reinterpret our previous experiences in order to accommodate the previously non-experienced (see Weick, 1995). This process of sensemaking Weick outlines in terms of seven properties: (1) grounded in identity construction, (2) retrospective, (3) enactive of sensible environments, (4) social, (5) ongoing, (6) focused on and extracted by cues, and (7) driven by plausibility rather than accuracy (Weick, 1995, p. 17).

Epistemological Potentials

Given Queneau's contribution to the field of literature and the insights proffered by Weick, the epistemological potentials of writing (about) organization and management could be released by two distinct but interrelated approaches. On the one hand, writing could be approached as an arbitrary activity, constrained by textual devices such as discourses, genres, styles, and conversations; on the other hand, writing could be approached as an abductive and sensemaking activity, constrained by the reader's prior and evolving (inter)subjective experiences.

The former approach suggests that empirical material very well could be (re)presented in many different forms, at least to some extent reflecting the myriad ways that reality is socially constructed by and through language. The approach requires the author to, in the text, accommodate many different voices and linguistic styles of (re)presentations, but it also requires the author to display a great sensitivity towards linguistic differences. Seeking inspirations from Queneau's *Exercises in Style* could in this sense be a safeguard against (re)presenting empirical material in an omnipotent and realist manner, as well as ordering different accounts of reality into a grand narrative.

The latter approach suggests that empirical material very well could be (re)presented as open for the reader to interpret. Because no matter how empirical material is (re)presented by an author, the right of interpreting the material in the end belongs to the reader – and is subject to the reader's (inter)subjective and evolving experiences. These experiences cannot be controlled for, at least not entirely, by the writer, even if most writers adapt different strategies to close their texts to subjective interpretation (cf. Eco, 1992), such as ordering the empirical material in a strong chronology or making use of authoritarian plots. *One Hundred Thousand Billion Poems* in this regard highlights the creative aspects of reading – and the powers that are attributed to the reader, once the writer gives the text away. It is the reader who ultimately is in charge of arranging the material and imposing a meaningful order onto the material.

In the following, an attempt is made to combine the two approaches by presenting ten different versions of "the same event" without any ready-made chronology, narrative, or plot. This is up to you, the reader, to create by arranging the different versions into a specific reading sequence – and by interpreting the material abductively, as cues in relation to frame. In and during the reading your (inter)subjective experiences will most probably evolve, and this evolvement will be constrained – and enabled – by the specific reading sequence you have chosen. Reading the versions from one to ten will evoke a specific sense; reading the versions backwards from ten to one will create another sense and so on.

As you will see, the different versions of "the same event" are different both linguistic- and content-wise, and also in terms of time. The different versions are simply not bound to a specific time (and place). I have thus gone somewhat beyond the confines of *Exercises in Style* and replaced Queneau's synchronic writing with a diachronic one. The reason for this is my ambition to translate Queneau's literary legacy into the area of organization and management, making it more meaningful in relation to the empirical dynamics that organization and management scholars most often face.

The material I present is purely "fictional"; the event I present – and the different versions of it – has not occurred in "real" life. This is not, however, to say that the material is without relation to "real" life: it is based on my (inter)subjective experiences, and as such, the material bears the potentials of being empirically plausible rather than realistically accurate.

3,628,800 Ways of Writing Organization and Management

1. *The Press Release*

Anna Isberg appointed CEO of Scandbusiness

The former CFO Anna Isberg has been appointed CEO of Scandbusiness. The appointment is effective immediately. The former CEO, John Buridan, will by mutual agreement assume the role of consultant to the board.

"I am really proud and excited to lead Scandbusiness into the future. Our company already has a strong reputation in the business, and together with our highly dedicated personnel, it is my intention to develop Scandbusiness's market positions," says Anna Isberg.

"John Buridan has done a fantastic job on Scandbusiness's behalf. It is thanks to his visionary leadership that the company has gone from being on the brink of ruin to being the market's most profitable and well-managed company, and it is thanks to Buridan's stubbornness that the company today is well equipped to conquer the European market. The board's assessment, however, is that the challenges Scandbusiness now are facing require a new leadership," says Christian Thorneck, chairman of the board.

In accordance with the agreement, John Buridan retains his salary during the period of notice, which is set at twenty-four months. Thereafter, a severance pay of SEK 4.3 million, corresponding to twelve months of salary, is payable.

2. *On the Shop Floor*

"Did you hear that the 'mule' has been sacked?"

"Yeah. I actually saw when he was led out by the company guards. Thorneck ran before them and showed the way."

"No, he didn't?!"

"Yes, he did! And he didn't look too happy, I can say – Johnny B, that is. Thorneck looked pretty amused, if you ask me. But the 'mule' will probably laugh all the way to the bank. Ten mill without lifting a finger!"

"Get out of here!"

"Well, that's for sure. He earned in a month, what you and I do in a year."

"Now what?"

"Who knows. Business as usual. Anna Isberg is a tough cookie."

3. *The Nine O'Clock News*

The Board of Directors of Scandbusiness today announced that the company's CEO, John Buridan, is leaving the company immediately. The announcement comes after the disclosure earlier this week by the *Evening Paper* that Mr. Buridan has earned large sums on insider trading. John Buridan also has used the company's aircraft for private pleasure trips. The Nine O'Clock News has sought John Buridan for a comment, but with no results.

4. *In the Boardroom*

"Thorneck, my dear old friend, I must say you have really acted promptly and wisely today!"

"Thank you! I'd rather be roughly right than slow, as Percy used to say. As soon as I realized that the media was onto us, I thought it was time for a pawn's sacrifice. A bone to the dogs, so to speak."

"Mmm... and it is not as if that our man goes empty handed from all of this."

"Nah, he knew very well what he had gotten himself into."

"Right. And the nice thing of it all, is that the stock is booming!"

"I know! It seems as if Pangloss was right, after all."

5. *At the Comedy Club*

Listen to this! The CEO of Scandbusiness, John Buridan, has been fired because of "insider trading." He himself is completely baffled: "What do you mean by insider trading? I bought the stuff at the outdoor parking behind Walmart!"

Then it is rumoured that he is stubborn as a mule. If he doesn't get what he wants, he simply goes berserk. He is so stubborn that when he visited an animal farm as a little boy, all the mules went out on strike because he was making them look incompetent.

"But he got a pretty nice parachute, you have to say: 10 mill. Asked what he intends to do with all the money, he says: "I'm taking it to the laundry on Monday!"

6. *The Memoir*

In early 2020, many years ago, I had to leave the position of CEO for Scandbusiness. Some say it was dramatic. But it wasn't for me. The board considered that a new captain was needed at the helm, and I felt that I had done what I could for the company. I had led Scandbusiness into the new economy and taken the company further out in Europe with fantastic results for both owners and customers. Now it was time to make room for a new force. And on that, Christian Thorneck, the man of honour of Scandbusiness's board, and I totally agreed. All the drama in the media was simply nothing but a tempest in a teacup. I turned the page and got a great opportunity to develop parts of myself that I had to downplay in my business career. On the one hand, my passion for opera, and on the other, my desire to do good and contribute to a humanistic society.

My interest in opera developed early. Even as a six-year-old boy, when I was sitting in the salon of my grandparents' fantastic summer house in the Stockholm archipelago waiting for dinner to be served, I remember how I was drawn into the music by the seductive tones – it must have been something from *La Traviata* – that were flowing out of the radio. It left me spellbound, blissfully expecting...

7. The Great Poet on Twitter

Oh,
but for a moment
listen to the surges
of sinking ships
and at the beach of eternity
sprinkle banknotes in the wind
#blessed #Scandbusiness

8. The Professor of Organization and Leadership

There is no research that shows that a golden parachute in any way contributes to increased efficiency or profitability. Researchers instead agree that such parachutes encourage increased risk taking and unethical action. From the CEO's position, it can indeed be seen as a safety net, and as a trampoline from which one can bounce back into the business world. For the company, however, it poses a delicate agency dilemma, not the least if the parachute is released due to misconduct. Ultimately, it is the chairman of the board who has to resolve this dilemma – and to face the consequences of it. On the other hand, it is the chairman of the board who is ultimately responsible for installing defective compensatory schemes in the first place, and therefore, it might be a good thing to remember that the function of the executive always is commissioned by the board.

9. The Talk Show

The talk show host (cheerful): John Buridan, a warm welcome from us here at *Under Pressure*. It is great to have you here as a guest. Let me start by asking you... (deliberate pause): Are you a crook?

John Buridan (outraged, on the verge of leaving the TV studio): What kind of question is that? No, I really am not!

The talk show host (looks John Buridan in the eyes, waits a couple of seconds): Do you think others see you as a crook?

John Buridan (sighs heavily): Yes, it is very possible... considering what has been written about me in the press. But all those stories have very little to do with what actually happened.

The talk show host (eagerly): What happened then?

John Buridan (almost sad): Well, I think that... No, I don't know what happened, anymore. Everything went so fast. I was negotiating with one of Scandbusiness's major customers in Germany, and then all of a sudden I received a call from Christian, who said that I had to leave the company. Immediately. I did not understand anything. I thought that we had an agreement...

10. Wikipedia

John Buridan, born 15 March 1957, in Finland, is a Swedish business executive, board professional, and cultural patron.

Buridan was born in Turku, Finland, but grew up in Djursholm, outside of Stockholm, Sweden. After studies at the Stockholm School of Economics, Buridan was headhunted to the Bergwall Group. In 1988, he became CFO at Järnverket, one of the subsidiaries within the Bergwall Group, and in 1992 he was promoted to CEO. In 2002, Buridan left the Bergwall Group to become CEO of the Bank Consortium. In 2008, he became CEO of Scandbusiness, the flagship within the Bergwall Group.

In February 2020, Buridan was dismissed as CEO of Scandbusiness after disclosures about financial misconduct. However, this never came to trial, as the Swedish Economic Crime Authority closed the preliminary investigation.

His memoir, *In the Womb of Culture* (Bonniers, 2023), aroused some controversy, as intimate details from an extramarital relationship with a "woman in the arts" were revealed. This woman has not yet been identified.

John Buridan is the son of banker William (Wille) Buridan from his marriage to actress Inga Buridan (née Bergman).

In Queneau-land?

So, what do you say? Did my Queneauan writing attempt make any sense? Can you say that you know what happened? Can you tell what the "event" really is? And what it was all about? Questions like these do not have any clear-cut answers. They are dependent on your sociocultural trajectory and position in life, and the intersubjective experiences that follow in your footsteps. Some might find the protagonist to be a "nice guy," whereas others will object to such a characterization; some might find John Buridan's name to be meaningful, whereas others will be blind to such intertextual references; and some might have come up with a reading sequence that frames the cues as a tragedy, whereas others might have construed a romantic plot. In this sense, I hope, my writing attempt is an example of an open text, that is, a text that can be interpreted in many different ways – just as the empirical world is open to a plenitude of interpretations.

Opening up academic texts for interpretation, and inviting the reader to be part, perhaps even in charge, of the sensemaking process could be conceptualized as impressionist writing (Van Maanen, 1988). Seeking inspiration from impressionist painters such as Renoir, van Gogh, and Monet, John Van Maanen argues in favour of an ethnographic style of writing that sketches the vivid, fragmented, and unusual aspects of life, instead of presenting detailed and complete still-life portrayals of the ordinary. Queneauan writing and impressionist writing in this regard indeed have much in common: they both search for speculative reading effects, and they both reject the notion of grand narratives. Impressionist writing, the way Van Maanen characterizes it, is, however, basically a postmodern construct, whereas Queneauan writing is sprung from the surrealist movement. This intellectual (and artistic) movement might very well be worth investigating for organization and management scholars interested in alternative writing, sensemaking, and representation, and not just for its potentials in regard to the use of metaphors, fantasy, and dream coding (cf. Carr, 2007).

Queneauan writing also can be seen as a supplement to David Boje's (1995) inquiries into "Tamara-land." Inspired by the play *Tamara*, in which the audience,

> [i]nstead of remaining stationary, viewing a single stage ... fragments into small groups that chase characters from one room to the next, from one floor to the next, even going into bedrooms, kitchens, and other chambers to chase and co-create the stories that interest them the most.
>
> (pp. 998–999)

Boje formulates a theory of plurivocality in organizations and argues that *Tamara* could be used as a metaphor for a storytelling organization. Boje and Queneau both share the fascination of factorial reasoning. *One Hundred Thousand Billion Poems* is in this sense matched with 479,001,600 stories that the *Tamara* audience could co-create with a dozen stages and a dozen storytellers (Boje, 1995, p. 999). However, the similarities between them end there. Whereas Queneau is interested in the potentialities of writing, Boje is interested in the empirical potentialities of (alternative) storytelling. Or, put slightly differently, Queneau is on a quest to destabilize (the French) language, whereas Boje is searching to understand and challenge the language-mediated boundaries and practices of (post)modern organizations. A fruitful avenue for future research within organization and management would thus be to combine the two, conducting empirical research in Tamara-land and writing in Queneau-land.

References

Alvesson, M., & Sköldberg, K. (2000). *Reflexive methodology: New vistas for qualitative research.* London, UK: SAGE.

Boje, D. M. (1995). Stories of the storytelling organization: A postmodern analysis of Disney as 'Tamara-land'. *Academy of Management Journal, 38*(4), 997–1035.

Carr, A. N. (2007). "Art as" The Great Refusal": Lessons for organization studies and management. *Tamara: Journal for Critical Organization Inquiry,* 6(1), 12–35.

Czarniawska, B. (1999). *Writing management. Organization theory as a literary genre.* Oxford, UK: Oxford University Press.

Duncan, D. (2019). *The Oulipo and modern thought.* Oxford, UK: Oxford University Press.

Eco, U. (1992). *The role of the reader. Explorations in the semiotics of texts.* Bloomington: Indiana University Press.

Gergen, K. J. (1999). *An invitation to social constructionism.* London, UK: Sage.

Hagström, L. (1990). Foreword. In R. Queneau (Ed.), *Stilövningar.* (Exercices de style) (pp. 3–5). Lund, Sweden: Bakhåll.

Motte, W. F. (Ed.). (1986). *Oulipo: A primer of potential literature.* Lincoln and London, UK: University of Nebraska Press.

Potter, J. (1996). *Representing reality: Discourse, rhetoric and social construction.* London, UK: Sage.

Queneau, R. (1947/1981). *Exercises in style.* New York, NY: New Directions.

Queneau, R. (1961/1983). *One hundred thousand billion poems.* Paris: Kickshaws.

Shorley, C. (1985). *Queneau's fiction.* Cambridge, UK: Cambridge University Press.

Van Maanen, J. (1988). *Tales of the field. On writing ethnography.* Chicago, IL: University of Chicago Press.

Weick, K. (1979). *The social psychology of organizing.* New York, NY: Random House.

Weick, K. (1995). *Sensemaking in organizations.* Thousand Oaks, CA: Sage.

14 Is a Culture-Forming Interaction between Art and Management Possible and on What Conditions?

Mateusz Falkowski

The Problem

The question about the relationship between art (as well as aesthetics) and management (as well as organizational theory and practice) arises, of course, at a specific historical moment. Diagnosing and identifying its nature would probably allow us to lay down precise guidelines for developing a meaningful relationship between artistic activity – or, more broadly, artistic approach – and management activities – or, more broadly again, a certain managerial ethos. The three questions that immediately come to mind are: *has such a relationship already existed? What is the purpose of maintaining it or establishing a new one, or in other words, why do art, management, or something else even want such a relationship and why should they want one? What are the real (that is, historical) and core conditions to be able to establish such a relationship?* It is worth addressing in particular the latter question – which is a strictly philosophical, yet seemingly abstract one – as we have currently found ourselves in the potentially critical moment when we are being flooded with demands and calls to establish a brand new relationship between the two disciplines that seem so disparate. Therefore, the point is whether these ties – existing or future ones – can only be external by nature and can only function as a temporary alliance or, perhaps, they are actually close and touch the very cores and realities of both disciplines, thus, transforming them or nudging them towards previously unreachable or undiscovered terrain.

Encounters

There is no doubt that management, in the broad sense of the term, has been present in art for a long time, mainly as the elementary practice aimed at making the functioning of institutions (e.g. the court), people (happy buyers and paid artists), artworks, and tools (within the framework of the supply chain system) effective. As time went by, with the development of the "artistic market," the establishment of museums and collections, the opening of art galleries and auction houses, the development of numerous new functions and positions – such as antiquarians, curators, and investment counsellors – and, finally, with the growing number of diverse forms of exposition – such as fairs, exhibitions, festivals – management was gradually improving its position and status and was becoming increasingly professionalized, which manifested itself best in the full-blown academic system as well as the education of cultural and arts managers or the managers of the art market. Art is eager to take advantage of these benefits, even if it sometimes puts up more or less sincere resistance to them. In turn, it has already managed to become a set of tools and techniques used in management, or if not in management itself, then at least certainly in the aspect of it that relates to promotion, advertising, and marketing. These encounters – however intense, desired, or effective – are of an external nature, that is, they are usually based on an exchange of competencies, information, and skills specific to each discipline.

Management and Art Today

One might remark – quite pointedly – that the scope and depth of management's interference in art, even if it more often happens through specific practices rather than through a mass transfer of managers, is far greater than the penetration of management by art. Thus, we could say – even though it might be a little exaggerated, it still reveals certain tendencies – that these results from the dominating role of management within late modern social structures, their continuous bureaucratization, institutionalization, and a tendency to regulate everything in legal terms, as well as a growing number of interactions between countries, groups, and individuals or between them and objects (both material and nonmaterial) contribute to us living in consumer (Baudrillard, 1998), knowledge (Drucker, 1994), and risk societies (Beck, 1992). For in all these areas – including those of production, ignorance, and security (perceived as positive and autonomous rather than the reverse sides of their supposed opposites, as if playing the part of essence of the contemporary world) – what counts the most is management, organization, control, and optimization (see Deleuze, 1992; Foucault, 1995). Everything can and ought to be managed – a family business, a nursery school, a concert, a religious community, leisure time, and one's own emotions. To put it slightly excessively: *today, management is a significant part of the social "base."*[1] Speaking more philosophically: while all that exists (from individual lives to the earth, from intellectual capacities of citizens to countries' energy potential) becomes a resource, it makes itself available to us mainly through its management.

On the other hand, specific ideas, strategies, and phenomena stemming from art or at least developing within the field of art – such as creativity and self-creation, aesthetization, shock, seduction, rebelliousness, experiment, visual attractiveness, or editing – have achieved the status of a universal code with which our societies speak about themselves and to each other. It comes as no surprise given that presumably no other discipline – not politics, not religion, not education, not even science or economics – has done as well during the period of late modernity. That is to say, no other discipline was as sophisticated, creative, clever, and truly profound in keeping distance when needed, while also being fiercely critical on other occasions, reacting with wit and gravitas, realism and idealism, as well as behaving quite interestingly in the most shameful of moments. These are, of course, qualities that act in art's favour, but they do not account for the real origins of art's transformation into an important code of contemporary times, the fact that – to yet again resort to a hyperbole – today, *art has become a significant part of the social "superstructure."*

Side Note: Design as an Encounter

Before we take a closer look at this issue, let us consider the following hypothesis: in our times, it is *design* that acts as the intersection where the base and the superstructure meet, that is, management as the basic attitude towards the world and art as the basic language of communication. It is an intersection that has been increasingly emphasized at least since the beginning of the twenty-first century. This, so to speak, "inflation of design" (see Bryl-Roman, 2009) – of its various forms and fields of application – can be viewed as a powerful testimony to the rules of co-existence between art and management. Even though it is certainly not a prevalent phenomenon, even though there is a significant amount of elitism and exceptionality about it, even though it is often a principle applied merely selectively or pointwise, only in specific disciplines, or, in other words, even though it is often a phenomenon that can be seen or heard of in theory rather than in practice, its universal and egalitarian aspirations are plainly visible. First of all, we can and – in a world that requires constant organization and control – must design everything. Second, we all do it to a certain extent, we do it better or worse, but we do it all the time (see Lawson, 2006; Matthwes & Wrigley, 2017). Third, we can all learn how to do it and how to do it better. And, what is more, contemporary advanced design uses tools and strategies typical of art conceived and treated as a certain anthropological phenomenon. Inspiration, games of imagination, blundering, working with lack of knowledge and emotions, experimenting, repetition – these tricks that artists have been perfectly comfortable with using in their work and that are, at the same time, part of the natural repertoire of the Homo sapiens species have now been included into the general pool of problem-solving strategies. Finally, this is because design, and, what follows, management itself, is nothing but problematization: a reinterpretation of the world as a universe of problems.

On another note, let us remark that such a vision of reality as one made out of problems (rather than, for example, things) is not, of course, unproblematic. Even if only due to its historicity, it is tied up in conjunctures of historical events. The most naive, but also the most important, question to pose would be about the conditions of possibility in creating such a vision – conditions founded in both real history and knowledge. For, on the one hand, it is the world itself that had to become something made out of problems; on the other, transformations of cognition, also in the field of sciences (social sciences, the humanities, and engineering), led to the formation of problem as the central object, so that it could even present itself to cognition.

Strategies of Requested Transfer

What assumptions underlie the ideas and demands clearly aimed at establishing a new relationship between art and management, and, more specifically, opening the latter to the possibilities offered by the former (Guillet de Monthoux, 1993; Strati, 1999)? An opening which, as should be emphasized, would reach beyond the relationships that have already been developed, such as the ones that enable the organization of the art market, the functioning of the institutions related to art, the development of careers, and the promotion of events. This time, the transfer would have to take place in the opposite direction: it would not be about managing art, but about leaving management at the mercy of art.

Self-criticism

Management – up to now based on the instrumental model of goal-oriented rationality (to use Weber's term: *Zweckrationalität*) – would hence be able to notice the limits of such a self-definition and also the limits of its own practices measured by efficacy, countability, and control. Regardless of the specific accusations directed at itself, this type of approach is based on the *strategy of self-criticism.* If criticism, understood in the classical Kantian sense, means acknowledging and setting limits, then a generous but radical interpretation of the demands discussed here forces us to perceive these demands as proof that they are more than just accidental limitations resulting from a misapplication of theory or from insufficient skill. On the contrary, it is precisely the perfectly realized, if anything, virtuosic management, and thus management itself, that will never be able to overcome the limitations of its own rationality.[2] We should therefore abandon such rationality itself.[3]

Selection

Recipes like that are usually more moderate – perhaps also due to the peculiar nature of instrumental rationality. As is well known, Kant's description of critique – or, more precisely, self-critique – of reason invariably leads to a change of its domain. As a result, problems that cannot be solved by means of theoretical reason are reformulated by practical reason, where some hypotheses that have not yet been confirmed operate in "as if" mode: although we cannot possibly *know* whether freedom exists, as ethical beings we can, or even must, *assume* it does. Moreover, this is actually precisely what we do assume all the time. In other words, from the point of view of cognition, no evidence of freedom can be *seen* in the world. This is something that lies beyond the phenomenal order. Hence – to apply that logic of self-criticism to what is of interest to us – from the point of view of rationality of management, we *cannot see* something that is non-instrumental. Taking this even further, perhaps, from the perspective of a different discipline, such as art, we can assume that something like this exists, or, what is more, we can demonstrate that in reality this is precisely what we are doing even while managing.[4] It seems, however, that more often than not we are dealing with a *selective strategy*: the incorporation of certain aspects considered typical of art into the theory and, especially, the practice of management. This would be a reversal of the Kantian formula: instead of changing perspective to see what we had been unable to see until now from that point of view, we remain in our position and assume that we can see something that is beyond our view – and, what is more, we are capable of adapting that to our existing conditions. Direct proof of this is in the aforementioned selectivity[5]: taking an interest in specific qualities rather than adopting a different viewpoint or *asking about the possibility of looking at management from the perspective of art*. Therefore, it is not preposterous to pose another question at this point: does "art" remain *art* when we selectively use some aspects of it? This issue, as it shall turn out, takes on an interesting meaning especially in the light of historical deliberations.

Pragmatism

Self-criticism and selection indicate what is actually at stake in the practice discussed here, which, as should be remembered, is only examined theoretically and, more specifically, in terms of its basic premises, guidelines, and strategies. Incorporating art into management is expected to bring about specific *effects*: it is supposed to humanize managerial practices and "materialize" them, that is, soften the sharp contrast between spirit and matter or, finally, restore balance between rational technocracy and everyday experience (see Linstead & Höpfl, 2000; Strati, 1999). This is the *pragmatic strategy*. Again, potential accusations of the instrumentalization of art should be preceded by the question whether art can even be instrumentalized – more specifically, whether it can be used to change or bring about something.

To sum up: art in self-critical management is supposed to perform a therapeutic and correctional function – it is meant to be a box of (selected) tools which is expected to be effective.

Art: Idea versus Reality

A Brief Course for Managers

In order to properly assess such projects, it is worth taking a closer look at what *vision of art* underlies the potential alliance initiated by management. What type of art takes people into account, develops sensitivity, broadens horizons, restores balance, and risks at most – if overly functionalized – turning into kitsch and becoming ideological (Kostera, 1997; Pelzer, 2006)? From what specific perspective can *such* art be seen and is it the perspective of *art*? Or, perhaps, the perspective of *today's* art?

Art history has been going to great lengths to assure us that, despite all changes, there is such a thing as art – embodied in several fundamental institutions (the artist, the artwork, the art viewer... and also ultimately the market, administration offices, academies, etc.). On the other hand, contemporary times – times *after* "the end of art," thus also *after art as such* – offer us access to art as a certain whole, precisely because of that end, which also means fulfilment, completion, closure – in the mode of more or less illusory, yet reproduced ahistoricity. Here lies art – merged into one unified whole and yet visible in all its shapes and forms – in front of us and at our disposal. It is not difficult to notice that this art is *different* from the one that was before – the question is: with which one does management crave to and is *able* to build a relationship; which one promises to deliver the expected results?

Anyhow, at the centre of our discussion is the issue of relationship, the shape of the "and" which is supposed to link management with art. In what way – one might ask – has art ever established any relationships? Which aspects of art have enabled references to the external world? We know from other sources that the absolute key event and aspect that shapes modern art is the struggle for its autonomy and later also its gradual sanctioning and persistent reproduction (see Bourdieu, 1996). At least up until that point, the relationship with the exterior had been the subject of strategic choices and decisions, often a pretext for obvious manifestations and certainly one of the highest stakes played for in art today. Managers should not forget about it – these issues had already been considered long before modern management settled in for good.

Poetics and Expression

Treating the matter not entirely historically – that is, perceiving the subsequent phases also as certain models that did not necessarily follow one another, but sometimes merged or formed hybrids[6] – we can say that the initial tension, crucial from the point of view of the relationship with the exterior under discussion, was generated between poetics and expression. Artistic creation, even if it has always been engaged in multiple relations with politics, religion or social life, has nonetheless followed a more or less clearly defined set of rules and norms. A potential breach or expansion of those norms have never undermined the fundamental value of techne as a skilled craft and knowledge, the knowledge of rules determining their contribution to perfection. Poetics or its remains – depending on the artistic domain – have most likely survived until today (in the form of academisms, as well as handbooks), but, in the meantime, art has discovered truly subversive forms of exterior. Genius, sentiment, nation, folklore, earth, energy – art as a tool of expression of various phenomena rather than fulfilment of norms (even if norms of expression itself became necessary; see, for example, the Stanislavski system applied in theatre and acting) has achieved the status of something exceptionally important, as well as something strictly instrumental. Frequently, *only art* was capable of *only expressing* something.[7] Artists have not really ever taken it seriously, all too aware of the difficulties related to the creation process – nevertheless, the value of authenticity or sincerity, just like the concept of the artist-as-medium or, finally, the issue of the "message" carried by an artwork, have become so strongly attached to art and its calling that sometimes sincere expression alone was enough to testify to its artistic value. In specific cases, "classicism" (faithfulness to poetics) and "romanticism" (the cult of expression) were commonly mixed together in reasonably fair proportion so that, in the end, their mixture became part of the popular view of art as a tool for *skillful* expression of *important* (non-artistic) themes. A distant echo of former tensions can be found in the disputes, occasionally arising here and there, over the primacy of either content or form or – on the contrary – over school-like commitment to combine them adequately. It is clearly visible that the extraordinary status of the artist is reaffirmed here: the artist as the provider of something initially and usually unavailable, perhaps even unnecessary, which has the opportunity to become visible only in its best versions. Elevation of artistry makes it all the more burdensome. It is no longer just a profession. It involves a considerable risk: you need to possess talent not only to make things, but also to express them, and, in consequence, also to get in touch with what is being expressed. An artist, as someone who is as if "from a different world", not only inspires awe, but is also forced to constantly prove his or her position in "this world". They should be both naive and strong, sensitive and resilient, detached from reality, as well as unbeaten by it. Therefore, they always risk being accused of excessive pageantry which overshadows the essence of art. However, by no means can they remain invisible. An ideal artist would be one who is focused on the essence of the matter, which would be revealed almost in passing, as if without the artist's involvement. This is why unrecognized geniuses receive such exceptional attention. Their secrecy is the measure of their artistry.[8]

Autonomy of the Artwork

It is true that the artist has the work of art at their disposal – a work of art located directly in the space of expression. In fact, the artwork is yet another medium, equally at risk of being accused of pushiness or casting aside the true goal: the message, the content, the genius... Discovering unrecognized works of art is actually no different to rehabilitating forgotten artists. We often confuse these two in popular reception: the artist is appreciated for their ability to produce brilliant works of art, whereas works of art are admired as proof of brilliant creators. A continuation of this dialectical tension between importance and unimportance is the relationship between the viewer, the artist/the artwork, and that what is expressed by the artist/the artwork. On the one hand, the artist and the artwork are intermediaries that – since they are unique and exceptional – inflict violence on viewers by transferring the message (ultimately, even the form of the artwork can be the message, as it is irrelevant). Genius and quality are measured in terms of efficacy. Which is precisely why both the artwork and the artist are jointly left at the mercy of all the mechanisms and conditions that can guarantee efficacy. What is more, they should not – when forcing the main content of the message – force themselves upon the audience (by, for example, overly exposing the techniques of such forcefulness). The nexus between "classicism" and "romanticism," between poetics and expression provides, at the same time, the greatness and insignificance, the power and weakness, the indispensability and redundancy, as well as the gravitas and shallowness of art. The strength of this nexus is practically synonymous to the so-called death of art.[9]The moment when this correlation came into existence – that is, around the nineteenth century – was also the time when first attempts were made to break it off in the name of autonomy of art, its independence from all transcendental instances. This was the end of poetics and expression. Putting it cautiously: everything that has so far defined art from the outside, not so much as disappears, as it is meant to emerge as the result of and, more importantly, during the process formerly called "creation." For it is rather difficult to call it "creation" without any reservations. It should rather be called "work," whose aim is to enable a spontaneous generation of what, although still often called an "artwork," is not just a creation, a message, a medium, or an expression. Or even if it is, it is such only in its own right, unbeknownst to anyone – at best, it can only be revealed.[10] This is the reason for the quasi-scientific, research-oriented, experimental nature of artistic activity. Lack of guidelines and a new freedom require the highest degree of precision – this is why a modernist artist (as they are who we are discussing[11]) becomes a victim, a worker putting all his effort and sacrificing his entire life in the name of something that *must and can happen by itself.*[12] Is this synonymous with art's detachment from the world (detachment of content, themes, viewers, problems, etc.)? Art has certainly developed numerous distancing techniques, but only so that the entire world (politics, the society, feelings...) can be woven from it – in its painted, aural, or written version. This world was by no means non-existent, fictional, or entirely random; rather, art was carefully establishing the uneasy relationship between its own means and the world. This could perhaps be the only problem of such art: how to make it possible for that real world to emerge within this artistic one; how to turn the relationship with the exterior into a subject of art? It does not imply a return to the eternal question of finding adequate form for pre-assigned content. The content itself must still come into shape, sometimes remaining shapeless.

Violence and Force

This art is probably not the most viewer friendly. However, from a certain point of view, the viewer finds themselves in a situation similar to that of the artist, rejected by the artwork with no more subtlety than any other person. Perhaps, the rejection is even stronger if, after years of being next to what they are being consistently denied, they are aware of their mutual strangeness. In that regard, the oblivious viewer hits the wall of, at the most, incomprehensibility, without being exposed to the entire cruelty of the everyday closeness. Paradoxically, incomprehensibility protects them from far fiercer violence. Most importantly, from the violence of sovereignty itself. Autonomy quickly became synonymous with loss of control, and mostly one's control over the fate of their artwork, that is, relationships that the artwork develops, that one establishes with it; in other words, what it does and what is being done to it – ultimately, control over the fact of whether the *artwork works*.

It is an ancient truth, but what is important is that it was rediscovered within the context and on the grounds of the "modernist" cult of the work of art and the simultaneously increasing autonomy of art (in the form of the market, but also a discipline of social activity and a group of people of a certain status, standing, and way of life). To simplify matters: art fully reveals its power and impact at the exact moment when it has only just fully defined its absolutely sacred territory. Paradoxically, from that moment onwards, all excursions into foreign territory, provocations, or interventions risk being neutralized by the all-to-easy gesture: "it is just art." So-called freedom of art can quickly fall victim to pacifying indifference, which is the reverse side of the guarantee of freedom of speech "for artistic purposes." A response to this indifference – and, in spite of appearances, not a bad one either – is downplaying: in the world of forces, head-on clashes, arguments, and confrontations, this neutralizing gesture, which is supposed to protect from the effects brought about by the acts of artistic agency, presumes too big a distance between the artwork and the action; in fact, it does not acknowledge their identities. Of course, nothing is determined or defined once and for all – the struggle not only takes place on the level of real acts, but also on the level of interpretation of their status ("just art" versus actual agency). This struggle can be interpreted either as an expression of the jactitation of artists who crave to leave the closed circle of the once secured autonomy or as the testimony of fear on the world's part. However, the sheer violence of these disputes seems to prove how real this conflict is.

In any case, abandoning the primacy of the artwork and discovering active force within it and underlying it provide a whole spectrum of new forms of involvement – initiating action, intervention, creating situations, arranging events; some do not necessarily have to lead to a lasting "artwork" (sometimes, a recording is enough, even though it is not itself an artwork in the classical understanding of the term). The autonomy gained during the "artwork era" now proves to be an opportunity and a condition for the freedom to penetrate all areas – not only in order to create something artistic within the field of art, but also to dis- or reassemble forces in other fields. What this means is mainly the (potential) renouncement of the formula of a work of art – insofar as all creations are acts of interference and carriers of forces. Thus, the artist becomes an activist in the strict sense of the term, and also in the sense that their main working materials are alliances with the non-artistic fields, strategies of forging said alliances, social change, mobilizing, and so on.

Culture Forming

Thanks to that, as it is easy to notice, art has the chance to regain its highly equalizing character. Old relationships with so-called low or popular art – which have entered the "cultural world," like the space of artists, the proper norms, trends, and tastes, somewhat through the back door[13] – are developed through the reapplication of existing means and accomplishments to different purposes: not art forming but culture forming. What happens is a slight redefinition or broadening of the activist's mission. The activist – as an analyst and diagnostician – has transformed the world, each time changing, even if only slightly, the balance of forces (within communities, individuals, institutions, and discourses), simultaneously intercepting tools from other disciplines (e.g. propaganda or science). Such art has been interdisciplinary and revolutionary by nature. However, as long as a counter-interception is possible – which, after all, occurs in politics, in advertisement, as well as in design – it opens up a possibility to perform actions across disciplines enjoying equal rights, without the need for special certifications and sanctions, actions carried out also purely for fun. Such counter-interception takes place when art not only offers up its tools and techniques by forming alliances, but also creates a model of gift giving for other disciplines. In other words, it goes far beyond the statement that "everyone can be an artist." It happens when art is everywhere, becoming a language of sorts,[14] which, as we know, can be used in different ways.

Let us use the world "culture" to describe the peculiar, yet quite real, space – almost indistinguishable from the space of contemporary media, which are culture's pars pro toto or its caricatures – where any fields or disciplines meet or can potentially meet.[15] Thus, we have currently lived to see the times when the famous "autopsy table," which until recently remained surreal, is now becoming reality.[16] What we can find on this table are tools, strategies, and artistic devices. We can use them to do business, to problematize and to improve the world, and, finally – by blurring the distinction between artists and viewers, senders and receivers, designers and clients, insiders and outsiders – to add new layers on top of the pre-existing ones, initially only showing how it is done, without the need to refer to the norms, the "message," the durability of the artwork, or the power of its impact. All of it is done in order to make what is difficult available to everyone – unlike in the world where even what is simple is available only to a few.

Management in the Name of What?

At last, we should pose the question: how can management establish a relationship with thus understood art and what relationships could it forge? First of all, if management resorts to art, it should probably be aware of the multitude of models and formulas of its functioning. Second, this will allow it to break not so much with instrumentalization of artistic tools (which art very often encourages and a possibility of which it has been working towards) as with instrumentalization of the extremely traditional model of art. Management would be able not to participate in preserving the official vision, status, and position of art. Third, perhaps instead, it is worth following art's example in terms of breaking with hitherto ways of its own functioning – not by borrowing from it, but by adopting a different approach to one's own techniques, methods, and means. To put it briefly, art has lost its innocence and it is high time that management lost it too. There is no point in defending its past functions and roles by emphasizing the obviously different nature of art as an activity that is selfless, exclusive, entertaining, located in the social sphere, as well as incidental and therefore having the luxury of allowing itself to transform. Nothing of this is a universal truth or something lying at the very heart of art. However difficult or odd it might be (especially in the context of the economic and symbolic position of managers in the contemporary world), management could be a little more easygoing about its goals, its social function and status. Why? In the name of what? Well, fourth, just like any other domain, management can also contribute to the creation of the cultural space and therefore it has the full right to interact closely with it – just like art, which at some point had the ambition to penetrate and change reality, which in consequence led it to be transformed itself. In the specific case of the relationship between management and art, we can imagine a certain bold interference – let management enter art before it modestly welcomes art on its own territory by selectively applying those measures that are supposed to ease its rationalism and technocracy. Paradoxically, this is precisely what the necessity to question the basic conditions of professionalism, knowledge, and initiation into knowledge might mean, as long as it forces a departure from the trusted territory of hitherto actions and, as it were, leaves its own tools and ways of thinking at anyone's disposal. Fifth, it will teach us not to sacralize art. Sixth, and last, such actions could be carried out especially at the stage of managerial education – by working together with artists to design events that would be neither just art nor just management; on the contrary, every time they would require laying down rules of cooperation, defining goals – not purely artistic or strictly managerial – as well as constantly showing what is being done and how, reporting the assumptions made, the forms and the results of such an interaction. We should remember: just like creating works of art is no longer the sole purpose of art, the goal of management does not have to be merely organization and control. The safest and most general name for such a type of endeavor is, at least for now, culture forming.[17]

Notes

1 Management is the element that directly increases "productivity," it is a source of skills and techniques of organizing production, as well as a real factor that shapes all relations (including those of production). By no means does it imply a negation of the role of economic relations, especially their capitalist version – on the contrary; insofar as contemporary management seems much bigger and considerably more serious than merely a "new spirit," an ideology, or a "culture" of capitalism (see Boltanski & Chiapello, 2005; Stachowiak, 2014).

2 It seems that reformers – even if they do not state it explicitly – unanimously reject the possibility of solving these problems by increasing and spreading instrumentalization – in keeping with Hegel and Siemek's baffling diagnosis/recipe according to which, instead of looking for a *different* rationality (like Habermas's communicative rationality), we ought to rationally acknowledge that the instrumental mind produces downright non-instrumental effects, especially if we were to look at it from a longer, historical perspective: relations built on recognition (Siemek, 1998).

3 The question is: to what extent would it be tantamount to a rejection of proper management, that is, to what extent can we modify or supplement the instrumental mind? It is not about remaining essentialists and defending the purity of the field at all costs. In the end, there is nothing preventing us from incorporating various elements into the field of management. It is possible

that the know-how of breeding aquarium fish might prove extremely beneficial in managing. By its very nature, an interdisciplinary approach knows no limits. For it is not really a matter of loss of identity ("this is no longer management"), but – on the contrary – it is about superficial changes that do not touch the core in any way (instrumentalization of the interdisciplinary approach). Paradoxically, this often does not indicate its durability or resilience against change, but the fact that it is an empty sign, a pure form that is supposed to conceal real forces controlling the domain that uses the sign of a seemingly unchangeable identity as its name and guise (the instrumental mind as an overt opponent but not a real one).

4 This would mean an attempt to reinterpret, at least partly, the field of management from the point of view of aesthetics (see Guillet de Monthoux, 1993).

5 What exactly are we trying to seize from art? Which aspects of art – its epistemology, its concepts, its attitudes? In turn, what aspects do not spark any interest? Which artistic disciplines serve as a model for its understanding? All of these questions, which will not be answered in this chapter, require further research.

6 As a matter of fact, these are the models of functioning of not only art itself (as an artist–artwork–message–receiver–world... system), but also its possible interpretations (also as the effect of the changing position and status of art, of the accompanying ideology, of current educational models...).

7 Dialectics expressed in this double "only" is probably the shortest definition of priesthood as being "in the second place" or "second after God." Such a combination of subordination and inalienability, of servitude and rank is art's permanent temptation, even in the times after its "death."

8 However, the opposite is often true – it is fame that suffices to indicate some talent: in extreme cases, it can even be a talent for finding fame or, in our times, shaping one's image. And this should not necessarily be perceived as fraud – has not one's image become the most contemporary form of a multimedia installation, undermining the traditional status of the artwork and its materiality, as well as questioning the traditionally understood roles of artist and viewer?

9 Indubitably, all of the elements and values listed here have found adequate expression in money, which can not only measure all the qualities of the artist and his artwork or their rank etc., but also intensify and mobilize them.

10 Such a primacy of the self-disclosure of an artwork entails an increasingly clearer distinction into: signs sent by the work of art during the process of creation, into reading of which the artist must put a lot of effort in order to proceed, and signs emitted into the world by the finished artwork. This difference is particularly sharp in the case of the so-called performative arts – when the virtuoso performer (be it musician, actor...) follows a piece of art and must create it as they go, simultaneously using acquired techniques of such a procedure, which are at the same time techniques from being on "stage" or against "the world". As if two parallel communication channels existed: between the artwork and the artist, as well as between the artist/artwork and the viewers. Structure and matter. Probably in the attempt to abolish this dualism or, more precisely, to eliminate the unsettling power of the signs directly touching the audience, Gould gave up on giving concerts for the sake of recording only in a recording studio (disappearance from stage). Kafka might have sensed this tension even within the so-called productive arts – the ominous act of *demonstrating* not only that one writes, but also that one writes *well*. Is this why he asked to burn his writings?

11 Again, more in the sense of a certain attitude, although its dominance definitely occurred in a specific time for art history – from the mid-nineteenth century up until the end of the last century.
12 The most complete manifesto, a summary, and a philosophical explanation of thus understood modernism could be Blanchot's *The Space of Literature* (1982).
13 One of the characteristic features of democracy of the "cultural industry," in which a popular artist, a distinguished artist, a journalist, a celebrity, a curator, and the head of a supporting institution can all meet, is the fact that not everyone has easy access to it. Equality existing in this world – sanctioned by the media – is truly Olympian.
14 Gould expressed his deep contentment with the fact that music – even in what seems like its most primitive forms (such as muzak) – has been gradually achieving a language status: something that (a) everyone uses, (b) is widely available, (c) makes it impossible for artists to maintain the privileged status of sacrosanct sources, (d) develops as if by itself, without control, exerting which actually becomes impossible (see Gould, 1966).
15 More about the archaeology of thus understood culture, which – in such a universal and universalizing role – replaces "a human being" even in the field of the former humanities, can be found in Florczyk (2015).
16 Without a doubt, also due to the equalizing power of abstraction that is characteristic of money and the market in its modern, capitalist version – regardless, however, of the issues of influence, direction of dependence, and a potential primacy of economic factors – the space under discussion is by no means tantamount to the so-called culture as the discipline of "spiritual and intellectual" activity, which is the responsibility of the "ministry of culture." It is rather a space where material, ideological, economic, and artistic elements are brought together; it is not only a space of battle or of negotiation, but also of coexistence and expression, stagnation, repetition, contemplation, and nonsense. Something very similar to life itself or to politics (taken from the famous slogan "everything is politics") – the difference being that while these two would define the domain of original production and genesis, culture would be the domain of secondary reproduction, a reconstructing and deconstructing process. It would be a garbage bin rather than a factory.
17 I want to thank all the cultural and media management students who participated in the course "Laboratorium: sztuka, estetyka, kreatywność" [Laboratory: art, aesthetics, creativity] that I taught in the second semester of 2018/2019 at the Institute of Culture at Jagiellonian University in Kraków and during which we discussed, among others, the concept of culture forming. I want to thank them for daring to take the risk of cooperating with artists – they were the ones who carried most of the burden and suffered the biggest cost, which is inevitable for any pioneers.

References

Baudrillard, J. (1998). *The consumer society. Myths and structures.* London, UK: Sage.

Beck, U. (1992). *Risk society: Towards a new modernity.* New Delhi, India: Sage.

Blanchot, M. (1982). *The space of literature.* Lincoln: University of Nebraska Press.

Boltanski, L., & Chiapello, È. (2005). *The new spirit of capitalism.* London, UK, New York, NY: Verso.

Bourdieu, P. (1996). *The rules of art*. Stanford, CA: Stanford University Press.
Bryl-Roman, W. (2009). Inflacja design. *Kultura współczesna, 3*(61), 18–30.
Deleuze, G. (1992). Postscript on the societies of control. *October, 59*, 3–7.
Drucker, P. (1994). *Post-capitalist society*. London, UK and New York, NY: Routledge.
Florczyk, M. (2015). Fikcje I, II. Projekt archeologii humanistyki radykalnej. w M. Falkowski, K. Pacewicz, & C. Zgoła (red.) *Foucault: źródła / ujścia*. Warszawa, Kraków, Poland: Eperons-Ostrogi.
Foucault, M. (1995). *Discipline & punish. Birth of the prison*. New York, NY: Vintage Books.
Gould, G. (1966). The prospects of recording. *High Fidelity Magazine, 16*(4), 46–63.
Guillet de Monthoux, P. (1993). Det sublimas konstnärliga ledning: Estetik, konst och företag. Stockholm, Sweden: Nerenius & Santerus.
Kostera, M. (1997). The kitsch organization. *Studies in Cultures, Organizations and Societies (Culture & Organization), 3*, 163–177.
Lawson, B. (2006). *How designers think*. Oxford, UK: Elsevier.
Linstead, S., & i Höpfl, H. (2000). Introduction. w S. Linstead & H. Höpfl (red.), *The aesthetics of organization* (pp. 1–11). London, UK, Thousand Oaks, CA, and New Delhi, India: Sage.
Matthews J., & Wrigley, C. (2017). Design and design thinking in business and management. *Higher Education Journal of Learning Design, 10*(1), 41–54.
Pelzer, P. (2006). Art for management's sake? A doubt. *Culture and Organization, 12*(1), 65–77.
Siemek, M. J. (1998). Ku krytyce nie-instrumentalnego rozumu. w M. J. Siemek (Eds.), *Hegel i filozofia* (pp. 50–66). Warszawa, Poland: Oficyna Naukowa.
Stachowiak, J. (2014). O koncepcji nowego ducha kapitalizmu w ujęciu Luca Boltanskiego i Ève Chiapello. *Przegląd socjologiczny, 4*(63), 9–43.
Strati, A. (1999). *Organization and aesthetics*. London, UK, Thousand Oaks, CA and New Delhi, India: Sage.

15 Prologue to Filmic Research(ing)

Hugo Letiche

Introduction

No one expects that the workers on the assembly line in a Ford factory really have much of anything to say about the models. They may have preferences for colours or accessory packages, but none of that has any significance for what gets produced or sold. Bernard Stiegler calls this "proletarianization" (2017), when those who manufacture the product or service lose (all) control over what actually gets made. Many of us feel that higher education has been proletarianized – the instructors are assigned to deliver standard predetermined content, which is not meant to be contextualized or individualized. Similarly, research is focused on getting published in a four-star (or as many stars as possible) journal, requiring meeting someone else's demands (so-called peer review), and/or delivering what was promised to get the research grant (funding) in the first place. Without grants and articles there will be no tenure, and without more grants and articles, there will be no promotions or pay rises.

I am not talking about research that is really meant to say something, but an activity created to retain employment. Such research is not actually intended to make a social or an intellectual difference; in fact, the articles are not even written to be read. The research is not a product of a process of challenging investigation and critical understanding, but of survival and desperation. Indeed, instead of critically studying neoliberal competition and labour conditions, far too much research has become an instance of the worst characteristics of these tendencies. The university as a community of discussion, thought, and awareness, has to a significant degree been superseded by a learning factory of student consumers and the faculty's pursuit of commercially focused research contracts. Granted, conditions are a lot worse in the United Kingdom and less bad on the European continent, but everywhere, academe seems to be in "survival mode" and little able to transcend the contradictions between its own conditions of work and its supposed goals of social justice, community development, and the pursuit of creative uses of human effort (Letiche et al., 2017; Bikram et al., 2020).

All too often, research has been reduced to the application of quantitative methods and well-trodden themes of pseudo-questions. The unknown is avoided – after all it may not produce anything of value and it almost always creates resistance. The highly individual or original is taboo – the editors may not like it, senior colleagues may disdain it, and the funding bodies certainly will not fund it. In this context, it takes a strong will and much imagination to entertain research that is authentic or relevant. But despite the context, I believe that interesting and valuable initiatives do seem (occasionally) possible. In this contribution, I want to describe such efforts. I certainly do not want to say that what follows outlines what research has to be, but only point to an option of what it might sometimes be(come). My catchphrase is "filmic," that is, research that has (some) film-like characteristics. I will not, here, produce filmic research, but I will propose a set of characteristics and possibilities for the filmic. This is thus a prologue to the filmic, based upon the writing strategies of filmic texts – texts that read like images in motion. Such texts appear in one's mind's eye, like film; that is, as if one was seeing circumstances and events that are to be responded to affectively. There may be a voiceover, but no authorial "I" dominates – the world, as seen, felt, and heard, is what comes first – commentary, conclusions, and instruction (if present) follow.

Academic articles are normally dominated by the authorial "I" of science – the reader does not experience circumstances but is told what the (supposedly, mostly hidden) truth of the situation studied amounts to. Social science assumes that naïve awareness or everyday consciousness is at best incomplete, and most of the time, utterly inadequate. You need science's proven insights to know what really is. The "being" of circumstances as lived is false, and objectively established lines of causality are real. The social scientist assumes the voice of objectivity and provides the authorial "I" of scientific authority. Phenomenal experience is mostly shut out, excluded, and debunked. Linear relationships are to be studied, categorized, and defined. The filmic flies in the face of all of this. Film-like awareness depends on direct affective relatedness to make its point. But to pose a crucial question in Husserlian terms, am I trying to "return to the things themselves," or much worse, to replace social science by a primitivism grounded in common sense or the "natural attitude"? I trust that it will be evident that my project is not in defence of naïve untheorized work. I do not assume that there is a life-world that is opposed to a system-world and that is self-evidently accessible to researching and is unquestionably true. But I do wish to argue that social research needs to be intuitively engaging and intellectually relevant to its readers.

In this contribution, I describe what I mean by the "filmic," illustrate how it could operate as a research form, and try to address questions about its social and experiential legitimacy.

What Is the "Filmic"?

I have chosen the term "filmic" to refer to multifaceted and layered inquiry. The word "film" has, since the nineteenth century, referred to an opaque layer on top of a surface, and in particular, the light-sensitive gel that served as the base to photography. In its origins, a "vel" (Dutch) or "fell" (German) (which are the etymological origins of the word "film") is a thin membrane or hide that covers a surface – the substance of layeredness. Research, I submit, puts an additional coat or deposit onto whatever it examines. It adds text – words and metaphors – followed by meanings, reflections, concepts, and observations onto an object of regard. The common metaphor for research entails going down deeper into the object of study – penetrating down into its origins, fundaments, or principles in order to reveal basic generalizable laws. Two principles reign: those of proof and simplicity. Incontrovertible evidence is required for the affirmation of a theory and/or of the efficacy of some proposed action. Social science is supposed to reveal simple generalizable rules for how persons and societies function.

Instead, I am making a plea for adding levels of reflection, awareness, and thought to whatever is observed; that is, for covering the surfaces of circumstance with a rich film of ideas, speculation, and possibility. This is a plea for complexification, rich description, and variations of perspective. The social–sexual metaphor of "penetrating" down to the essence of matters perpetuates an ideology of mastery and control. Things being "covered up" is traditionally portrayed as deceit opposed to truthful insights. I want to argue for a reversal – adding layers of "film"; that is, ideation, creativity, thought, text, and reflection is to be seen here to be a desired research goal.

In organization and business studies we investigate "text." The texts can entail accounting reports, strategic decisions, financial results, project management, research and development, marketing, human resources, leadership and entrepreneurship, innovation and creativity, et cetera. And the materials examined can include documents, interviews, participant observation, (auto-)ethnography, audio–visual material, et cetera. Thus, there are many sorts of "text" involved. Researchers collect, select, and classify "text" to examine, analyze, and comment on it.

I propose to employ the following structuration of layeredness (Figure 15.1):

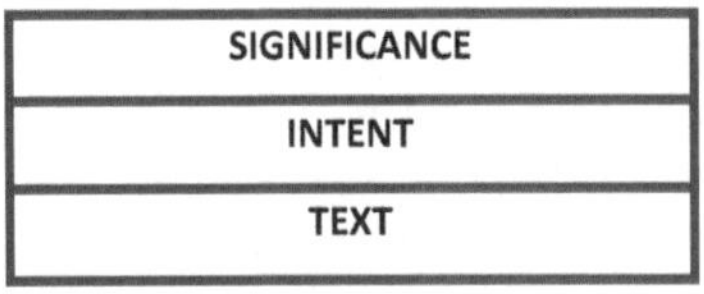

Figure 15.1 Levels of text.

Throughout, the research is meant to question actant intent. What did these persons, this group or organization intend? What was their purposiveness, why did they make the choices they made, and what were the results? Thus, the researcher has to establish which texts are going to be studied and then to answer the question, what was intended to be achieved? Finally, the researcher has to ask "So what?" – what is there to be said about the actions intended and the actual deeds that resulted? What significance do the texts, collected and structured into a report, and the analysis of intent reveal? Research that only produces texts with no revealing of intent amounts to data dumps, where the research is meaningless. Research that displays activity and reports on its intentions, but does not question the significance of what has been researched, is superficial and really has next to nothing to reveal. But all too often in business studies, intent is not analyzed; often because principle actants do not want their goals revealed. And discussion of significance is often neglected because it might bring the researcher(s) into conflict with the researched, jeopardizing access and funding. Of course, the structuring of the research task, into firstness, secondness, and thirdness, as I do here, is nothing new, and I acknowledge the debt to Roland Barthes (1977). But the focus on research structuration is not commonplace. As each layer succeeds the other, and the research moves back and forth in iterative cycles, a "filmic" result can emerge, which is my theme here.

What drives the progression from text to intent, to significance? Is it merely a matter of progression in abstraction, from the concrete to the theoretical? If so, why is the more abstract somehow superior to the less abstract? Is the progression, thus, just another example of conceptual ideation? Is, then, research really just a matter of rationalization, where the more abstract the level of thought the better? And crucially, do we need to see this effort at rationalization as what Alison Baily calls "privilege evasive epistemic pushback" (2017); that is, the effort not to see the nitty-gritty of hurt, discrimination, and partisanship. One can make pain, exploitation, and gender-related violence invisible by insisting upon a high enough abstraction level, whereby gender, class, and ethic difference simply disappear. Indeed, at a certain level of abstraction, all differences simply cease to exist. Radical philosophy of conceptual creativity, for instance as aspired to by Deleuze, can discuss flow, the rhizomatic, identity, difference, and repetition at such a level of metaphysical abstraction, that proximal issues simply disappear too often in a sort of intellectual patriarchy (Thorton, 2019).[1] As Andrea Nye (1990) claimed, the philosophical focus on logic and rationality is not neutral, but is a power strategy, wherein alternative options are blocked and strategies of dominance are defended.

Let us take stock. The structure of text/intent/significance does not predetermine which significances or what loyalties will be developed and put on display. The firstness, secondness, thirdness triad is not just a patriarchal form of structuralism all over again, where the more general (powerful or dominant) principle(s) govern the less so. What is aimed at here is quite different from the constant prioritization of the abstract above the concrete, the rulers above the ruled, the dominators above the dominated. But up to now, my perspective has been very "readerly." The focus has been much more on the reception of the research text than on the production of that text. I did begin with a dystopic description of the situation of the contemporary university researcher, but I then focused on the layered construction of rich experiential text. Even the official research assessment machinery has discovered that the incessant demand for researchers to produce more four-star journal articles leads to conformity and very little real "impact" (Letiche et al., 2017). Counting how often successful academics quote one another has only worsened matters. Defining "impact" as managerial utilitarianism, or how often academic work is "used" or "applied" by managers, may work as a sort of over-the-top consequentialism of cost–benefit analysis, but to continue in the terminology of ethics, it falls down on deontological and virtue criteria. Thus, I acknowledge that this chapter is, in a sense, about research ethics – as the significance to the reader, researcher and researched, of research. Current research ethics is more focused on harm not to be done to the researched, often more in the form of avoiding legal liabilities of the university, than examining whether the research has any virtuous or principled value. In my way of thinking, "research ethics" centres on the values, commitments, and regard characteristic of the research. All of which leads me to assert that the "filmic" follows the pattern set by an ethics of the "turn-to-affect."

Spinoza's *affectus* centres on the ability to affect and be affected. My assertion is that research needs to be about *affectus* – about how the researcher can be moved by the researched, and how the research can affect the reader (including the researched and researcher).[2] In Spinoza's ethics (2002), affect either increases or decreases the aliveness of those involved, and the ethics assumes the desirability of the increase in aliveness and the undesirability of the decrease. Affect comes in intensities, and it is innate (Massumi, 1987, 2002). In other words, there is an inherent proclivity to reactivity – the principle of responsiveness is ontologically given. An ethics of research, questions which responsiveness, how communicated, and when shared; these are the key issues that "filmic" research needs to answer to.

Exemplars of the "Filmic"

This chapter has been very long in coming. It started in 1965 when Alan Berube (2000, 2011) organized a photo essay in a hallway of a student residence of the University of Chicago. We, the residents, pitched in to choose and, in effect, to curate a photographical exhibit by ordering what was hung. A sterile bureaucratic hallway was transformed into a pop-up gallery. James Agee's *Let Us Praise Famous Men* (2001) was our point of reference, which for me has been accompanied, thirty years later, by Kathleen Stewart's *A Space on the Side of the Road* (1996) – her account of studying the same territory Agee had explored. Alongside Agee and Stewart, there are Alphonso Lingis's theoretical demonstrations of multilayeredness (2000, 2004, 2007). And, the last two years, I have explored the texts of Édouard Louis and Annie Ernaux. These two French writers[3] combine form(s) of auto-ethnography, social science, and social philosophical thought in descriptive excellence. I have studied them in reverse chronological order: I began with Édouard Louis and then backtracked to read Annie Ernaux, whose work is an important source for Louis. I will once again, here, follow that reverse order.

Édouard Louis's oeuvre is all about identity. He was born Eddy Bellegueule: "Eddy" being a very lower class Christian name, and Bellegueule is not much better, as it translates to "pretty face" or "nice snout." His first book (2014), which was an instant bestseller, was entitled *En finir avec Eddy Bellegueule*, wherein he tells why and how he became someone else. The theme of changed identity may have sparked my interest from my personal background: my father was a Jewish boy, born (1918) Yannick Letichevsky in Uman the Soviet Union (it is now in the Ukraine), and died (2017) John M Letiche, a secular Californian and retired academic. Louis's transformation entails a settling of accounts with his social class background and sexual identity. He was born into a poverty trap where the cycle of weak schooling, poorly paid factory jobs, and macho compensation for low social standing, was all powerful. No one escaped. The poverty was very real: from housing to food, transport to clothing. There was no money for much of anything more than ensuring minimal survival. His father, through a work-related accident, was unemployed for a long time; the government only cut his welfare benefits further and further. Life was gritty, merely a sort of minimal existence; there was no perspective of betterment. Louis was effeminate as well as an excellent student – all things he really was not supposed to be. But he was even more ashamed of his family's poverty, than of his sexuality.

Eventually, Louis escaped his origins and, as a university-trained sociologist, worked in the team of Pierre Bourdieu. From Bourdieu, Louis has taken his sense of how social position reproduces itself irrespective of personal will. All of Louis's texts are autobiographical, and he insists that there is no fiction anywhere in them. The actual, he asserts, is too important and too demanding of documentation, for fantasy to be justified. Being beaten up, teased, or bullied for his homosexuality required witnessing. Existence with no escape from poverty, social inferiority, and repressed self-destructive anger is too important a theme to go and make up something else.

In his second book, *Histoire de la violence* (2016), Louis described being homosexually raped. He allowed himself to be picked up by a North African young man who offered to come back with him to Louis's apartment. Sex, theft, and violence ensued. Thereafter, Louis had to decide whether or not to go to the police, who he sees as his class enemy. After reporting the incident, the medical examinations followed. Ultimately, the young man turned out to have come from another country and to have a totally different background than he had told. Identity is destabilized here on many levels: Louis has become the citizenry that the police protects; his pickup turns out to be false in many ways; fear and shame seem inescapable.

Louis's third book, *Qui a tué mon père* (2018), describes him coming to terms with his father, a father who could not really value a son who was so different from himself and everybody around them. A father who had sunk into alcohol and self-defeatism as the fate of social class and poverty closed in on him. But a man who came round in the end to respect Louis's political opposition and fight.

Obviously, what I offer here are only very brief sketches of what the books are about. Their excellence is grounded in how close they bring the reader to the experiential or phenomenological life-world (as understood by Merleau-Ponty[4]) that they render. The food, the ever-present TV, the sense of no-way-out, seeing existence as a constant fight to survive, the self-guilt and perception of lost chances; everything that defines situated consciousness is powerfully rendered. Existence as socially and geographically located circumstance is vividly described. On the one hand, there is superb writing and descriptions, but on the other, it is not the personal subjectivities but the collective and shared social condition that is really the subject. Louis remains a witness, even of his own rape and its aftermath. There is text or rich description of place and circumstance, and there is intent in the revealing of how social stratification is enacted and reproduced. The reader is forced to witness that the political and economic elite's flaccid clichés about individual responsibility and economic opportunity are false. But what do we make of it? I for one was enormously impressed by Louis's authenticity – I never doubted that the world he describes exists for him as he says it does. For once, I read something where I did not feel deceived, or felt that the raw, problematic, tragic, and unaccountable had been expunged or even lied about. Nor, I need to stress, is the text negativist: Louis insists that he has moved on to be who he now is, thanks to the help, solidarity, and friendship of others. There is a basic assertion about human goodness and respect for Other in his writing. In fact, in the third book the reconciliation with the father, or the coming to terms with the Other, is a motif equal to the social critique, which earned the book disapproval from (some of) Louis's politicized public. Thus, in the potential conflict between the humanist ethics of care and friendship and the critique of social injustice and call for radical politics, Louis positions himself in a complex manner, which raises questions and doubts. Or, put more simply, his writing evokes issues about how we position ourselves as persons in regard to social–economic abstractions. Louis is deeply influenced by Bourdieu and certainly takes the reproduction of social and economic injustice very seriously, but he is also a witness to relatedness and the immediacy of relationship. His "filmic" thus has to do with how these two levels of "truth" at times bite one another, disaggregate our awareness, and set us up for existential problems. The more literal sense of "filmic" is significant here – we "see" circumstances and situations via the writing. There, indeed, is an interaction between the visual and very experiential level of the text via the ideas, issues, and concepts at play. But above and beyond that sense of the "filmic," there are multiple layers of signification and awareness that are placed one above another, creating the complex possibility for reflection and judgement.

Annie Ernaux has written at least twenty books, and there is ample secondary literature (1983, 1993, 2008, 2014, 2016; Best et al., 2014; Fort & Houdart-Merot, 2015). Thus, I will have to be selective as well as brief. An obvious choice is *L'usage de la photo* (2005) as the "filmic" is relevant here in the metaphorical sense as I have been using it in this chapter, but also in a more explicit and visual manner, as photographs play a key role in the book. The book is literally multi-voiced: while most of it was written by Ernaux, there are sections written by a second person, her then lover, Marc Marie. The book is constructed on at least four levels. First there are the photos that introduce each chapter. They are photos of the clothes of a man and a woman thrown onto the floor. We are told that they are the clothes of Annie and Marc caste down as they abandoned themselves to sex. The photos were taken the morning after, without any rearranging. Second, Annie and Marc later agreed to write texts to accompany the photos. These texts were not at first to be shared; only after the project was completed would they get to see each other's writing. Third, Ernaux witnesses that she was suffering at the same time from breast cancer and underwent chemo therapy, lost her hair, wore a wig, and feared for her life. Finally, and lastly, Ernaux as a cancer patient tries to think her (pending?) inexistence. She writes about herself, her body, her feelings of fear and jealousy, her exaggerated sense of smell; he writes about her, how he sits at her writing desk, normally forbidden to him, when she is in the hospital or how in the relationship he is ambivalent about doing household chores because she hates the idea of "the couple." Her fascination for colour, composition, and sex determines what we are brought to see in the photos, and it is her metaphor of the photos, similar to evidence in a police investigation, that sets the stage. Ernaux stresses that photos have no duration: the difference between life and death, flow and finitude is absolved in the photograph, just as in her mindset as a cancer patient. Crucial to the photos is the disappearance of the bodies – there are only clothes and never the persons who wore them. And this parallels death – there are human remains but consciousness and thought disappear. There is the corpse, but what of the corpus (for instance, of her writing)? There is absence as death, but also as jealousy – she wonders where he is and with whom he is, when he is absent. The book ends both with Ernaux's cancer and lover in remission, and she is about to read his texts, fearing to discover his alterity.

That the book is characterized by multiple texts – hers/his, that of the photos, sex versus cancer, affect versus death – is evident. The intent of this layered text is less evident. It is certainly about things that pass us by. The concreteness of the objects only serves as evidence of their existential emptiness. Is it "Being" that is temporary? I propose to examine more of Ernaux's writing in order to come to a statement about the book's significance.

Ernaux's best-known book is probably *Les années* (2008). It starts with the statement "Toutes les images disparaîtront" (All images will disappear) and ends with "Sauver quelque chose du temps ou l'on ne sera plus jamais" (Salvage something from the time, when one will be no more). It is a project of memory and remembrance, recording ideas and attitudes from the 1930s to 2006. It is not a standard personal text or memoire – nowhere in the 250 pages is there an "I." Circumstance is seen in the third person singular, as "she," or the third person plural as "one." Ideas and sensations, attitudes and events are paraded before the reader pretty much as they would have existed for someone of the leftist intelligentsia of the period. Ernaux is intensely class conscious – her youth was defined by her modest social background; her adult life by having achieved middle-classness. There are two dominant "logics" to the text – the social–cultural–economic one and the sexual. This is contemporary history as a bio-sociological exposé. One's place in the social structure and the attitudes thereby imposed upon one and one's emotive–sexual drives are the determinant factors. It amounts to Ernaux's way of doing sociology – there are crucial influences, but it is very much a strategy that is almost hers alone.

The book is structured around old visual material of Ernaux (black and white and colour photographs, scenes from home movies and videos) put in chronological order. Each time, Ernaux describes the visual material – her expression, clothing, and the setting, anyone else present, who took the picture – and then she extrapolates to discuss the social–emotive context. In this way, she links remembrance to context. But nowhere does she write subjectively; it is not an introspective text. Nor is it a text about subjective relationships or felt emotions. For instance, she marries, has two children, moves with her family from the Savoie to the Parisian region, and then divorces – all without ever naming either her husband or her sons. We learn that there was a bit of haggling over furniture and the car at the divorce and also that she and her husband had stopped having sex, but that is about it. What sort of companions they were, or were not; what they discussed, thought; how they interacted; what they had to say to one another; or what they felt about one another is not in the (or for that matter, any other Ernaux) book. What we learn about the family pertains to the cultural milieu: they were PSU (socialists who were opposed to the war to retain Algeria), vaguely sympathized with May 68 but did not play a role, had a car and TV, took vacations, shopped at the shopping centre, that is, profited from growing middle-class prosperity. We know more about what she read than who their friends were or what they felt for one another or for others. She read Bourdieu, de Beauvoir, Foucault, Sartre, and Camus; watched Bergman films; read the French "nouveau roman"; and never liked teaching (her profession). Ernaux describes the person "elle" (she) as a social object and not as a consciousness. We do not come to know what the various writers evoked in the reader, what the films meant to the cinema goer, or how "elle" interacted with pupils or colleagues.

In *Les années,* Ernaux describes her existence in France from the late 1940s to the early twenty-first century. Repeatedly, she combines three elements. Passages firstly begin with a description of a photograph of herself; as her clothes change, the context evolves, her expression (or lack thereof) varies. She refers to growing up, going to university, getting a job, evolving, and changing. It is the world of the life cycle: starting with relationships to one's parents and their world, evolving through a fragile sense of one's own self in youth, and moving on to adulthood and one's own generativity, ending in growing older.

A second element is formed by ideas and artefacts common to the period or the moment focused upon. Popular singers, political leaders, shared beliefs and attitudes pass the review. All of these are momentarily evoked; the reader has to fill in who or what is involved. For instance, if you do not know what happened in Paris on 17 October 1962, the reference to knowing or not knowing, acknowledging or not attending to events will be inexplicable.[5] Likewise references to Bergman's films, Jospin's politics, "les nouveau philosophes," Radio Luxembourg, et cetera, all depend on the reader recognizing them. An albeit changing world is evoked by naming persons, trends, and sometimes events that were talked about, all of which supposedly evokes memories in the audience, but the strategy will probably not work very well with persons born fifty years after Ernaux. The paradox is that it is a book of memory, meant to evoke a memory of "our times," but the book's strategy depends on the reader sharing the memories evoked. If one is an outsider to the memories, the strategy will only reveal the limits of memory and will not conjure up much of anything more.

Third, there is the movement of sexual desire and need. Throughout, Ernaux questions her physical and social relationship to her body and its sexuality. How society demands she relates to men and to her own sexuality is a constant theme, as is her juxtaposition to those demands. From the Catholic obsession with repressing female sexuality predominant in her youth, to her "affaires" in her forties and fifties, sexual drift and need remain a constant. Seemingly, social mores may change, but the physicality of sex does not.

In the book, social progression is clear. Ernaux grew up after World War II in a small poor provincial city where her parents owned a grocery store, adjunct bar. Their clients were working class, who often needed to buy food on credit. The loo was in the courtyard; everything they owned dated from before the war. Transport was by bicycle and life's pace indeed seemed to be that of the bicycle. Only in the 1950s did scooters become common. Then, canned fruit became more fashionable than fresh, Formica tables replaced wooden ones, change started to become visible. The 1960s arrived, with automobiles, shopping centres, and the beginnings of the consumer society. The year 68 came and went; the idea of a radically different society with more justice flowered and faded. By the 1980s, when Mitterand came to power, Ernaux is focused on herself, her identity as a woman, and her need for independence. Hers is an individualized world, where the Other, as a moral or ethical factor, plays a very limited role. And in the 1990s and 2000s, objects disappear as an issue: everybody has a car, TVs are all over the place, one can travel if one wants to. But work is all the more indefinite, unstable, and problematic. Throughout, Ernaux saw work as an imposed near necessity; she was a teacher who seems to have never really liked it. She never writes about teaching or schools as valuable or significant to her. Quite the opposite, writing is the one activity that she valued and all the rest was merely a distraction. Already from when she was a young girl, her diaries were the focus of her creative life. To write, for her, is to live, and that never changed.

Les années is an exciting experiment in social studies. What Ernaux has done is to assume that social/personal existence can be understood by describing it through the perspective of two sources: Pierre Bourdieu and Simone de Beauvoir. Ernaux integrates her version of these sources into who "she" is and what "she" knows, sees, and does, as portrayed in the text. Thus, my claim is that "she" is a social science experiment, carried out with noteworthy consistency. "She" states very clearly that the two sources have made a bigger impression on her than all others. Coming from Bourdieu, there is the triad of cultural (institutionalized) capital, social capital (the person's network), and economic capital (money and possessions). Ernaux's relationship to education is one of coming from a background with little or no cultural capital and being initiated, through the educational system, into higher and higher levels of cultural capital, ending with the PhD. But she seems to reject and/or to be rejected from belonging to the institutions of high cultural capital. She had a job on the periphery of higher education, in the world of distance learning, but never seems to have been integrated into the university system, and, in any event, she kept initiation into the French elite cultural system hidden in her writings. She has widely read literature and philosophy, followed politics, listened to music, seen many art films – thus, she has been an intensive consumer of cultural capital, but she never reports belonging to the institutions of high culture. For instance, her relationship to her editors and publishers is never mentioned. And while numerous seminars and conferences have been organized around her work, and in her presence, up to and including the very prestigious Cerisy (2012), that side to who she is has never been integrated into the "she" that she writes about.

Ernaux's social capital is also portrayed as very restricted. She has had several lovers and maintains some contact with her sons and their families – mainly portrayed in terms of family dinners – but friends and colleagues, neighbours and acquaintances are absent from her texts. Socially she has written about observing her neighbourhood and watching people, for instance, first in the metro and later in the RER (i.e. the subway and then the rapid train service), but again, the social is described minimalistically. Economically, she reports having a house in the Parisian working-class suburbs of Cergy and that is pretty much it. Thus, Ernaux's "she" as portrayed in terms of capital is very restricted. The texts are all about "capital-lessness" and that is their key foci. Whether the person Annie Ernaux is really as lacking in capital as the persona "she" in the books can be doubted. But for the social science experiment, which I claim forms the crux to Ernaux's oeuvre, this is a side issue. The experiment centres on the ability to describe contemporary existence in terms of the capital forms, for instance, without ever embracing the individualizing characteristics of psychology. Ernaux is insistently sociological – she does make references to "anomie," "spectacle society," and "consumerism," but all as sociological concepts.

From de Beauvoir, Ernaux gained support for her will to individual independence. From early girlhood to her later life, she has been determined to deny determination by a man. She radically does not want men to govern who she is, what she wants, or how she positions herself sexually. Passionate sexual engagement she values; intellectual partnership or artistic companionship is never developed as a possibility.

Les années I believe is an exceptionally successful "filmic" text. Combining Bourdieu's sociology of how capitalist societies of restricted freedom reproduce themselves and employ various forms of capital, wherein very few persons can ever master enough capital to really achieve influence, with de Beauvoir's focus on gender and how the feminine has been restricted and held down, Ernaux produces a powerful autobiography of "she." *Les années* reads convincingly. It was a bestseller, and I think there is no doubt that many recognized (at least partially) themselves in the text. Thus, as social studies I would argue it is a success – a textual rendering of contemporary society with significant analytic propositions to it, which puts a powerful perspective on display. The text has been taken up by its audience as significant. Furthermore, there is no split popular culture/high culture here: not only has the text proven popular, the multiple seminars and ample secondary literature reveal that the ideation has been accepted as serious by academe (Best et al., 2014; Fort & Houdart-Merot, 2015). Thus, *Les années* is a case of successful multilayered exposition. Whether the politics is too rigid and/or the lack of introspective subjective and affective relatedness is too extreme, is another matter.

Qua significance, I obviously see major problematic issues in Ernaux's viewpoint. What is important, here, is that her method produces what I would call "successful social studies" or a description of social reality that is experienced by audiences as credible and opens significant discussion about social reality and circumstances. Likewise, Louis's texts are convincing and about important issues of repression, identity, shame, and reconciliation. Louis's debt to Bourdieu is somewhat less rigorous than Ernaux's. Louis accepts much more relatedness, affect, and the psychological into his perspective than does Ernaux. But my goal here is not to produce an evaluation of their points of view or the "significance" of their ideas. My goal is methodological: it is to assert that another sort of researching and writing is possible and even ethically necessary than what the university system is now demanding.

Concluding/Opening the Manifesto

I have illustrated what I have called "filmic" or the creation of the multilayered text as a form of social studies. Ernaux uses another term: what I call "filmic" she calls *palimpsest*,[6] which is a word for text written on parchment over other (older) texts. I will stick to "filmic" because I want to stress that the texts are layered, and built the one upon the other; I believe that what is at issue is not just a matter of text upon text, but of text in relationship to other text.

Both Louis's and Ernaux's books are categorized in the bookstores as "literature" and not as social studies. Their way of studying social reality does not match the commonly acknowledged social science form. Do I have to call their work "art" and claim that art is what organizational studies requires? Literally, the "filmic" or ethnographic film and video are possible elements in the layering of understanding. And there have been a few scholars (Burrell, 1993; Linstead, 2018; Wood & Salovaara, 2019) who have made proposals in this sense, in the filmic direction. But their conceptual commitment to dealing with multiple layers of text, in the processes of both investigation and presentation, was nowhere as sharply pronounced as is the case with Louis and Ernaux. Thus, I chose for Louis and Ernaux, though their use of visual material is less exemplary. While the "filmic" can entail multimedia research, this is not the crux of the matter. It is not the means of layeredness that are essential, but the aim of matching complex social circumstances to multiple layered forms of representation.

Louis's rendering of his homosexual rape is an example of layeredness: a Parisian intellectual is confronted by a North African immigrant, in an incident involving race, violence, sexuality, exploitation, the law, politics, affect, revulsion, cynicism, hierarchy, hypocrisy, tenderness, friendship, (in)tolerance, and fear. The aporia of my prologue is that in comparison to Louis, my text is not really a layered text. Written material can be multiple, complex, evocative, and phenomenologically rich. The medium, I wish to assert, is *not* the message; what the author or researcher does with the medium is here the crux of the matter.

Filmic researching explores multiple layers of testimony, displays researchee voice, includes authorial commentary, reveals contingent circumstances, makes use of compounded testimony, investigates anecdotal declarations, is open to co-research and collaboration, and attends to theoretical complexity. Visual anthropology producing film and/or video research can be one dimensional and prescriptive; it is not by definition "filmic."

The "filmic" is not a methodology or technique; it is a call for research to be circumstantial and (re-)territorialized. The particular unicity of the researched and of the specificity of the social and historical moment and of the fears, hopes, and lives of those studied need to be returned to research. The filmic is tenaciously anti-reductionist: there is never one simple truth or principle to circumstance; there are always multiple facets, perspectives, and possibilities. Research, all too often, has become *reductio ad absurdum,* incapable of understanding otherness, difference, or deviance. Reductionism brings the logic with it of intolerance, hate, and fear. Instead of complex motives, diverse goals, and pluriform desires, business research seems all too often to assume that there is one optimal solution and a single model of effectiveness. Circumstance is sacrificed to defining and achieving the one best model, which is supposedly evidence based, universal, "true," and "scientifically" valid. Pluralism or social and human complexity are ideologically dismissed to the dustbin of irrelevance. Total belief in technocratic hegemony prevails.

The filmic entails openness to otherness, to difference, and to complexity. Research I maintain should reveal multifacetedness, opening us to multiplicity, choice, and possibility. Research is meant to open doors to awareness and not to close them. Openness, to even one Other, requires acknowledgement of difference, and the ability to accept that Other and self are not the same. In the contemporary culture, seemingly dominated by the model of the sociopath, acknowledgement of divergence and variance is problematic. The one-true-result model of research denies human complexity, social difference, and cultural disparity. The researcher does not really want to respect and learn to know the researched, but is determined to draw one result or truth out of the data set. Empathy is voided, affect denied, and unicity of person and circumstance ideologically rejected. Total performativity – understood as commercial effectiveness and efficiency – is embraced as the research goal. An episteme of intolerance, including hatred for difference and fear of Other, reigns. It is not just the extremes of populist politics that threaten humanist awareness; the prevailing research models have no more respect for Otherness, individuality, or phenomenal experience than they do. It is once again *Krisis (Krisis der europäischen wissenschaften,* Edmund Husserl, 1936), where it is necessary to struggle against lived awareness being sacrificed to prejudice, and where intolerance threatens to overwhelm the openness-to-Other necessary for doing research. The filmic, however, I hasten to clarify, is very different from Husserl's phenomenology because the filmic embraces circumstantial awareness and stresses the specificity of time, place, and community.

Affective awareness is not compatible with reductionism; empathy cannot support positivist scientificity. The filmic is an anti-methodology. If you (pre-)define your methodology, you, in effect, close yourself to the Other, to circumstance, and to the unexpected. The cry for methodology probably comes from researchers' fears of being overwhelmed, of being rendered speechless, of feeling lost in the field, and of not knowing what to do. Researchers fear and avoid the Other; they dread the unknown, the unpredictable, and the undisciplined. Groping for words adequate to circumstances is difficult. Earning your way to openness and awareness is very demanding. Research techniques that avoid all the pain, doubt, and insecurity of relatedness are very seductive. But by making research "easier," we have dehumanized it and made it socially destructive.

The goal of the filmic is to put awareness, relatedness, and complexity back into our investigation. It is a call to perceptual responsibility, which has an aesthetics and an ethics. Simplifying rationalizations, grounded in dualist, naturalist, or modernist assumptions, make "filmic" research impossible. Layered complex textuality answers to another aesthetic and ethics. Until "filmic" research is valued, I fear, multitudes of articles will continue to be produced that have no textual interest or valuable intent, whereby their significance is only to further their authors' careers. The something else called for here involves rich description, multiple perspectives, and variated forms of analysis. Does this amount to calling for art in the study of organization? Not necessarily, there is art that simplifies and is narrow in its literalness. Multi-perspectfulness in layered evocative work, coupled to raising theoretical issues and questions, supported by intensely affective writing, does not really have a name, and thus the choice for "filmic."

Notes

1 I refer to Gilles Deleuze here because he epitomizes seeing philosophy, thought, and text interpretation as a creative, always in motion, form of action (Deleuze & Guattari, 1988). Deleuze's experimentation in and of thought, and his efforts to create new ideas, has engendered new forms of relatedness and difference.

2 While Spinoza's ethics was written in the seventeenth century, its holistic emphasis on human affectivity as a basic ontological and ethical characteristic of human aliveness has reemerged as a crucial inspiration to contemporary thought.

3 They are both amply translated.

4 Maurice Merleau-Ponty (1969) was a leading phenomenologist, committed to understanding human--world relatedness as interactive and dynamic and not as mind–body dualism. In his late work, he focused on the "skin" as an inside/outside, as self but in the world, as alive but also a boundary phenomenon.

5 There was a police massacre of peaceful demonstrators for Algerian independence, where the number killed remained unclear for more than thirty years; the man responsible for the massacre, the then police chief of Paris, Maurice Papon, was ultimately convicted of crimes against humanity, dating from World War II, in 1998.

6 The object-oriented philosopher Graham Harman has also used the term *palimpsest* much as it is developed here.

References

Agee, J. (2001). *Let us now praise famous men.* New York, NY: Mariner Books.

Baily, A. (2017). Tracking privilege-preserving epistemic pushback. *Hypatia, 32*(4), 876–892.

Barthes, R. (1977). *Images music text.* London, UK: Fontana Press.

Berube, A. (2000). *Coming out under fire.* New York, NY: Free Press.

Berube, A. (2011). *My desire for history.* Chapel Hill: University of North Carolina Press.

Best, F. et al. (2014). *Annie Ernaux: le Temps et la Mémoire.* Paris, France: Stock.

Bikram, C., Cordery, C., Letiche, H., & de Loo, I. (2020). The spectacle of performance measurement and accounting academics (published ahead-of-print 14.04.20). *AAAJ Accounting Auditing & Accountability Journal.*

Burrell, G. (1993). Eco and the bunnymen. In J. Hassard & M. Parker (Eds.), *Post-modernism and organizations* (pp. 71–82). London, UK: Sage.

Deleuze, G., & Guattari, F. (1988). *A thousand plateaus.* London, UK: Athlone.

Ernaux, A. (1983). *La Place.* Paris, France: Folio Gallimard. [*A man's place* (1992) New York: Seven Stories Press].

Ernaux, A. (1993). *Journal du dehors.* Paris, France: Folio Gallimard. [*Exteriors* (1996) New York: Seven Stories Press]

Ernaux, A. (2008). *Les années.* Paris, France: Folio Gallimard. [*The Years* (2018) London: Fitzcarraldo Editions]

Ernaux, A. (2014). *Le vrai lieu.* Paris, France: Folio Gallimard.

Ernaux, A. (2016). *Regarde les lumières mon amour.* Paris, France: Folio Gallimard.

Ernaux, A., & Marie, M. (2005). *L'usage de la photo.* Paris, France: Folio Gallimard.

Fort, P. L., & Houdart-Merot, V. (Eds.). (2015). *Anne Ernaux Un engagement d'écriture*. Paris, France: Presses Sorbonne.
Husserl, E. (1970). *The crisis of European sciences and transcendental phenomenology*. Evanston, IL: Northwestern University Press. [Die Krisis der europäischen Wissenschaften und die transzendentale Phänomenologie: Eine Einleitung in die phänomenologische Philosophie, (1936)].
Letiche, H., Lightfoot, G., & Lilley, S. (2017). Classements, Capitalisme Académique et Affects des Chercheurs en Gestion. *Revue Francaise de Gestion 267*, pp. 97–115.
Lingis, A. (2000). *Dangerous emotions*. Berkeley: University of California Press.
Lingis, A. (2004). *Trust*. Minneapolis: University of Minnesota Press.
Lingis, A. (2007). *The first person singular*. Evanston, IL: Northwestern University Press.
Linstead, S. (2018). Feeling the reel of the real: Framing the play of critically affective organizational research between art and the everyday. *Organization Studies, 39*(2–3), 319–344.
Louis, E. (2014). *En finir avec Eddy Belleguele*. Paris, France: Points Editions du Seuil. [*The End of Eddy* (2018) New York: Macmillan).
Louis, E. (2016). *Histoire de la violence*. Paris, France: Points Editions du Seuil. [*History of Violence* (2018) London: Harvill Secker].
Louis, E. (2018). *Qui a tué mon père*. Paris, France: Editions du Seuil. [*Who Killed my Father?* (2019) London: Harvill Secker].
Massumi, B. (1987). "*Translator's foreword: Pleasures of philosophy.*" In G. Deleuze & F. Guatarri (Eds.), *A thousand plateaus* (pp. *ix–xix*). Minneapolis: University of Minnesota Press.
Massumi, B. (2002). *Parables for the virtual*. Durham, NC: Duke University Press.
Merleau-Ponty, M. (1969). *Visible and invisible*. Evanston, IL: Northwestern University Press.
Nye, A. (1990). *Words of power*. London, UK: Routledge.
Spinoza, B. (2002). *Spinoza: Complete works*. Cambridge, UK: Hackett.
Stewart, K. (1996). *A space on the side of the road*. Princeton, NJ: Princeton University Press.
Stiegler, B. (2017). The proletarianization of sensibility. *Boundary, 44*(1), 5–18.
Thorton, E. (2019). Deleuze and Guattari's absent analysis of patriarchy. *Hypatia, 34*(2), 348–368.
Wood, M., & Salovaara, P. (2019). The terrifying thing about film as business education. In H Letiche & J. L. Moriceau (Eds.), *Turn to films* (pp. 129–151). Leiden, Netherlands: Brill.

Index

Note: *Italic* page numbers refer to figures and page numbers followed by "n" denote endnotes.